A
EDITOR'S
BURIAL

WES ANDERSON was born in Houston, Texas. His films include *Bottle Rocket*, *Rushmore*, *The Royal Tenenbaums*, *The Life Aquatic with Steve Zissou*, *The Darjeeling Limited*, *Fantastic Mr. Fox*, *Moonrise Kingdom*, *The Grand Budapest Hotel*, and *Isle of Dogs*. His latest film is *The French Dispatch*.

SUSAN MORRISON has been the Articles Editor of *The New Yorker* for twenty-three years.

DAVID BRENDEL is a New York-based screenwriter, journalist, and documentarian.

AN

EDITOR'S BURIAL

JOURNALS AND JOURNALISM
FROM
THE NEW YORKER
AND OTHER MAGAZINES

EDITED BY DAVID BRENDEL

PUSHKIN PRESS

Pushkin Press
71–75 Shelton Street
London WC2H 9JQ

An Editor's Burial was first published by Pushkin Press in 2021
Selection of contents © 2021 Pushkin Press
Full permissions acknowledgments on pp. 351–52

1 3 5 7 9 8 6 4 2

ISBN 13: 978-1-78227-664-7

Designed and typeset by Tetragon, London
Printed and bound in the United States

www.pushkinpress.com

CONTENTS

THE PILOT LIGHT

(Or: Missing Something Left Behind)

A CONVERSATION BETWEEN
WES ANDERSON AND SUSAN MORRISON

SUSAN: Your movie "The French Dispatch" is a series of stories that are meant to be the articles in one issue of a magazine published by an American in Paris. When you were dreaming up the film, did you start with the character of Arthur Howitzer, Jr., the editor, or did you start with the stories?

WES: I read an interview with Tom Stoppard once where he said he began to realize—as people asked him over the years where the idea for one play or another came from—that it seems to have always been two different ideas for two different plays that he sort of smooshed together. It's never *one* idea. It's two. "The French Dispatch" might be three.

The first idea: I wanted to do an anthology movie. Just in general, an omnibus-type collection, without any specific stories in mind. (The two I love maybe the most: "The Gold of Naples" by de Sica and "Le Plaisir" by Max Ophuls.)

The second idea: I always wanted to make a movie about *The New Yorker.* The French magazine in the film obviously is not *The New Yorker*—but it was, I think, totally inspired by it. When I was in 11th grade, my homeroom was in the school library, and I sat in a chair where I had my back to everybody else, and I faced a wooden rack of what they labeled "periodicals". One had drawings on the cover. That was unusual. I think the first story I read was by Ved Mehta. "Letter from Delhi." I thought, "I have no idea what this is, but I'm interested." But what I was most interested in were the short stories, because back then, I thought that was what I wanted to do—fiction. Write stories and novels and so on. When I went to the University of Texas in Austin, I used to look at old bound volumes of *The New Yorker* in the library, because you could find things like a J.D. Salinger story that had never been collected. Then I somehow managed to find out that UC Berkeley was getting rid of a set, forty years of bound *New Yorkers*, and I bought them for $600. I would also have my own new subscription copies bound (which is actually not a good way to preserve them). When the magazine put the whole archive online, I stopped paying to bind mine. But I still keep them. I have most every issue starting in the 1940s. Later, I found myself reading various writers' accounts of life at *The New Yorker*—Brendan Gill, James Thurber, Ben Yagoda—and I got caught up in the whole aura of the thing. I also met Lillian Ross (with you), who, as we know, wrote about Truffaut and Hemingway and Chaplin for the magazine and was very close to Salinger, and so on and so forth.

The third idea: a French movie. I want to do one of those. An anthology, *The New Yorker*, and French. Three very broad notions. I think it sort of turned into a movie about what my friend and co-writer Hugo Guinness calls reverse emigration. He thinks Americans who go to Europe are reverse emigrating.

SUSAN: When I saw the movie, I told you how much Lillian Ross, who died a couple of years ago, would have liked it. You said that Lillian's first reaction would have been to demand, "Why *France*?"

WES: Well, I've had an apartment in Paris for I don't know how many years. I've reverse emigrated. And in Paris, any time I walk down a street I don't know well, it's like going to the movies. It's just entertaining. There's also a sort of isolation living abroad, which can be good or it can be bad. It can be lonely, certainly. But you're also always on a kind of adventure, which can be inspiring.

SUSAN: Harold Ross, *The New Yorker*'s founding editor, was famous for saying that the history of New York is always written by out-of-towners. When you're out of your element, or in another country, you have a different perspective. It's as if a pilot light is always on.

WES: Yes! The pilot light is always on.

SUSAN: In a foreign country, even just going into a hardware store can be like going to a museum.

WES: Buying a light bulb.

SUSAN: Arthur Howitzer, Jr., the editor played by Bill Murray, gathers the best writers of his generation to staff his magazine, in Paris. They're all expatriates, like you. In this book, you've gathered the best *New Yorker* writers, many of whom lived as expatriates in Paris. There is a line in the movie: "He received an Editor's Burial," and several of the pieces in this book are obituaries of Harold Ross.

WES: Howitzer is based on Harold Ross, with a little bit of William Shawn, the magazine's second editor, thrown in. Although they don't really go together particularly. Ross had a great feeling for writers. It isn't exactly respect. He values them, but he also thinks they're lunatic children who have to be sort of manipulated or coddled. Whereas Shawn seems to have been the most gentle, respectful, encouraging master you could ever wish to have. We tried to mix in some of that.

SUSAN: Both Ross and Shawn came from the Midwest; Howitzer is from Liberty, Kansas, right in the middle of America. He moves to France, to find himself, in a way, and he ends up creating a magazine that brings the world to Kansas.

WES: Originally, we were calling the editor character Liebling, not Howitzer, because the face I always pictured was A.J. Liebling's. We tried to make Bill Murray sort of look like him, I think. Remember, he says he tricked his father into paying for his early sojourn in Paris by telling him he was thinking of marrying a good woman who was ten years older than he, although "Mother might think she is a bit fast..."

SUSAN: There are lots of similarities between your Howitzer and Ross. Howitzer has a sign in his office that says, "No crying." Ross made sure that there was no humming or singing or whistling in the office.

WES: They share a general grumpiness. What Thurber called Ross's "God-how-I-pity-me!" moods.

SUSAN: But you see a little bit of Shawn in Howitzer, as you mentioned. Shawn was formal and decorous, in contrast to Ross's bluster. In the movie, when Howitzer tells the writer

Herbsaint Sazerac, who Owen Wilson plays, that his article is "too seedy for decent people," that's very Shawn.

WES: I think that might be Ross, too! He was a prude, they say. For someone who could be extremely vulgar.

SUSAN: In Thurber's book "The Years with Ross," which is excerpted here, there's a funny part where Ross complains about a writer trying to sneak in a reference to menstruation, by having a woman character use the code phrase "I fell off the roof." I'd never heard that euphemism! I had to look it up.

WES: "We can't have *that* in the magazine."

SUSAN: Thurber also compared him to "a sleepless, apprehensive sea captain pacing the bridge, expecting any minute to run aground and collide with something nameless in a sudden fog." You publishing a collection of stories as a companion piece to a movie feels like a literary version of a soundtrack. You can read this book the way you might read E.M. Forster before taking a trip to Florence. What made you decide to put this together?

WES: Two reasons.

One: our movie draws on the work and lives of specific writers. Even though it's not an adaptation, the inspirations are specific and crucial to it. So, I wanted a way to say, "Here's where it comes from." I want to announce what it is. This book is almost a great big footnote.

Two: it's an excuse to do a book that I thought would be really entertaining. These are writers I love and pieces I love. A person who is interested in the movie can read Mavis Gallant's article about the student protests of 1968 in here and discover there's much more in it than in the movie. There's a depth, in part because it's much longer. It's different, of course. Movies have their own thing. Frances McDormand's character, Krementz, comes from Mavis Gallant but Lillian Ross also gets mixed into that character, too—and, I think, a bit of Frances herself. I once heard her say to a very snooty French waiter, "Kindly leave me my dignity."

I remember reading Pauline Kael on John Huston's movie of "The Dead." She said Joyce's story is a perfect masterpiece, but so is the movie. It has strengths that the story can't have, simply because: actors. Great actors. There they are. Plus, they sing!

SUSAN: Wouldn't it be cool if every movie came with a suggested reading list?

WES: There are so many things we're borrowing from. It's nice to be able to introduce people to some of them.

SUSAN: "The French Dispatch" is full of references to classic French cinema. There are lots of schoolboys in capes skittering around, like the ones in Truffaut and Jean Vigo movies.

WES: Yes! We wanted the movie to be full of all of the things we've loved in French movies. France, more or less, is where the cinema starts. Other than America, the country whose movies have meant the most to me is France. There are so many directors and so many stars and so many styles of French cinema. We sort of steal from Godard, Vigo, Truffaut, Tati, Clouzot, Duvivier, Jacques Becker. French noir movies, like "Le Trou" and "Grisbi" and "The Murderer Lives at Number 21." We were stealing things very openly, so you really can kind of pinpoint something and find out exactly where it came from.

SUSAN: When is the movie set? Some of it is 1965.

WES: I love Mavis Gallant's piece about the events of May 1968, her journal. I knew that at least part of the movie had to take place around that time. I'm not entirely sure when the other parts happen! The magazine went from 1925 to 1975, so it is all during those 50 years, anyway.

SUSAN: I see. I'd wondered if you have a particular affinity for the mid-sixties. You were born in 1969. There's a psychological theory that says what we tend to be most nostalgic for is a period in time that is several years before our own birth—when our parents' romance might have been at its peak. The technical term for the phenomenon is "cascading reminiscence bump."

WES: I like that! I came across a good jargon-type phrase after we had made the movie. We do this thing where sometimes we have one person speak French, with subtitles, and the other person answers in English. I kept wondering, "Is this going to work?" Of course, we do it in real life all the time. The term I came across is: "non-accommodating bilingualism." When people speak to each other, but don't switch to the other person's language. They stay in their own language, but they understand. They're just completely non-accommodating.

SUSAN: The Mavis Gallant story feels like the heart of the movie. Francine Prose, the novelist, is a big Gallant fan. She has described her as "at once scathing and endlessly tolerant and forgiving."

WES: There's nobody to lump her in with. Writing about May 1968, she has a totally independent point of view. It's a foreigner's perspective, but she's very clear-sighted about all of it. Clarity and empathy. She went out every day, alone, in the middle of the chaos.

SUSAN: Gallant was Canadian, which I think gave her a kind of double remove from America. Canadians in the United States have the pilot light, too. I think it's why there are so many comedians from Canada. They have an outsider's take. The great fiction writers from the American South also have it.

WES: She lived to be 91. In Paris. She lived in my neighborhood, less than a block away from our apartment, but I never met her. She died five years ago. I do feel like I almost knew her. I just missed her. It would have been very natural to me (at least, in my imagination) to say, "We have dinner with Mavis on Thursday." So forceful and formidable a personality, and a very engaging person.

SUSAN: This book includes a beautiful piece by Janet Flanner, about Edith Wharton living in Europe. She writes about how Wharton kept "repeatedly redomiciling herself," and ended up a permanent "prose exile." Is there a trace of Flanner in Krementz?

WES: Yes, there is some Janet Flanner in there. Flanner wrote so many pieces, sometimes topical in the most miniature ways. The smallest things happening in Paris in any given week. She wrote about May 1968, too. Her piece on it is good, and not so different from Mavis Gallant's, but Flanner wasn't standing out there with the kids in the streets so much.

She was 76 then, and maybe a bit less sympathetic to the young people.

SUSAN: Gallant is also sympathetic to their poor, worried parents. But there's a toughness to her as well. You can tell that the Krementz character in the movie has sacrificed a lot in order to pursue her writing life. Her emotions only seem to surface as a result of tear gas.

WES: I have the sense that Gallant was one of those people who could be quite prickly. From what I've read about her, she seems like she was a wonderful person to have dinner with, unless somebody said something stupid or ungenerous, in which case things might turn dark. I think she might have been someone who, in certain situations, could not stop herself from eviscerating a person who had offended her principles. She was not going to stand for nonsense.

SUSAN: You mention Lillian Ross, too.

WES: Yes, as you know, Lillian had a way of poking right through something, needling, with a deceptively curious look on her face. I first met her when Anjelica Huston brought her to the set of "The Royal Tenenbaums." You were there with her.

SUSAN: Yes, at that glass house designed by Paul Rudolph, in the East Fifties. Ben Stiller's character lived there in the movie.

WES: I said to Anjelica, "Lillian Ross is going to come visit? That's incredible." She said, "Yes. Be careful." Anjelica has so much family history with Lillian starting, obviously, when she wrote "Picture." Anjelica and Lillian were great friends.

SUSAN: In your movie, the showdown between Krementz and Juliet, one of the revolutionary teenagers, is intense.

WES: Krementz scolds the kids, but she admires them. There are lines in Frances's dialogue, as Krementz, that are taken directly from the Gallant piece: "The touching narcissism of the young." There are some non-sequiturs in the script, some things totally unrelated to the action, that I put in only because I wanted to use some of Mavis Gallant's actual sentences. Timothée Chalamet's character, the teen revolutionary, says, at one point, "I've never read my mother's books." In Gallant's piece, she says that about the daughter of her friend. Also, "I wonder if she knows how brave her father was in the last war?" Just to call it "the last war"—our most *recent* world war—maybe we wouldn't say it that way now. I mean, is there another one coming? We don't know.

SUSAN: In the movie, the student protest begins because the boys want to be allowed into the girls' dormitories. During the screening, I remember thinking, "Oh, that's such a Wes Anderson version of what would spark a student uprising!" Then when I read up on the history of the conflict, I saw that it actually was the original issue.

WES: Daniel Cohn-Bendit in Nanterre. That was one of his demands. Maybe the larger point was, "We don't want to be treated like children," but literally calling for the right of free access to the girls' dormitory for all male students? The sentence sounded so funny to me. And then the revolutionary spirit spreads through every part of French society and ends up having nothing to do with girls' dormitories. By the end, no one can even say what the protests are about anymore. That's what Mavis Gallant captures so well, that people can't quite fully process what's happening and why.

SUSAN: It's a world turned upside down. There are workers on strike, professors who want a better deal, people angry about the Vietnam war.

WES: And Gallant is trying to figure out: what can end this chaos, when the protesters can no longer clearly articulate what they're fighting for? She asks the kids, and the answer seems to be: an honest life, a clean life, a clean and honest France.

SUSAN: It reminds me of something that William Maxwell, Gallant's *New Yorker* editor, once said about her stories: "The older I get the more grateful I am not to be told how everything comes out." You know, the film captures an interesting aspect of the writer–editor relationship. When a writer turns in a new story, it's like an offering to the editor. There's something intimate about it. Howitzer and his magazine function as a family for all of these isolated expatriates. Krementz, in particular, seems to use the concept of "journalistic neutrality" as a cover for loneliness. What does the chef say at the end?

WES: Yes, Nescaffier, the cook played by the great Stephen Park, describes his life as a foreigner: "Seeking something missing, missing something left behind."

SUSAN: That runs through all of these pieces, and also through the lives of all of these writers. People have been calling the movie a love letter to journalists. That's encouraging, given that we live in a time when journalists are being called the enemies of the people.

WES: That's what our colleagues at the studio call it. I might not use that exact turn of phrase, just because it's *not* a love letter. It's a movie. But it's about journalists I have loved, journalists who have meant something to me. For the first half of my life I thought of *The New Yorker* as primarily a place to read fiction, and the movie we made is all fiction. None of the journalists in the movie actually existed, and the stories are all made up. So I've made a fiction movie about reportage, which is odd.

SUSAN: The movie is like a big otherworldly cocktail party where mashups of real people, like James Baldwin and Mavis Gallant and Janet Flanner and A.J. Liebling, are chatting with subjects of *New Yorker* articles, like Rosamond Bernier, the art lecturer, who was profiled by Calvin Tomkins. In the story about the artist in prison, Moses Rosenthaler, Bernier is the inspiration for the character that Tilda Swinton plays, J.K.L. Berenson. Or Joseph Duveen, the eccentric buccaneer art dealer played by Adrien Brody in the same story.

WES: Duveen sold Old Masters and Renaissance paintings from Europe to American tycoons and robber barons. The painters were all dead, but we have a living painter, Rosenthaler. So that relationship comes from somewhere else. And so does the painter himself. Tilda's character, inspired by Rosamond Bernier, ends up being sort of the voice of S.N. Behrman, the *New Yorker* writer who profiled Duveen. It's a lot of mixing.

SUSAN: Duveen is such a modern character. He seems like somebody who works for Mike Ovitz.

WES: Or he could've been a *mentor* to Ovitz. Or Larry Gagosian. We have a rich art-collecting lady from Kansas named "Maw" Clampette, who is played by Lois Smith. In the Duveen book, there is a woman, a wife of one of the tycoons, I can't remember which one, who talks a bit like a hillbilly. We based "Maw" Clampette's manner of speech on hers, maybe. But the character was actually inspired by Dominique de Menil, who lived in my hometown of Houston. She's the most refined kind of French Protestant woman, a fantastically interesting art collector, who came to Texas with her husband and together they shared their art and their sort of vision. Her eye.

SUSAN: I guess "Clampette" is a reference to "The Beverly Hillbillies?"

WES: I feel yes.

SUSAN: The character of Roebuck Wright, who Jeffrey Wright plays in the last story, about the police commissioner's chef, is another inspired composite. He is a gay, African American gourmand, and he seems to be one part A.J. Liebling and one part James Baldwin, who moved to Paris to get away from the racism of the United States. That's a daring combination.

WES: Hopefully people won't consider it a daring, ill-advised combination. With every character in the movie there's a mixture of inspirations. I always carry a little notebook with me to write down ideas. I don't know what I am going to do with them or what they're going to end up being. But sometimes I jot down names of actors who I want to work with. Jeffrey Wright and Benicio Del Toro have been at the top of this list that I've been keeping for years. I wanted to write a part for Jeffrey and a part for Benicio. When we were thinking about the character of Roebuck Wright, we always had a bit of Baldwin in him. I'd read "Giovanni's Room" and a few essays. But, when I saw Raoul Peck's Baldwin movie, I was so moved and so interested in him. I watched the Cambridge Union debate between Baldwin and William F. Buckley from 1965. It's not just that Baldwin's words are so spectacularly eloquent and insightful. It's also *him*, his voice, his personality. So: we were thinking about the way he talked, and we also thought about the way Tennessee Williams talked, and Gore Vidal's way of talking. We mixed in aspects of those writers, too. Plus Liebling. Why? I have no idea. They joined forces.

SUSAN: There's a line from Baldwin's piece, "Equal in Paris," which reads like an epigraph for your movie. He writes, "the French personality had seemed so large and free… but if it was large, it was also inflexible, and, for the foreigner, full of strange, high, dusty rooms which could not be inhabited."

WES: If you're an American in France for a period of time, you know that feeling. It's kind of a complicated metaphor. When I read that, I do think, "I know exactly what you mean."

SUSAN: One of the things Howitzer is always telling his writers is "Make it sound like you wrote it that way on purpose." That reminds me of what Calvin Trillin says about Joseph Mitchell's style. He says that Mitchell was able to get the "marks of writing" off of his pieces. Where did you get your line?

WES: I guess I was thinking about how there's an almost infinite number of ways to write something well. Each writer has a completely different approach. How can you give the same advice to Joseph Mitchell that you would give to George Trow? Two people doing something so completely different.

I was trying to come up with a funny way to say: please, attempt to accomplish your intention perfectly. I don't know if that's very useful advice to a writer.

SUSAN: It's good. Basically, it's just, "Make it sound confident."

WES: When you're making a movie, you want to feel like you can take it in any direction, you can experiment, as long as it in the end feels like this is what it's meant to be, and it has some authority.

SUSAN: There's an unnamed writer mentioned in the movie, described as "the best living writer in terms of sentences per minute." Who is that a reference to?

WES: Liebling said, of himself, "I can write better than anybody who can write faster, and I can write faster than anybody who can write better." We shortened it so that it would work in the montage. There's maybe a little bit of Ben Hecht, too. There are a few other writers mentioned in passing. We have the faintest reference to Ved Mehta, who I've always loved, especially "The Photographs of Chachaji." The character in the movie has an amanuensis. I learned that word from him, I think!

SUSAN: And then the "cheery writer" who didn't write anything for decades, played by Wally Wolodarsky? That's Joe Mitchell, right?

WES: That's Mitchell, except Mitchell had an unforgettable body of work before he stopped writing. With our guy, that doesn't appear to be the case. He never wrote anything in the first place.

SUSAN: That's wonderfully Dada. I became friendly with Joe Mitchell late in his life. I was trying to get him to write something for me at *The New York Observer*. He hadn't published in thirty years. He never turned anything in, but we talked on the phone every week and he would sing sea shanties to me.

WES: The character that Owen Wilson plays, Sazerac, is meant to be a bit like Mitchell. He writes about the seamy side of the city. And Sazerac is on a bicycle the whole time, which is maybe a nod to Bill Cunningham, but also Owen is always on a bike in real life. It wouldn't be unheard of, if you were in Berlin or Tokyo or someplace, to see Owen Wilson riding up on a bicycle. Sazerac also owes a major debt to Luc Sante, too, because we took so much atmosphere from his book "The Other Paris." He is Mitchell and Luc Sante and Owen.

SUSAN: The Sazerac mashup is especially inventive. Joseph Mitchell was the original lowlife reporter. He went out to the docks and slums and wandered around talking to people. And Luc, whose books, "Low Life," about the historical slums of New York, and "The Other Paris," about the Paris underworld of the nineteenth century, is more of a literary academic. He finds his gems in the library and the flea market.

WES: Mitchell is more, like, "I talked to the man who was opening the oysters, and he told me this story."

SUSAN: Mitchell is what we call a shoe-leather reporter. You've included Mitchell's magnum opus on rats in this book. There's a line in it, about a rat stealing an egg, that feels like it could be a sequence in one of your movies: "A small rat would straddle an egg and clutch it in his four paws. When he got a good grip on it, he'd roll over on his back and a bigger rat would grab him by the tail and drag him across the floor to a hole in the baseboard."

WES: Maybe Mitchell picked that up talking to an exterminator. I remember an image from the piece about how, when it starts to get cold in the fall, you could see the rats running across Central Park West in hordes, into the basements of buildings, leaving the park for the summer. It was the first thing by Mitchell I ever read.

SUSAN: Have you been filing away these *New Yorker* pieces for years?

WES: I don't know. Not deliberately. I knew which writers I wanted to refer to. At the end of the movie, before the credits, there is a list of writers we dedicate the movie to. Some of the people on the list, like St. Clair McKelway and Wolcott Gibbs, or E.B. White and Katharine White, are there not because their stories are in the movie, but because of their roles in making *The New Yorker* what it is. For defining the voice and tone of the magazine.

SUSAN: Usually when *New Yorker* writers are depicted in movies, they're portrayed as just a bunch of antic cut-ups, rather than people who are devoted to their work.

WES: It's harder to do a movie about real people, when you already know who each person is meant to be—like the members of the Algonquin Round Table—and each actor has to then embody somebody who already exists. There's a little more freedom when you make the people up.

SUSAN: Have you ever made a movie before that drew on such a rich reservoir of material for inspiration?

WES: Not this much stuff. This one's been brewing for years and years and years. By the time I started working with Jason Schwartzman and Roman Coppola, though, it sorted itself out pretty quickly.

SUSAN: What order did you write them in?

WES: The last story we wrote was the Roebuck Wright one, and we wrote it fast. The story about the painter, I must've had something on paper about that for at least ten years. The Berenson character that Tilda Swinton plays wasn't in it yet, though.

SUSAN: Talk about the names of the two cities: Liberty, Kansas and Ennui-sur-Blasé.

WES: I think Jason just said it out loud: "Ennui-sur-Blasé." We wanted them to be sister cities. Liberty, well, that's got an American ring to it.

SUSAN: What do you think the French will make of the movie?

WES: I have no idea. We do have a lot of French actors. It's kind of a confection, a fantasy, but it still needs to feel like the real version of a fantasy. It has to feel like its roots are believable. I think it's pretty clear the movie is set in a foreigner's idea of France. I always think of Wim Wenders' version of America, which I love. "Paris, Texas," and also the photographs that he used to take in the West. It's just that one particular individual German's view of America. People don't necessarily like it when you invade their territory, even respectfully, but maybe they start to appreciate it when they see how much you love the place. But then again: who knows?

THE YEARS WITH ROSS

James Thurber

1957

H AROLD ROSS died December 6, 1951, exactly one month
after his fifty-ninth birthday. In November of the following year the *New Yorker* entertained the editors of *Punch* and
some of its outstanding artists and writers. I was in Bermuda
and missed the party, but weeks later met Rowland Emett for
lunch at the Algonquin. "I'm sorry you didn't get to meet Ross,"
I began as we sat down. "Oh, but I did," he said. "He was all
over the place. Nobody talked about anybody else."

Ross is still all over the place for many of us, vitally stalking
the corridors of our lives, disturbed and disturbing, fretting,
stimulating, more evident in death than the living presence
of ordinary men. A photograph of him, full face, almost alive
with a sense of contained restlessness, hangs on a wall outside
his old office. I am sure he had just said to the photographer,
"I haven't got time for this." That's what he said, impatiently,
to anyone—doctor, lawyer, tax man—who interrupted, even
momentarily, the stream of his dedicated energy. Unless a
meeting, conference, or consultation touched somehow upon
the working of his magazine, he began mentally pacing.

I first met Harold Ross in February, 1927, when his weekly
was just two years old. He was thirty-four and I was thirty-two.

The *New Yorker* had printed a few small pieces of mine, and a brief note from Ross had asked me to stop in and see him some day when my job as a reporter for the New York *Evening Post* chanced to take me uptown. Since I was getting only forty dollars a week and wanted to work for the *New Yorker*, I showed up at his office the next day. Our meeting was to become for me the first of a thousand vibrant memories of this exhilarating and exasperating man.

You caught only glimpses of Ross, even if you spent a long evening with him. He was always in mid-flight, or on the edge of his chair, alighting or about to take off. He won't sit still in anybody's mind long enough for a full-length portrait. After six years of thinking about it, I realized that to do justice to Harold Ross I must write about him the way he talked and lived—leaping from peak to peak. What follows here is a monologue montage of that first day and of half a dozen swift and similar sessions. He was standing behind his desk, scowling at a manuscript lying on it, as if it were about to lash out at him. I had caught glimpses of him at the theater and at the Algonquin and, like everybody else, was familiar with the mobile face that constantly changed expression, the carrying voice, the eloquent large-fingered hands that were never in repose, but kept darting this way and that to emphasize his points or running through the thatch of hair that stood straight up until Ina Claire said she would like to take her shoes off and walk through it. That got into the gossip columns and Ross promptly had his barber flatten down the pompadour.

He wanted, first of all, to know how old I was, and when I told him it set him off on a lecture. "Men don't mature in this country, Thurber," he said. "They're children. I was editor of the *Stars and Stripes* when I was twenty-five. Most men in their twenties don't know their way around yet. I think it's the goddam system of women schoolteachers." He went to the window behind his desk and stared disconsolately down into the street, jingling coins in one of his pants pockets. I learned later that he made a point of keeping four or five dollars' worth of change in this pocket because he had once got stuck in a taxi, to his vast irritation, with nothing smaller than a ten-dollar bill. The driver couldn't change it and had to park and go into the store for coins and bills, and Ross didn't have time for that.

I told him that I wanted to write, and he snarled, "Writers are a dime a dozen, Thurber. What I want is an editor. I can't find editors. Nobody grows up. Do you know English?" I said I thought I knew English, and this started him off on a subject with which I was to become intensely familiar. "Everybody thinks he knows English," he said, "but nobody does. I think it's because of the goddam women schoolteachers." He turned away from the window and glared at me as if I were on the witness stand and he were the prosecuting attorney. "I want to make a business office out of this place, like any other business office," he said. "I'm surrounded by women and children. We have no manpower or ingenuity. I never know where anybody is, and I can't find out. Nobody tells me anything. They sit out there at their desks, getting me deeper and deeper into God knows what. Nobody has any self-discipline, nobody gets anything done. Nobody knows how to delegate anything. What I need is a man who can sit at a central desk and make this place operate like a business office, keep track of things, find out where people are. I am, by God, going to keep sex out of this office—sex is an incident. You've got to hold the artists' hands. Artists never go anywhere, they don't know anybody, they're antisocial."

Ross was never conscious of his dramatic gestures, or of his natural gift of theatrical speech. At times he seemed to be on stage, and you half expected the curtain to fall on such an agonized tagline as "God, how I pity me!" Anthony Ross played him in Wolcott Gibbs's comedy *Season in the Sun*, and an old friend of his, Lee Tracy, was Ross in a short-lived play called *Metropole*, written by a former secretary of the editor. Ross sneaked in to see the Gibbs play one matinee, but he never saw the other one. I doubt if he recognized himself in the Anthony Ross part. I sometimes think he would have disowned a movie of himself, sound track and all.

He once found out that I had done an impersonation of him for a group of his friends at Dorothy Parker's apartment, and he called me into his office. "I hear you were imitating me last night, Thurber," he snarled. "I don't know what the hell there is to imitate—go ahead and show me." All this time his face was undergoing its familiar changes of expression and his fingers were flying. His flexible voice ran from a low register of growl to an upper register of what I can only call Western quacking. It was an instrument that could give special quality to such Rossisms as "Done and done!" and "You have me there!" and "Get it on paper!" and such a memorable tagline as his farewell to John McNulty on that writer's departure for Hollywood: "Well, God bless you, McNulty, goddam it."

Ross was, at first view, oddly disappointing. No one, I think, would have picked him out of a line-up as the editor of the *New*

Yorker. Even in a dinner jacket he looked loosely informal, like a carelessly carried umbrella. He was meticulous to the point of obsession about the appearance of his magazine, but he gave no thought to himself. He was usually dressed in a dark suit, with a plain dark tie, as if for protective coloration. In the spring of 1927 he came to work in a black hat so unbecoming that his secretary, Elsie Dick, went out and bought him another one. "What became of my hat?" he demanded later. "I threw it away," said Miss Dick. "It was awful." He wore the new one without argument. Miss Dick, then in her early twenties, was a calm, quiet girl, never ruffled by Ross's moods. She was one of the few persons to whom he ever gave a photograph of himself. On it he wrote, "For Miss Dick, to whom I owe practically everything." She could spell, never sang, whistled, or hummed, knew how to fend off unwanted visitors, and had an intuitive sense of when the coast was clear so that he could go down in the elevator alone and not have to talk to anybody, and these things were practically everything.

In those early years the magazine occupied a floor in the same building as the *Saturday Review of Literature* on West 45th Street. Christopher Morley often rode in the elevator, a tweedy man, smelling of pipe tobacco and books, unmistakably a literary figure. I don't know that Ross ever met him. "I know too many people," he used to say. The editor of the *New Yorker*, wearing no mark of his trade, strove to be inconspicuous and liked to get to his office in the morning, if possible, without being recognized and greeted.

From the beginning Ross cherished his dream of a Central Desk at which an infallible omniscience would sit, a dedicated genius, out of Technology by Mysticism, effortlessly controlling and coördinating editorial personnel, contributors, office boys, cranks and other visitors, manuscripts, proofs, cartoons, captions, covers, fiction, poetry, and facts, and bringing forth each Thursday a magazine at once funny, journalistically sound, and flawless. This dehumanized figure, disguised as a man, was a goal only in the sense that the mechanical rabbit of a whippet track is a quarry. Ross's mind was always filled with dreams of precision and efficiency beyond attainment, but exciting to contemplate.

This conception of a Central Desk and its superhuman engineer was the largest of half a dozen intense preoccupations. You could see it smoldering in his eyes if you encountered him walking to work, oblivious of passers-by, his tongue edging reflectively out of the corner of his mouth, his round-shouldered torso seeming, as Lois Long once put it, to be pushing something invisible ahead of him. He had no Empire Urge, unlike Henry Luce and a dozen other founders of proliferating enterprises. He was a one-magazine, one-project man. (His financial interest in Dave Chasen's Hollywood restaurant was no more central to his ambition than his onetime investment in a paint-spraying machine—I don't know whatever became of that.) He dreamed of perfection, not of power or personal fortune. He was a visionary and a practicalist, imperfect at both, a dreamer and a hard worker, a genius and a plodder, obstinate and reasonable, cosmopolitan and provincial, wide-eyed and world-weary. There is only one word that fits him perfectly, and the word is Ross.

When I agreed to work for the *New Yorker* as a desk man, it was with deep misgivings. I felt that Ross didn't know, and wasn't much interested in finding out, anything about me. He had persuaded himself, without evidence, that I might be just the wonder man he was looking for, a mistake he had made before and was to make again in the case of other newspapermen, including James M. Cain, who was just about as miscast for the job as I was. Ross's wishful thinking was, it seems to me now, tinged with hallucination. In expecting to find, in everybody that turned up, the Ideal Executive, he came to remind me of the Charlie Chaplin of *The Gold Rush*, who, snowbound and starving with another man in a cabin teetering on the edge of a cliff, suddenly beholds his companion turning into an enormous tender spring chicken, wonderfully edible, supplied by Providence. "Done and done, Thurber," said Ross. "I'll give you seventy dollars a week. If you write anything, goddam it, your salary will take care of it." Later that afternoon he phoned my apartment and said, "I've decided to make that ninety dollars a week, Thurber." When my first check came through it was for one hundred dollars. "I couldn't take advantage of a newspaperman," Ross explained.

By the spring of 1928 Ross's young *New Yorker* was safely past financial and other shoals that had menaced its launching, skies were clearing, the glass was rising, and everybody felt secure except the skipper of the ship. From the first day I met him till the last time I saw him, Ross was like a sleepless, apprehensive sea captain pacing the bridge, expecting any minute to run aground, collide with something nameless in a sudden fog, or find his vessel abandoned and adrift, like the *Mary Celeste*. When, at the age of thirty-two, Ross had got his magazine afloat with the aid of Raoul Fleischmann and a handful of associates, the proudest thing he had behind him was his editorship of the *Stars and Stripes* in Paris from 1917 to 1919.

As the poet is born, Ross was born a newspaperman. "He could not only get it, he could write it," said his friend Herbert Asbury. Ross got it and wrote it for seven different newspapers before he was twenty-five years old, beginning as a reporter for the Salt Lake City *Tribune* when he was only fourteen. One of his assignments there was to interview the madam of a house of prostitution. Always self-conscious and usually uncomfortable in the presence of all but his closest women friends, the young reporter began by saying to the bad woman (he divided the other sex into good and bad), "How many fallen women do you have?"

Later he worked for the Marysville (California) *Appeal*, Sacramento *Union*, Panama *Star and Herald*, New Orleans *Item*, Atlanta *Journal*, and San Francisco *Call*.

The wanderer—some of his early associates called him "Hobo"—reached New York in 1919 and worked for several magazines, including *Judge* and the *American Legion Weekly*, his mind increasingly occupied with plans for a new kind of weekly to be called the *New Yorker*. It was born at last, in travail and trauma, but he always felt uneasy as the R of the F-R Publishing Company, for he had none of the instincts and equipment of the businessman except the capacity for overwork and overworry. In his new position of high responsibility he soon developed the notion, as Marc Connelly has put it, that the world was designed to wear him down. A dozen years ago I found myself almost unconsciously making a Harold Ross out of one King Clode, a rugged pessimist in a fairy tale I was writing. At one point the palace astronomer rushed into the royal presence saying, "A huge pink comet, Sire, just barely missed the earth a little while ago. It made an awful hissing sound, like hot irons stuck in water." "They aim these things at me!" said Clode. "Everything is aimed at me." In this fantasy Clode pursues a fabulously swift white deer which, when brought to bay, turns into a woman, a parable that parallels Ross's headlong quest for the wonder man who invariably turned into a human being with feet of clay, as useless to Ross as any enchanted princess.

Among the agencies in mischievous or malicious conspiracy to wear Ross down were his own business department ("They're not only what's the matter with *me*, they're what's the matter with the country"), the state and federal tax systems, women and children (all the females and males that worked for him), temperament and fallibility in writers and artists, marriages and illnesses—to both of which his staff seemed especially susceptible—printers, engravers, distributors, and the like, who seemed to aim their strikes and ill-timed holidays directly at him, and human nature in general.

Harold Wallace Ross, born in Aspen, Colorado, in 1892, in a year and decade whose cradles were filled with infants destined to darken his days and plague his nights, was in the midst of a project involving the tearing down of walls the week I started to work. When he outlined his schemes of reconstruction, it was often hard to tell where rationale left off and mystique began. (How he would hate those smart-aleck words.) He seemed to believe that certain basic problems of personnel might just possibly be solved by some fortuitous rearrangement of the offices. Time has mercifully foreshortened the months of my ordeal as executive editor, and only the highlights of what he called "practical matters" still remain. There must have been a dozen Through the Looking Glass conferences with him about those damned walls. As an efficiency expert or construction engineer, I was a little boy with an alarm clock and a hammer, and my utter incapacity in such a role would have been apparent in two hours to an unobsessed man. I took to drinking Martinis at lunch to fortify myself for the tortured afternoons of discussion.

"Why don't we put the walls on wheels?" I demanded one day. "We might get somewhere with adjustable walls."

Ross's eyes lighted gloomily, in an expression of combined hope and dismay which no other face I have known could duplicate. "The hell with it," he said. "You could hear everybody talking. You could see everybody's feet."

He and I worked seven days a week, often late into the night, for at least two months, without a day off. I began to lose weight, editing factual copy for sports departments and those dealing with new apartments, women's fashions, and men's wear.

"Gretta Palmer keeps using words like introvert and extrovert," Ross complained one day. "I'm not interested in the housing problems of neurotics. Everybody's neurotic. Life is hard, but I haven't got time for people's personal troubles. You've got to watch Woollcott and Long and Parker—they keep trying to get double meanings into their stuff to embarrass me. Question everything. We damn near printed a news-break about a girl falling off the roof. That's feminine hygiene, somebody told me just in time. You probably never heard the expression in Ohio."

"In Ohio," I told him, "we say the mirror cracked from side to side."

"I don't want to hear about it," he said.

He nursed an editorial phobia about what he called the functional: "bathroom and bedroom stuff." Years later he deleted from a Janet Flanner "London Letter" a forthright explanation of the long nonliquid diet imposed upon the royal family and important dignitaries during the coronation of George VI. He was amused by the drawing of a water plug squirting a stream at a small astonished dog, with the caption "News," but he wouldn't print it. "So-and-so can't write a story without a man in it carrying a woman to a bed," he wailed. And again, "I'll never print another O'Hara story I don't understand. I want to know what his people are doing." He was depressed for weeks after the appearance of a full-page Arno depicting a man and a girl on a road in the moonlight, the man carrying the back seat of an automobile. "Why didn't somebody tell me what it meant?" he asked. Ross had insight, perception, and a unique kind of intuition, but they were matched by a dozen blind spots and strange areas of ignorance, surprising in a virile and observant reporter who had knocked about the world and lived two years in France. There were so many different Rosses, conflicting and contradictory, that the task of drawing him in words sometimes appears impossible, for the composite of all the Rosses should produce a single unmistakable entity: the most remarkable man I have ever known and the greatest editor. "If you get him down on paper," Wolcott Gibbs once warned me, "nobody will believe it."

I made deliberate mistakes and let things slide as the summer wore on, hoping to be demoted to rewriting "Talk of the Town," with time of my own in which to write "casuals." That was Ross's word for fiction and humorous pieces of all kinds. Like

"Profile" and "Reporter at Large" and "Notes and Comment," the word "casual" indicated Ross's determination to give the magazine an offhand, chatty, informal quality. Nothing was to be labored or studied, arty, literary, or intellectual. Formal short stories and other "formula stuff" were under the ban. Writers were to be played down; the accent was on content, not personalities. "All writers are writer-conscious," he said a thousand times.

One day he came to me with a letter from a men's furnishing store which complained that it wasn't getting fair treatment in the "As to Men" department. "What are you going to do about that?" he growled. I swept it off my desk onto the floor. "The hell with it," I said. Ross didn't pick it up, just stared at it dolefully. "That's direct action, anyway," he said. "Maybe that's the way to handle grousing. We can't please everybody." Thus he rationalized everything I did, steadfastly refusing to perceive that he was dealing with a writer who intended to write or to be thrown out. "Thurber has honesty," he told Andy White, "admits his mistakes, never passes the buck. Only editor with common sense I've ever had."

I finally told Ross, late in the summer, that I was losing weight, my grip, and possibly my mind, and had to have a rest. He had not realized I had never taken a day off, even Saturday or Sunday. "All right, Thurber," he said, "but I think you're wearing yourself down writing pieces. Take a couple of weeks, anyway. Levick can hold things down while you're gone. I *guess*."

It was, suitably enough, a dog that brought Ross and me together out of the artificiality and stuffiness of our strained and mistaken relationship. I went to Columbus on vacation and took a Scottie with me, and she disappeared out there. It took me two days to find her, with the help of newspaper ads and the police department. When I got back to the *New Yorker*, two days late, Ross called me into his office about seven o'clock, having avoided me all day. He was in one of his worst God-how-I-pity-me moods, a state of mind often made up of monumentally magnified trivialities. I was later to see this mood develop out of his exasperation with the way Niven Busch walked, or the way Ralph Ingersoll talked, or his feeling that "White is being silent about something and I don't know what it is." It could start because there weren't enough laughs in "Talk of the Town," or because he couldn't reach Arno on the phone, or because he was suddenly afflicted by the fear that nobody around the place could "find out the facts." (Once a nerve-racked editor yelled at him, "Why don't you get Westinghouse to build you a fact-finding machine?")

This day, however, the Ossa on the Pelion of his molehill miseries was the lost and found Jeannie. Thunder was on his forehead and lightning in his voice. "I understand you've overstayed your vacation to look for a dog," he growled. "Seems to me that was the act of a sis." (His vocabulary held some quaint and unexpected words and phrases out of the past. "They were spooning," he told me irritably about some couple years later, and, "I think she's stuck on him.") The word *sis*, which I had last heard about 1908, the era of *skidoo*, was the straw that shattered my patience. Even at sixty-four my temper is precarious, but at thirty-two it had a hair trigger.

The scene that followed was brief, loud, and incoherent. I told him what to do with his goddam magazine, that I was through, and that he couldn't call me a sis while sitting down, since it was a fighting word. I offered to fight him then and there, told him he had the heart of a cast-iron lawn editor, and suggested that he call in one of his friends to help him. Ross hated scenes, physical violence or the threat of it, temper and the unruly.

"Who would you suggest I call in?" he demanded, the thunder clearing from his brow.

"Alexander Woollcott!" I yelled, and he began laughing.

His was a wonderful, room-filling laugh when it came, and this was my first experience of it. It cooled the air like summer rain. An hour later we were having dinner together at Tony's after a couple of drinks, and that night was the beginning of our knowledge of each other underneath the office make-up, and of a lasting and deepening friendship. "I'm sorry, Thurber," he said. "I'm married to this magazine. It's all I think about. I knew a dog I liked once, a shepherd dog, when I was a boy. I don't like dogs as such, though, and I'll, by God, never run a department about dogs—or about baseball, or about lawyers." His eyes grew sad; then he gritted his teeth, always a sign that he was about to express some deep antipathy, or grievance, or regret. "I'm running a column about women's fashions," he moaned, "and I never thought I'd come to that." I told him the "On and Off the Avenue" department was sound, a word he always liked to hear, but used sparingly. It cheered him up.

It wasn't long after that fateful night that Ross banged into my office one afternoon. He paced around for a full minute without saying anything, jingling the coins in his pocket. "You've been writing," he said finally. "I don't know how in hell you found time to write. I admit I didn't want you to. I could hit a dozen writers from here with this ash tray. They're undependable, no system, no self-discipline. Dorothy Parker says you're a writer, and so does Baird Leonard." His voice rose to its level of high decision. "All right then, if you're a writer, write! Maybe you've got something to say." He gave one of his famous prolonged sighs, an agonized protesting acceptance of a fact he had been fighting.

From then on I was a completely different man from the one he had futilely struggled to make me. No longer did he tell White that I had common sense. I was a writer now, not a hand-holder of artists, but a man who needed guidance. Years later he wrote my wife a letter to which he appended this postscript: "Your husband's opinion on a practical matter of this sort would have no value." We never again discussed tearing down walls, the Central Desk, the problems of advertisers, or anything else in the realm of the practical. If a manuscript was lost, "Thurber lost it." Once he accused me of losing a typescript that later turned up in an old briefcase of his own. This little fact made no difference. "If it hadn't been there," he said, "Thurber would have lost it." As I become more and more "productive," another of his fondest words, he became more and more convinced of my helplessness. "Thurber hasn't the vaguest idea what goes on around here," he would say.

I became one of the trio about whom he fretted and fussed continually—the others were Andy White and Wolcott Gibbs. His admiration of good executive editors, except in the case of William Shawn, never carried with it the deep affection he had for productive writers. His warmth was genuine, but always carefully covered over by gruffness or snarl or a semblance of deep disapproval. Once, and only once, he took White and Gibbs and me to lunch at the Algonquin, with all the fret and fuss of a mother hen trying to get her chicks across a main thoroughfare. Later, back at the office, I heard him saying to someone on the phone, "I just came from lunch with three writers who couldn't have got back to the office alone."

Our illnesses, or moods, or periods of unproductivity were a constant source of worry to him. He visited me several times when I was in a hospital undergoing a series of eye operations in 1940 and 1941. On one of these visits, just before he left, he came over to the bed and snarled, "Goddam it, Thurber, I worry about you and England." England was at that time going through the German blitz. As my blindness increased, so did his concern. One noon he stopped at a table in the Algonquin lobby, where I was having a single cocktail with some friends before lunch. That afternoon he told White or Gibbs, "Thurber's over at the Algonquin lacing 'em in. He's the only *drinking* blind man I know."

He wouldn't go to the theater the night *The Male Animal* opened in January, 1940, but he wouldn't go to bed, either, until he had read the reviews, which fortunately were favorable.

Then he began telephoning around town until, at a quarter of two in the morning, he reached me at Bleeck's. I went to the phone. The editor of the *New Yorker* began every phone conversation by announcing "Ross," a monosyllable into which he was able to pack the sound and sign of all his worries and anxieties. His loud voice seemed to fill the receiver to overflowing. "Well, God bless you, Thurber," he said warmly, and then came the old familiar snarl: "Now, goddam it, maybe you can get something written for the magazine," and he hung up, but I can still hear him, over the years, loud and snarling, fond and comforting.

HERE AT THE NEW YORKER

Brendan Gill

1975

To me in my early weeks and months on the staff of *The New Yorker*, the most startling fact was the total absence of any camaraderie in the office. Among my family and friends, I was accustomed to a continuous manifestation of high spirits in the form of badinage, laughter, and intermittent bursts of song and whistling. At *The New Yorker*, I perceived that a show of high spirits was out of the question; it was not merely unwelcome but impermissible. The custom was to speak as little as possible, and then as dourly as possible. One never touched another person except by accident. Song was as strictly forbidden as whistling, which among reporters has always been thought to invite bad luck. I was willing to get along without whistling, but it was hard to get along without song; and to get along without conversation was surely impossible.

At the magazine, it was plain that *any* ordinary show of friendliness was thought to invite bad luck. No one invited me to pass the time of day with him. The editors and other writers on the staff appeared not to see me; against my will, I had become invisible to everyone except the elevator men. In those days, all four of our elevators were manually operated (now only one of them is, for Shawn's sake: he dislikes running any machine more dangerous than a typewriter), and the operators were, poor devils, the very dregs of the employment market, but oh, how grateful I was to them! They said "Hello," and "Have a good day," and "You too," and "Sure is," and so helped me to remain, though tenuously, a member of the human race.

Everyone I passed in the corridors of *The New Yorker* seemed to be feeling sick. Later, I learned that many of them *were* sick, with hangovers of varying degrees of acuteness. I was not a drinker in those days and so failed to recognize the many telltale signs of distress that have since become commonplaces to me—for example, the conviction that one can feel one's hair growing and that it hurts. In my innocence, I was misled into supposing that the entire staff must have contracted some obscure tribal contagion, for which there was no known medical cure. They glowered, they sulked, they passed one another in silence, or with an inarticulate snarl, and my only consolation in the presence of so much indurated misery was the discovery, made little by little, that none of it was directed at me personally; it was a universal expression of misanthropy and played no favorites. It turned out that another newcomer, E.J. Kahn, Jr., had been undergoing a somewhat similar initiation, but because he had begun on a lower level of buoyant good health than I, he was better adjusted to the grim sourness of the office air. For him that air was natural and even refreshing, and I found out why. Drinking and smoking, he played jazz all night with some friends in a flat off the Bowery, and one day he happened to describe his usual procedure on rising. "I get out of bed," he said, "and throw up and take a shower and shave and have breakfast..." "You throw up *every* morning?" I asked, in the bewilderment of a non-smoking, non-drinking, early-to-bed young man from Hartford. "Of course," Kahn said. "Doesn't everyone?"

As a newcomer of a slightly later period, John Bainbridge was as astonished as I by the coldness he encountered at the magazine. A Middle Westerner, brought up in the genial civilities of that part of the world, Bainbridge had always longed to write for *The New Yorker* and rub elbows with Ross, E.B. White, Wolcott Gibbs, and the other great men about whom he had read and heard. At last he found himself on the staff and with an office on the same floor as Gibbs. He knew Gibbs by sight, but had never spoken to him. Bainbridge was in the habit of getting to the office early, and so was Gibbs, on the days when he got there at all. On the morning of a day that happened to follow New Year's Day, Bainbridge stopped at the water-cooler for a drink. Gibbs came up and drew a couple of quick ones. Seizing this opportunity to make conversation, Bainbridge said, "Did you have a nice New Year's, Mr. Gibbs?"

"Fuck you," Gibbs said, tossed his paper cup into the basket, and walked back to his office.

Gibbs's rudeness was a function of his being extremely shy. Contrary to what many shy people like to think, shyness is not necessarily an attractive attribute. It is certainly not one that justifies bad manners; all the less so since there are cases of shyness as extreme as Gibbs's—I am thinking, of course, of

Shawn—that lead to the most solicitous good manners. Gibbs's rudeness was his way of keeping the world at a distance, out of fear, and this fear, especially in his youth, wore the mask of a continuous aloof scorn. Like any number of gifted and intelligent but ignorant young men, he affected to despise everything, thus guarding himself against unexpected entrapments by people more knowledgeable than he. Ingersoll recalls in his memoirs that no matter how interesting and perhaps even useful an observation someone in the office might offer, Gibbs would sneer, "Don't be banal!" He abandoned this childish device as he grew older and more confident of his powers and of the body of knowledge at his command, but he never outgrew the shyness and rudeness; they were intrinsic and therefore unalterable.

Gibbs's first principle in editing was to omit. It was a common practice with him to lop off the first two or three paragraphs of nearly any manuscript; he liked to say, "This will cut like butter," and it almost always did. When I first knew him, he was writing Notes and Comment for the first page of "Talk of the Town." He had succeeded White in this task, the Whites, at Andy's urging and with Katharine's reluctant consent, having retired to their farm in Maine; there White was playing countryman and writing monthly pieces for *Harper's*. (Mrs. White believed herself to be giving up the best job held by any woman in America when she followed her husband to Maine, and no doubt she was right. The retirement proved temporary, but Mrs. White was unable to regain her lofty place in the editorial hierarchy of the magazine.) As was to be expected, Gibbs felt that he would never be able to write Comment as good as White's, and as was also to be expected, it turned out that he did Comment brilliantly, if in a different fashion from his predecessor.

*   *   *

The New York World's Fair of 1939–40 was Ross's idea of a big event, and how thoroughly we covered it, with covers, drawings, Profiles, "Talk" pieces, and maps, in a continuous outpouring of celebratory particularities! The New York World's Fair of 1964–65 was such a bungle that it has tended to cast a shadow backward over its brilliant predecessor, but for those of us who all but lived on the fairgrounds during the long summer days and nights of 1939, it was indeed an incomparably happy time. We young reporters, with our passes and, therefore, with easy access to such sell-out exhibits as the General Motors Futurama, were much sought after. I scarcely dare glance at the thousand trifling episodes that jostle one another in my memory, pleading for mention: the newspaper cartoonist Denys Wortman arriving at the fair dressed and bewigged as George Washington and bearing an awesome resemblance to Lillian Hellman; Peter Arno having drinks at the French Pavilion with Brenda Frazier, most conspicuous of debutantes; the Cornelius Rathbornes hanging helpless in space, their parachute at the Parachute Jump having become entangled in its own shrouds; woebegone Admiral Byrd seated among a few equally woebegone Antarctic penguins at a concession he had opened in the so-called Amusement Area; nearby, and far more popular than the penguins (though less popular than a display of premature babies in shiny oxygen tanks), a hapless nudie show, sneaked into the fair under the sacred name of education. The girls were allowed to go bare-breasted because they were teaching us the customs of the ancient Amazon warriors and so, by extension, giving us a glimpse of that lost classic world so precious to our elders and betters. From time to time, one or another of the girls would lift a silvery papier-mâché spear and toss it listlessly at some enemy offstage; we would watch her rosy nipples rise and fall, and sigh with gratitude at having our minds so much improved.

It was nonsense, and much of it was charming nonsense; still, contemporary young people might well wonder how we young people of that day could have been so willing to be charmed on the very brink of the greatest and bloodiest war in history; did we not perceive the doom that was then plainly hanging over the world? The answer is that although we perceived it and tried to pay proper attention to it, it was often rendered unreal by a spontaneous sense of personal and national well-being. The world that stood on the brink of war was emerging from a prolonged depression and seemed also to stand on the brink of that mingling of peace and prosperity that the fair had been calculated, however meretriciously, to embody. Surely there *was* some exhilarating promise in the air, even as the leaves of the trees turned belly-up and the sky darkened. We were like a man dying of cancer, who, on a sunny morning, rejoicing to find himself still so intensely alive, begins to doubt the reality of his own pain. It was evident that something terrible might be about to happen in Europe, and most of the Americans I knew, though by no means most of the Americans throughout the country, assumed that if England were to be drawn into a war, the United States would be sure to follow. In the summer of 1939, we were intermittently aware that we faced difficulties, but the degree of the desperation we might eventually be confronted with was only beginning to be imagined; we were far from taking an accurate measure of our future, though there were plenty of signs of imminent disaster even at the fair. In a few months, for example, the lovely Polish Pavilion would stand as a silent witness to the fact that the country of Poland no longer existed, having been overrun by its two adjacent tyrannies.

*　　　*　　　*

Ross liked to be thought an exemplar of common sense, but all the evidence of his life is to the contrary. He was a reckless and improvident gambler who preached prudence. Very early in my career on the magazine, he gave me a lecture about money, prompted no doubt by my being in want of it. The lecture began on the expected didactic note—"Gill, you don't know a goddam thing about money"—and proceeded to tick off the various means by which I might acquire a mastery of it. I was to learn to draw up an annual budget of household expenses; I was to set aside certain sums for taxes; I was also to set aside a sum for medical emergencies; and so on and so on. It was an impressive program as he sketched it out for me, and I supposed that it was firmly grounded on his own experience. Not at all—it was a fantasy of how things ought to be with him, a goal that Ross, twenty-two years my senior, was even farther from reaching than I.

Though I didn't know it at the time, my lecturer was a man whose financial affairs were in a state of advanced and continuous disarray.

*   *   *

Ross's success as an editor had certain elements of the fortuitous about it; for example, it was a lucky accident that his unappeasable appetite for facts coincided with a similar appetite on the part of the public. During the Second World War, the volume of information dispensed by what were beginning to be called the media—newspapers, magazines, books, movies, and, a few years later, TV—multiplied to an extent that nobody has been able so far to make an accurate reckoning of. It was a change so great that even the remotest illiterate hermit could not fail to be altered by it; for the first time, with astonishment and sometimes with dismay, one sensed that a Niagara of news was flooding unstoppably in upon us, not by the week and day but by the hour and minute. People sat by their radios and listened with satisfaction to news bulletins, infinitesimally rewritten as they were repeated, about victories and defeats throughout the world, and then went out and bought newspapers and magazines and gorged themselves on the same information for a tenth or twentieth time.

The Second World War was the most thoroughly reported event in history; it implicated hundreds of millions of people in both hemispheres, and the services of literally millions of reporters, editors, broadcasters, cameramen, printers, and distributors were required to keep abreast of it. The news magazines flourished as never before, and so did *The New Yorker*. Far from destroying the magazine, as Ross had noisily predicted, the war helped bring about its transformation into something far more complex and interesting than it had ever been. The transformation was bound to have taken place—impossible to imagine Shawn, intellectually so much more ambitious than Ross, remaining content with the magazine as he had first known it—but the war hastened the event. From a publication deliberately parochial in range and tone, consisting of a few funny drawings, some funny short pieces, an occasional serious short story, and the Profiles, limited enough in both length and intentions to deserve to be called profiles, it became a publication in which it was natural to look for the highest quality of reporting in almost any field of activity, from almost anywhere on earth.

Ross protested continually that he didn't want to see his magazine turned into a goddam *Saturday Evening Post*; as if to spite him (and Ross was a man who had no difficulty discovering in success signs of a conspiracy bent upon destroying him), the magazine expanded into a national institution and then an international one. Even its suspicious founder was impressed to learn during the war that it was being read, and thought highly of, at Number 10 Downing Street; he could scarcely object to having Churchill among his readers, and, for that matter, the King as well. Washington came to see that the magazine, far from being a luxury for wealthy civilians, was an indispensable part of the war effort; a small-size, twenty-four-page "pony" edition, printed by photo-offset and containing no advertising, was made available to the armed forces, as *Time* and *Newsweek* were. By the end of the war, the pony edition had a larger circulation than its parent. By then, too, our readers were accustomed to datelines more exotic than the two old foreign standbys, London and Paris. From the beginning, the magazine's notion of its geographical boundaries had implicitly embraced these cities, as places that New Yorkers frequented and felt happy in. With the passing of years, reluctantly, room was found inside our boundaries for Washington, a city that kept gaining in importance without ever acquiring a style. Until recently, no New Yorker would think of simply visiting Washington; one went there because one had some substantial professional reason for doing so and not otherwise.

The war broadened our physical horizons; it also taught us as writers how to be harder on ourselves, and so broadened our literary horizons. The extent of our newly acquired excellence can be sampled in *The New Yorker Book of War Pieces*, which came out in 1949 and which many critics and historians have called the finest collection of war-reporting ever published in a single volume. Among the contributors were A.J. Liebling, Mollie Panter-Downes, E.J. Kahn, Jr., Rebecca West, St. Clair McKelway, Janet Flanner, Mark Murphy, Walter Bernstein, John Hersey, Daniel Lang, S.N. Behrman, Philip Hamburger, and Joel Sayre.

*   *   *

Shawn's attitude toward writing, and by extension toward writers as a class, has always been that of reverence. There have been circumstances—never involving oneself, of course, but involving some of one's fellow-writers—in which it has been hard to credit this attitude, but the evidence is that it is genuine. Certainly it has survived decades of work on manuscripts of remarkable ineptitude (in the old days more than now, there were contributors to the magazine who delivered what Hamburger used to call great bundles of wet wash), and if Shawn were only pretending to be reverent, his mask would have slipped at least once or twice during all those years.

Shawn's method in dealing with a writer is to convey such a high regard for a given piece of work that once it has been put in type and the moment comes for the editor to challenge certain phrases and seek certain necessary changes, the writer is pretty well convinced that the corrections will cost Shawn as much pain as they do him—indeed, that the corrections are being made, at no matter what expense of spirit, only in order to bring a masterpiece from near-perfection to perfection. No author can fail to recognize the attractive logic of this proposition. The hazard in such cases is not, as it was with Ross, that one will pick a quarrel but that one will give way too quickly and easily. Shawn's delicacy is a negative brute force that gets greater results than Ross's positive one. Because most writers would do anything rather than hurt Shawn's feelings, they begin to babble premature agreements; they hear themselves apologizing for the gaucherie of a phrase that had seemed, up to a few minutes before, a stroke of genius.

The following passage is an exaggeration of Shawn's oral editing technique. It is an attempt to indicate with words what Shawn indicates with silences, hesitations, sidelong glances of his very blue eyes, tentative baton-like strokes in air of his dark-green Venus drawing pencil. Questioning a comma, he will shake his head and say in his soft voice that he realizes perfectly well what a lot of time and thought have gone into the comma and that in the ordinary course of events he would be the first to say that the comma was precisely the form of punctuation that he would have been most happy to encounter at that very place in sentence, but isn't there the possibility—oh, only the remotest one, to be sure, and yet perhaps worth considering for a moment in the light of the care already bestowed on the construction—that the sentence could be made to read infinitesimally more clearly if, say, instead of a comma a semicolon were to be inserted at just that point? And the author, touched by Shawn's sympathy, aghast with admiration for the skill of his circumlocutions, and determined at all costs to prevent Shawn from suffering the humiliation of having his proposed semicolon rejected, throws up his hands and exclaims, "Much clearer your way!"

THE OTHER PARIS

Luc Sante

2015

PARIS was a fortified city from at least around 1200, when Philippe-Auguste's wall was erected (there may well have been earlier, unrecorded walls), until 1670, when Louis XIV, in the fullness of his royal self-confidence, decided to tear down the fortifications and lay boulevards in their place. The word itself reflects this step, since *boulevard* derives from the same root as *bulwark*. Before a century had elapsed, however, the open-city plan had revealed its weakness. The lack of a wall made it difficult to enforce collection of the *octroi*, the much-hated tax levied upon goods entering the city for immediate local consumption, wine in particular. To that end the Farmers-General (who were not farmers but rich and powerful tax collectors), beginning in 1785, built a new wall that had no military purpose, was only about ten feet high, and was meant to be breached by sixty tollgates. Only fifty-four were built, because the architect was the visionary Claude-Nicolas Ledoux, whose vivid if rather supererogatory *propylaea* were ridiculously expensive to build.*

---

* Only four survived the revolution and still exist: the rotundas of La Villette and Monceau and the gates of the Trône, on Avenue de Vincennes, and d'Enfer, on Place Denfert-Rochereau

The wall did not prevent smugglers from tunneling beneath it, nor did the decree stipulating that nothing could be built within three hundred feet of the wall on the far side preclude a lively, free-flowing commerce flourishing in *guinguettes* (a name given to slap-up wine-shops, generally outdoor and rusticated) as close to the boundary as was practicable. The *octroi*, which lasted until 1943, during the Occupation, and was formally repealed after the war, created a semipermanent black market economy, with housewives purchasing their soap and salt and flour in the *banlieue*, where such things were considerably cheaper, and sneaking through the contraband dissimulated in heaps of rags and the like. As with so many laws of its type, the *octroi* pushed masses of otherwise blameless citizens to petty criminality, and arguably did much to foster and perpetuate the famously defiant attitude of the Parisian proletariat with regard to the constabulary and its servants.

The tollgates, known as *barrières*, remained functioning long after many of their Ledoux structures had been demolished by the revolutionary

The *barrière* Montmartre, future site of Place Pigalle, in 1855

"On more than one occasion, as he left the masked ball, M. de ** was arrested by the guards." Illustration by J.J. de Grandville, from *Scènes de la vie publique et privée des animaux*, 1842

masses. On the Left Bank, where construction south of the Latin Quarter and Saint-Germain was still haphazard at best in the early nineteenth century, the *barrières* were incongruous outposts of officialdom in the depopulated and anarchic wilderness. Victor Hugo, writing of the 1820s, noted that

> Forty years ago, the solitary walker who ventured into the wasteland of the Salpêtrière and descended the boulevard toward the Barrière d'Italic came upon places where you could say that Paris had disappeared. It wasn't empty, since there were passersby; it wasn't the countryside, since there were houses and streets; it wasn't a city, since the streets had ruts where grass grew, as on rural turnpikes; it wasn't a village, since the houses were too tall. What was it, then? It was an inhabited location where there was nobody, it was a deserted place where there was somebody; it was a boulevard in the big city, a street in Paris, that was wilder at night than a forest, gloomier in daylight than a graveyard.

The southern *barrières* became a byword for menace, obscurity, obscure menace. The term *rôdeur de barrières* (*rôdeur* means "prowler") came to designate a sort of urban highwayman, leaping out from behind the vegetation to accost passersby and relieve them of their negotiable goods, and it remained in the language as a generalized epithet long after urbanization had rendered this sort of banditry impracticable. Various sensational murders occurred around the *barrières*, with psychopaths taking advantage of the absence of potential eyewitnesses to kill by chance and at random. In the Parisian imaginary, place-names such as Glacière, Grenelle, Montsouris, even Montparnasse, and perhaps especially the Tombe-Issoire (an ancient if murky sepulchral title, now attached to a long, nondescript street in the Fourteenth, coincidentally near the Catacombs) became a sort of *in partibus infidelium*, a vague landscape of gnarled trees and blasted heaths, populated by beings whose heads grew below their shoulders.

Furthermore, in 1832 the guillotine was moved from its longtime emplacement on Place de Grève (now Place de l'Hôtel-de-Ville) to the *barrière* Saint-Jacques (now the site of the Saint-Jacques Métro station). It was a convenient location, since prisoners condemned to death were then kept at Bicêtre, just a few miles southeast. Hugo complained of it as an "expedient of philanthropists for hiding the scaffold, a shabby and shameful Place de Grève for a society of shopkeepers and burghers who shrink before the death penalty, daring neither to abolish it magnanimously nor to impose it authoritatively." In any event, in 1836 the city built the panoptic prison of La Roquette, near the Bastille, and both death row inmates and their instrument of termination were shifted

Sheet music for Berthe Sylva's "Rôdeuse de barrière," 1931

The guillotine in an early nine-teenth-century woodcut

there. Despite its brief term—only forty-one persons met their end there—the emplacement at Saint-Jacques nevertheless left a significant dent in collective memory as the execution site of the romantic murderer Pierre-François Lacenaire and the would-be regicides Louis Alibaud and Giuseppe Fieschi, not to mention the fictional Le Chourineur, antihero of Eugène Sue's *Mysteries of Paris* (1842–43).

But the association of exurban wasteland with public executions was already cemented in the Parisian mind, as from the thirteenth to the seventeenth centuries the municipal gibbet had been located at Montfaucon, reasonably distant from the city then, now a bit west of the Buttes-Chaumont, roughly on the site of the Bolivar Métro stop. Hanging was the standard method of disposal at the time, and the edifice at Montfaucon, which was somewhere between two and four stories high, could accommodate as many as fifty gallows birds at once. It was situated on a rocky mount just off a road, assuring that no one in the surrounding region could miss the sight. Although the last executions were held there around 1629, the impression the place left on the Parisian mind was sufficiently indelible that, for example, Serge Gainsbourg could casually allude to it in his song "Laissez-moi tranquille" (1959).

Before the gibbet even existed, and long after it ceased to be, Montfaucon was the site of an immense garbage dump, which persisted after the city's six other dumps were closed down by order of the king in the early seventeenth century. The site incorporated a knackers' yard and a manufacturer of *poudrette*, a manure that combined excrement with charcoal and gypsum—the gypsum quarries were conveniently adjacent. Animal bones were burned and the ash was used in building walls; the hides were picked up by tanners. Soon, chemical plants were established to make use of other by-products, and their runoff flowed in the open a quarter mile or more toward the nearest sewer. Some twenty-five hundred cubic feet of human excrement were carted there every day; at any given time the carcasses of twelve thousand horses and more than twenty-five thousand dogs, cats, goats, and donkeys were left to rot. These along with miscellaneous trash covered the ground in heaps up to five feet high, and of course there were rats, "in such numbers that if the carcasses of quartered horses were left in some corner on a given day, by the following they would be completely stripped; the rats mined the nearby hills and brought down entire houses." The ecosystem could be impressive: fish bait was produced by allowing carcasses to draw maggots; then the maggots drew flies; the flies drew large swarms of swallows; and these in turn drew hunters. In summer, the stink of Montfaucon could sometimes travel as far as the Tuileries.

The gibbet at Montfaucon, a nineteenth-century representation of the fifteenth century

"The border of the *ville lumière*." An *octroi* gate, 1930s

Complaints were lodged by the town councils of Belleville, Pantin, and Romainville, which depended on tourists from the city coming out to enjoy their fresh country air. Although a new dump farther away from the city was mandated in 1817, Montfaucon wasn't finally closed until 1849.

By then the city had moved much closer. In 1841, Louis-Philippe decreed that a new military wall should be built, and engaged Adolphe Thiers (1797–1877) to carry out the work. The fortification was to be a belt some twenty-four and a half miles long, with fifty-two gates, which would be closed at night with iron grilles. Inside the wall was a 500-foot-wide buffer that in 1860 became the *boulevards des maréchaux*. On the outside, the wall projected a *glacis*, an artificial 100-foot-wide slope, and beyond that lay another buffer, an 820-foot-wide ribbon of terrain that was designated a *zone non aedificandi*, "not to be built upon." The wall's circumference included a number of villages that would not be incorporated until 1860, and also "amputated" parts of the villages of Clignancourt, Montmartre, La Chapelle, Saint-Denis, and Saint-Ouen. Its dimensions, which more than doubled the previous size of Paris, established the city limits as they still stand—the present Périphérique highway follows the inner border of "the Zone"—although initially the wall simply imposed itself willy-nilly across blameless farmland and assorted wastes, its circumference determined by calculating the safest range to shield the city proper from artillery fire. The Prussian army proved otherwise in 1871, and demolition of the wall began to be discussed a decade later, although the process wasn't begun until 1919 and took another decade to achieve completion.

In the meantime the wall and its nimbus took on a life of their own. A lithograph by Daumier shows a peasant couple, standing outside their tiny shack, surrounded by undulating emptiness. In the far distance lies a dome: Panthéon, Val-de-Grâce, or Invalides. They look pleased with themselves. "And to think we're Parisians now," the woman says. Many improbable scenes and landscapes were now folded into the urban sphere: beet fields and vineyards, isolated *folies* and hunting lodges from the eighteenth century, railroad marshaling yards, rural villages that would not have looked out of place in Normandy or Champagne, wayside crucifixes, gypsy camps, scores of *guinguettes* that had thrived outside the tax wall just months earlier, overgrown cemeteries, the huts of rabbit trappers and beekeepers, and numerous stretches of unused land in various conditions of arability and desolation, of uncertain ownership.

"And to think we're Parisians now." Illustration by Honoré Daumier, from *Le Charivari*, 1852

An old hunting lodge on Boulevard d'Italie, circa 1900

Urbanization proceeded at different rates at different points of the compass. At first there were recognizable streets going right up to the wall only in a few places, in Montmartre and the Batignolles to the north and around the Point du Jour in the southwest, for example. Soon enough, many of the gates sprouted businesses catering to truckers, primarily wineshops, cafés, and brothels, and hodge-podge neighborhoods of tiny houses made of plaster, wood, brick, tin, clinker (residue from coal combustion), or stacked sardine cans filled with dirt, or any combination thereof. These coexisted with the parts of Belleville and the Batignolles that were being built up conventionally, using material salvaged from Haussmann's demolitions in the center, and with clusters of the horse-drawn trailers used by the Roma and other travelers who migrated according to the seasons, and with wilder stretches inhabited by the sorts of people who preferred it not be known they were inhabited. There were few paved streets, no streetlights, no sewers or, for that matter, plumbing, and water had to be fetched from pumps or streams sometimes a considerable distance away. As construction and land speculation within the wall proceeded apace, the more impoverished or legally compromised or simply contrary of those who lived on its interior fringes began gradually to move out to the Zone, which was not to be built upon but did not remain so for long.

Initially the Zone was a sort of tundra, empty grassland with the occasional lone tree, crossed by trails like deer runs, two-story buildings visible here and there on the far horizon. It was documented more by painters than by photographers. Vincent van Gogh's *The Outskirts of Paris* (1887) shows a vast plain with a windmill and a few barnlike structures in the distance, in the foreground the confluence of two muddy paths, a tumbledown fence, and, incongruously, a cast-iron lamppost. Jean-François

Raffaëlli made many paintings of the Zone as desolate farmland, featuring maybe a spavined horse and a few skinny chickens tended by an old woman in black, some unpainted hovels in the middle distance with wash lines strung between them, factory chimneys miles away, the scene perhaps interrupted by a man running past with a loaf of bread under each arm, looking back over his shoulder. Where the Zone was breached by the important roads bound for Italy or Flanders or the sea, there might be newspaper kiosks and perhaps an outdoor urinal plastered with advertising, on a tended surface with no neighboring structures.

The Outskirts of Paris. Painting by Vincent Van Gogh, 1887

Faubourgs parisiens. Painting by Jean-François Raffaëlli, 1880s

The ragpickers were the first to colonize the space. Ragpickers had been an integral part of city life since its unrecorded dawn, but they had never had an easy time of it. Besides the financial precariousness of the trade, there were successive waves of persecution by the authorities. In 1635 the sale of old clothes was prohibited in Paris, forcing ragpickers to work clandestinely or outside the walls. In 1701 heavy fines and corporal punishment were imposed

A ragpicker, 1840s

63

on ragpickers found on the streets at night. In 1828 the city began licensing ragpickers, but in 1832 it attempted to institute municipal trash collection, impinging on their trade. In 1835 a new police prefect allowed ragpickers a permanent market within Les Halles, but a few years later the order was rescinded, and by 1860 they were actively being chased from even their traditional corners. The final blow came in 1884, when Eugène Poubelle, prefect of the Seine, decreed that all houses be supplied with lidded containers for refuse, their contents to be collected by municipal authority; *poubelle* soon became, and remains, the word for "garbage can." Fifty thousand ragpickers demonstrated, but to no avail.

There was a hierarchical caste system among the ragpickers, who might be hereditary members of the professional tribe, or bohemians, or miserable, homeless alcoholics who slept under bridges or in abandoned houses and drank *casse-poitrine* (chest breaker) or *tord-boyaux* (gut twister). The highest-ranked of them, called *placiers*, drove horse carts and were often allowed to skim the trash in houses before it was put out on the street. They generally earned about ten times as much as the ordinary pickers, who collected not only rags and paper but also dead animals. The rags and paper were used for making paper and cardboard; bones went toward the manufacture of charcoal and blacking; broken glass was remelted; animal hides were tanned and the hair bought by wig makers. The *placiers*, however, might find valuable discards, which they would bring directly to market, either at the biannual fairs (the ham fair at Place de la République or the scrap iron fair at the Bastille) or else at the street market on Place d'Aligre or at the ancient Marché des

Patriarches on Rue Mouffetard, which
according to legend was sanctioned by
the church after beggars saved the life
of the bishop of Paris around 1350,
in return being given the right to sell
"untraceable goods and objects."

A flea market, circa 1910

Although these markets endured
for another century (and the one on
Place d'Aligre in some fashion still
exists), around 1860, ragpickers began
moving out to the Zone, where they
were generally free from police harass-
ment and enjoyed unlimited space to
spread their wares. At first the pickers
set down their bundles directly off the

Vendors awaiting the opening
of the Marché du Temple, circa
1910

path through the Plaine de Malassis,
where strollers would come by and
bargain. Professionals began organ-
izing markets in the 1880s, charging
rent to newcomers, who built shacks
from available litter, such as old wagons.
Saint-Ouen, bordering on the Zone to
the north, had been renowned for its
delicate white wine, which could not be
exported, so that it became a resort of
wineshops and *guinguettes*, but after phyl-
loxera (plant lice) destroyed the vines in
1900 the space was entirely given over
to what was just then beginning to be

Police Magazine, July 1935

called the "flea market." Soon it grew so large it merged with the neighboring market at Clignancourt, while others opened at Les Lilas and Quatre-Chemins (La Villette) in the northeast, Montreuil in the east, Bicêtre in the southeast, and Vanves in the south.

Of these, Montreuil, Vanves, and Saint-Ouen/Clignancourt still exist, the latter grown enormous. Over time the bourgeoisie came in search of antiques; painters such as the young Picasso bought old canvases they could scrape clean and reuse; Apollinaire and later the Surrealists sought peculiar and poetic objects; revivals of bygone styles were initiated through flea market finds. But the inventory of a vendor in the 1890s suggests a more typical display: two fragments of Turkish carpet, some bracelets made of hair, a lot of watches and chains in need of repair, three portraits of Napoléon, a compass, a tobacco grater, a shell box ornamented with a picture of Louis XVI inspecting a pot of lilies, a bust of *L'Intransigeant* editor Henri Rochefort, a chromo based on a painting by Édouard Detaille, and two meerschaum pipes, heavily colored and garnished with "immodest" nymphs.

Meanwhile, the Zone was still, as in Aristide Bruant's song "À Saint-Ouen" (1908), a field "where the harvest was of broken bottles and shards of china." The titular heroine of Edmond and Jules de Goncourt's 1865 novel *Germinie Lacerteux* takes a trip outside the walls, along "little gray trampled paths" through grass "frizzled and yellowed," across the railroad bridge, where she shivers at the "evil ragpickers' encampment and the stonemasons quarter below Clignancourt," where the houses are built of stolen construction materials, "sweating the horrors they concealed." She feels they hold "all the crimes of the night." But she is able to relax on the mound of the fortifications themselves, since there are children, and a brass ring game, and cafés and wineshops and fry joints, and a shooting gallery, and flags. Sixty years later the tireless flâneur André Warnod went to Montreuil on a Sunday, where

> surrounded by an attentive audience, a blindfolded man predicts the future. Peddlers hawk their junk, probably the same trash travelers try to bribe Africans with—but they, too, are doing a roaring business ... Behind canvas banners depicting grand tragic hunt scenes, for five sous you can see a live eagle, king of the beasts, poor fallen monarch who has a terribly hard time fitting his beak and his clipped wings into a horrible little cage.

He drinks "rude" red wine at the *guinguette* Aux Petits Agneaux, which is painted red like the wine. Wine-red or blood-red buildings keep recurring in accounts and reminiscences of the Zone. In Zola's *L'assommoir* the

Sheet music for Damia's "La guinguette a fermé ses volets," 1935

miserable hotel where we meet Gervaise and Lantier, a two-story hovel next to the Poissonnière gate, is painted "wine-dregs red."

On the private side the Zone had many faces, most of them hidden. It was a community of squatters, after all, who never knew when some political decision might result in their being rousted. And then there were those who preferred to remain anonymous anyway, because of bank robberies or incendiary leaflets or incendiary devices or religious or sexual persuasion or embezzlement or morals charges or skin disease. You had to know your way around. Blaise Cendrars took Fernard Léger to a gypsy camp in 1924:

> I took a path that zigzagged between the tarps, the farmyards, the henhouses, the little gardens, the vacant lots of the *zoniers*, enclosed in walls topped with broken bottles, delimited with barbed-wire fences and old railroad crossing gates, filled with furious dogs with nail-studded collars, their chains running along a strung wire that allowed them to go crazy from one end of their bare hutch to the other, leaping, barking, drooling with rage, among the empty, dented, crumbling tin cans, the stoved-in barrels, the jagged bits of sheet metal, the bed springs poking up from the slag, broken china and pottery, split soup cans, piles of obsolete household appliances, cannibalized vehicles, disemboweled trash bags, all surrounded by spruces, by scant tufts of lilacs, or else dominated like a Golgotha by the skeleton of a tree, a stunted elder, a tortured acacia, a diseased runt of a linden tree, the stump of its branch capped by a chamber pot, its pollarded top crowned by an old tire.

All sorts of people hunkered down in the Zone, which could resemble the streets of the old Cité spread flat across a gnarled ring of dead ground, and forecast the bidonvilles and favelas and refugee camps of a later era. By the time it was fully incorporated into the Parisian imaginary around 1900, however, the "Zone" evoked in potboilers and the popular press had a radius that extended back into the city itself, annexing big chunks of Belleville and Montmartre and the nebulous neighborhoods in the far south. It became a catchall slum where everything sensational and sleazy and prurient could be relegated. The Zone was frequently cited as the home of the criminals who were called *apaches* at the beginning of the twentieth century, and is nostalgically evoked in Jacques Becker's 1952 film *Casque d'Or*, the romantic apotheosis of fin-de-siècle criminality—although there were *apaches* all over the city, and the actual story behind the movie occurred in Belleville, around the Bastille, near Les Halles, and in the southern suburb of Alfortville. The mature prostitutes photographed by Eugène Atget in the 1920s standing in front of their doorways

Gypsy wagons and bombed-out houses in the Zone, 1920s

A murder in the Zone, 1930s

are often described as denizens of the Zone, although they lived and worked in Fort-Monjol, a flesh market on a street that no longer exists southwest of the Buttes-Chaumont, a considerable distance from the wall. But the Zone, besides the shadowy menace implicit in its very name, was indisputably a convenient place for people to go to ground when they were wanted by the cops, and the fortifications, with their elevation and unobstructed views, presented an ideal neutral spot for knife fights.

All this is exploited with mythmaking verve in Francis Carco's 1919 novel *L'équipe*, subtitled *Roman des fortifs*. The story, nearly generic now, was less so a century ago: a gang leader is released from prison only to find that his gang has been taken over by a rival; a protracted struggle between the two men ensues. The geography is as stunted as it would have been in the minds of the characters' prototypes: the world is confined to Belleville, the fortifications, the Zone, and a few miles of outlying suburbs. The men on the street are

> fugitive personalities whose eyes lit up and went out rapidly. In that sector where the plaster shanties, isolated among vacant lots, gave an oblique appearance to everything, they added to that impression … The green shutters—a washed-out green—alternated with little shacks of a sickly yellow, their walls carved up with graffiti, and with the shuttered fronts of unfinished new houses, and when night fell the collection of things incomplete or already dead gave off a feeling of emptiness and weighty unease … The flat roofs of banal houses cut a silhouette against the sky that was only occasionally relieved by small chimneys that looked like still-smoking cigarette butts someone had glued there.

Even Carco's unsentimental camera eye could not dislodge the romance of the fortifications. After the wall was demolished in the 1920s its shadow haunted the city for decades. Until the construction of the Périphérique (1958–73), its site, according to Jean-Paul Clébert, was "a filthy ribbon of grass and piles of dirt, but where there remains under the big sky a restful view of loamy hillocks where laughing, grimy kids play all week long and of small, trampled footpaths like those worn down by animals headed to the watering hole." Its fame endured in memoirs and old postcards and in Georges Lacombe's 1928 documentary *La Zone*, in which you can see Toulouse-Lautrec's favorite model, La Goulue, a denizen of the place in her old age, along with a variety of other characters, among them a formidable woman called *mère aux chiens*, "mother of dogs." Its final monument, though, was Fréhel's 1938 song "La chanson des fortifs," the deep-dish sentimentality of which is balanced by the resolute strength of her delivery. All the childhood heroes of the Zone have been translated to other existences:

"Mother of dogs" in the Zone, 1920s

Music on the fortifications, Saint-Ouen, circa 1910

P'tit Louis, the strongman, now owns a garage; Julot is being measured for an endowed chair; and Nini married somebody and acquired a château. The old embankment is now covered by six-story apartment houses with elevators and central heating. "Gone are the fortifications / and the little saloons by the gates. / Goodbye to the scenery of all the songs / the pretty songs of long ago."

Because while the Zone was a netherworld, a gray area, a borderland teeming with the sorts of shadowy activities that thrive on margins, it also at the same time represented a door to nature. Not everyone was comfortable in the heavily regulated parks; even the relative vastness of the Bois de Vincennes might have felt too constricted to people from the wrong part of town. In the Zone you could own the outdoors. You didn't risk being run down by the carriages of the bon ton, weren't subject to constant surveillance by the constabulary. You could drink and dance and smoke and swear while surrounded by garlands of flowers and Japanese lanterns under the trees. People could gather escargots in the trenches of the fortifications and herbs on its mounds, and after the wall came down parts of its site were occupied for decades by a patchwork of tiny garden plots worked by slum dwellers who might have to walk considerable distances to get to them. And then beyond the Zone was the *banlieue*.

Before the twentieth century the *banlieue* was primarily farmland punctuated by villages. Its waterways (the Seine, the Marne, the Oise) attracted boaters and day-trippers, familiar to us with their striped jerseys and straw hats in a long continuum that stretches from Manet's rowers at Argenteuil (1874) to Seurat's bathers at Asnières (1883–84) and loungers on the island of

La Grande Jatte (1884–86) to Jean Renoir's wedding party in *Boudu Saved from Drowning* (1932) to Cartier-Bresson's picnickers on the banks of the Marne (1936) and Renoir's holidaymakers in *Partie de campagne* (also 1936). There were *guinguettes* everywhere, from the classically minimal shack with a few tables under the trees to more elaborate installations with full restaurant service that might also include seesaws, swings, courts for *boules*, pedal-driven boats for hire, polished dance floors with bandstands, and even fairground rides. In 1848, in the southern suburb of Plessis-Piquet, an enthusiast of Johann David Wyss's *Swiss Family Robinson* (1812) was inspired to build a *guinguette* in the form of an elaborate tree house. Competitors erected their own tree house bistros, and before long the village's popularity as a Sunday destination was such that in 1909 it was officially renamed Plessis-Robinson. Although those establishments are long gone, some that are nearly as old survive today, such as Chez Gégène, on the Marne in Joinville-le-Pont, which dates back to somewhere in the pre-1914 mists and was repeatedly

A pleasure boat dock in Nogent-sur-Seine, circa 1910

Le Vrai Arbre, the first café in the trees, in Robinson, circa 1910

photographed by Robert Doisneau in the 1940s and '50s; it looks much the same as it ever did.

The permanent population of the *banlieue* was all the while steadily rising, with much of the influx coming from the city. Some went out to Pantin or Aubervilliers or Malakoff to buy their *octroi*-free staples and wound up staying. Ex-convicts were often declared *interdit de séjour* (forbidden to enter the capital) and while some became vagabonds, others chose to settle on the fringes. People with just a little bit of money built *bicoques* (shanties) of wood or plaster or concrete blocks, with names such as Malgré Tout, Ça Me Suffit, Mon Bonheur,* that served as summer retreats and represented the dream of retirement. Now and again some member of the Parisian minor bourgeoisie would round up sufficient cash to indulge a long-standing baronial fantasy and build himself a crenellated castle in the middle of nowhere.† The suburban experience manifested itself embryonically, first in the form of aspirational villas and then, after the First World War, as patchy developments of cheaply built *pavilions* aligned in neat rows, much like the pre-Levittown tract home enterprises in the United States.

In the unregulated *banlieue* these coexisted with muddy fields, gasworks, marshaling yards, stockyards, warehouses,

---

* "Despite Everything," "Enough for Me," "My Happiness."
† An early model was Alexandre Dumas père's Château de Monte-Cristo in Le Port-Marly, north of Versailles, a lavish Renaissance-style palace with Moorish touches, with an adjacent studio in the form of a miniature Gothic castle, the whole surrounded by English gardens with follies, grottoes, and waterworks. Dumas, flush with success, initiated construction in 1844, celebrated its completion in 1847 with a banquet for six hundred, but then, debt-ridden, was forced to sell in 1848. It still stands.

slaughterhouses, military depots, abandoned factories, working factories, acres of rubble, illegal dumps, soccer pitches, convents, orphanages, hospitals where patients stood by the gates to sell their medications, and old-age homes where the inmates waited outside to sell their tobacco allowances. And everywhere there were bars, of every description, some of them corner establishments made of brick, intended to anchor a street of shops that may or may not eventually have been built; some of them plywood shacks with tin roofs although minus the rustic amenities of a *guinguette*, kept afloat by a strictly marginal clientele who inhabited a notional extension of the Zone. And through the postwar years the area saw the emergence of bidonvilles— favelas, that is: whole communities built of scrap and inhabited primarily by immigrants from North Africa, which could vary dramatically in tone. There were reasonably stable hamlets where families predominated and people took pride in their dwellings, of the sort that Didier Daeninckx describes in his novel *Meurtres pour mémoire*, set in 1961:

The wall and the village of Saint-Ouen, circa 1910

She walked toward the water company buildings, where the first inhabitants of the bidonville had made their homes. The company for some obscure reason had let the land go to waste, in the process abandoning four rudimentary structures, big rectangular redbrick boxes. A few families had settled there, and had expanded their dwellings by building upper stories from boards and sheet metal. Over the course of months and years other families had joined them, and today the four structures formed the core and center of an agglomeration of shacks where five thousand people lived.

At the other extreme were encampments, essentially hobo jungles, congeries of single men where violence was perpetually imminent and—unsurprisingly, as their shacks were covered with tarpaper, and as kerosene was the source of both heat and light—fires could erase the whole patch at any time.

Meanwhile, the city of Paris had been attempting to address the problem of housing for the poor since at least the 1840s, and in 1894 the Siegfried Law, which stipulated financing and tax relief for such constructions, gave the impulse a practical footing. Not much was done until after World War I, however, when the housing problem began to reach crisis proportions, and the first proposals fell into two categories: garden cities, an idea borrowed from the British, and HBMs, or *habitations à bon marché*, or "cheap housing." These began to be built in 1928, two hundred thousand low-cost units in addition to eighty thousand medium-range, generally squat six-story orange-brick buildings, the first ones going up on the site of the former wall. The poet Jean Follain noted, with a touch of superciliousness, that "now an entire population aspires to a light-filled apartment.

The fairground wrestler, worn down, covered with hieroglyphic tattoos, wants nothing more in this fallen world than walls painted in soft colors." But it didn't take very long for these to decline, or at least for their mass-produced institutional lack of distinction to sap the spirits of their inmates. By 1933 the proletarian writer Eugène Dabit could describe "a circle of buildings, in the middle a courtyard with its flower beds filled with yellowed grass, a few flowerpots on a cement ground. Stairs and hallways all alike. When you were drunk you'd come home to some building, didn't matter which one. Whatever—it was all the same termite mound."

A bidonville in Saint-Denis, 1963

An old-style workers' *cité*, Île-de-France, circa 1910

But the HBMs could not adequately house even the forty thousand inhabitants of the Zone, all of them relocated by 1932. By then there were 2.1 million people living in the *banlieue*, as compared with 2.9 million in Paris itself; by the eve of the war the two populations were equal. After the war an enormous influx from the provinces further aggravated standing problems; there were bidonvilles within the city itself. And the *banlieue* terrified the municipal establishment—it was the "Red Belt," overwhelmingly working-class, reliably Communist at the polls, which editorial Cassandras foresaw seizing Paris in a pincer grasp, making a revolution from the outside in. And the inhabitants of the HBMs were increasingly unhappy. Cendrars surveyed the scene in the text he wrote to accompany Doisneau's photographs of the *banlieue*: "Everything is a sham in those big echoing barracks, from the broken elevators to the cellars where wine sours, turns to vinegar. The only real thing is misery: tuberculosis in proportion to the continual increase of children in cramped quarters, cuckoldry on every floor, worries drowned in drink, and women beaten like rugs."

In 1949 the HBMs became HLMs, *habitations à loyer modéré*, "reduced-rent housing," a telling move from plain speech and toward bureaucratic equivocation. The only possible direction was upward and outward, toward the *grand ensemble*, "the big set"—like a low-budget, reduced-scale version of Le Corbusier's apocalyptic cityscapes. The idea had already been tried out in the 1930s, in the Cité de la Muette in Drancy, which had buildings up to fifteen stories high.* Now, in the early 1950s, partly as a consequence of the agitations of Abbé Pierre, France's most prominent media cleric, who was incessantly leading crusades to bring attention to the plight of the homeless and the ill-housed, the mechanism swung into gear and, one after another, the *grands ensembles* arose: Arceuil, Orsay, Plaisance, Créteil, Massy-Antony, Melun-Sénart, Cergy-Pontoise, Marne-la-Vallée, Sarcelles-la-Grande-Borne, Saint-Quentin-en-Yvelines.

---

* Ten years later the Cité was converted into an internment camp for Jews, who were sent from there to Auschwitz.

And very soon the constructions moved beyond Île-de-France and encircled every major city in the land.

A *grand ensemble* represented by consumer goods, from Jean-Luc Godard's *2 or 3 Things I Know About Her* (1967)

The old *cités* had been rows of attached two-story houses with pitched roofs, grouped into courtyards and culs-de-sac, visually echoing the ancient layout of the walled farm as it can still be seen all over France. The new complexes looked like immense chests of drawers or speaker cabinets, like banks of Univac-style computers, like the Secretariat of the United Nations extended into a vast hedge. There were tower blocks with cross or tripod footprints, and some that were cylindrical, like silos. Their forward-looking architects eschewed the safe and familiar in favor of vanguard designs. Some had enormous walls of windows to which were assigned uniform drapes, while others had little slivers of windows in rows or stacks of two or three, meant more for the visual delectation of outsiders than for the use of the inhabitants. "The landscape being generally thankless, they've gone so far as to eliminate windows, since there is nothing to see," says the narrator of Maurice Pialat's short film *L'amour existe* (1960).

The title frame of Maurice Pialat's *L'amour existe*, 1960

Pialat, who had grown up before the war in one of the little detached *pavillons* in Courbevoie, made his movie as an elegy to the old *banlieue* at a time when it was being mercilessly reconfigured. He acknowledges the grayness and drabness and boredom of the *banlieue* as it was, the German bombs that cratered landscapes already unprepossessing as they were. He cites statistics: twenty-nine *lycées* in the city as compared with just nine in the *banlieue*, which by then had nearly twice the population. He notes that the new projects segregate not simply by class but by age and family status as well. He suggests that there are more than superficial similarities between the designers and builders of the new *cités* and those of the Todt Organization, the Nazi engineering outfit that gave Germany the Autobahn and the Siegfried Line and gave France the Atlantic Wall. He shows a street sign, flung down and trampled: RUE ORADOUR-SUR-GLANE, it reads. The street had been named after that village in the Limousin where, in June 1944, the Waffen SS massacred 642 men, women, and children—they had targeted another, similarly named village nearby but had gone to the wrong address. Around the fallen sign a group of young men are pummeling and kicking one another, smashing wooden crates on each other's heads, for no particular reason. Love still exists, Pialat's title says, but very little in his footage suggests where it may be found.

THIRTY-TWO RATS
FROM CASABLANCA

Joseph Mitchell

1944

I N NEW YORK, as in all great seaports, rats abound. One is
occasionally in their presence without being aware of it. In
the whole city relatively few blocks are entirely free of them.
They have diminished greatly in the last twenty-five years, but
there still are millions here; some authorities believe that in the
five boroughs there is a rat for every human being. During a
war, the rat populations of seaports and of ships always shoot
up. House rats left their nests in basements and began to dig
burrows in vacant lots and parks, particularly in Central Park,
earlier this spring than they have for many years. A steady
increase in shipboard rats began to be noticed in New York
Harbor in the summer of 1940, less than a year after the war
started in Europe. Rats and rat fleas in many foreign ports are
at times infected with the plague, an extraordinarily ugly disease
that occurs in several forms, of which the bubonic, the Black
Death of the Middle Ages, is the most common. Consequently,
all ships that enter the harbor after touching at a foreign port
are examined for rats or for signs of rat infestation by officials
of the United States Public Health Service, who go out in
cutters from a quarantine station on the Staten Island bank of

The Narrows. If a ship appears to be excessively infested, it is anchored in the bay or in one of the rivers, its crew is taken off, and its holds and cabins are fumigated with a gas so poisonous that a whiff or two will quickly kill a man, let alone a rat. In 1939 the average number of rats killed in a fumigation was 12.4. In 1940 the average rose abruptly to 21, and two years later it reached 32.1. In 1943, furthermore, rats infected with the plague bacteria, *Pasteurella pestis*, were discovered in the harbor for the first time since 1900. They were taken out of an old French tramp, the Wyoming, in from Casablanca, where the Black Death has been intermittent for centuries.

The biggest rat colonies in the city are found in rundown structures on or near the waterfront, especially in tenements, live-poultry markets, wholesale produce markets, slaughterhouses, warehouses, stables, and garages. They also turn up in more surprising places. Department of Health inspectors have found their claw and tail tracks in the basements of some of the best restaurants in the city. A few weeks ago, in the basement and sub-basement of a good old hotel in the East Forties, a crew of exterminators trapped two hundred and thirty-six in three nights. They nest in the roofs of some "L" stations and many live in crannies in the subways; in the early-morning hours, during the long lulls between trains, they climb to the platforms and forage among the candy-bar wrappers and peanut hulls. There are old rat paths beneath the benches in at least two ferry sheds. In the spring and summer, multitudes of one species, the brown rat, live in twisting, many-chambered burrows in vacant lots and parks. There are great colonies of this kind of rat in Central Park. The rat that Mrs. Zorah White Gristede, the critic of Park Commissioner Moses, pointed out for a newspaper photographer last week in the Eighty-fifth Street playground in Central Park was a brown rat. After the first cold snap they begin to migrate, hunting for warm basements. Herds have been seen on autumn nights scuttering across Fifth Avenue. All through October and November, exterminating firms get frantic calls from the superintendents of many of the older apartment houses on the avenues and streets adjacent to the Park; the majority of the newer houses were ratproofed when built. The rats come out by twos and threes in some side streets in the theatrical district practically every morning around four-thirty. The scow-shaped trucks that collect kitchen scraps from restaurants, night clubs, and saloons all over Manhattan for the pig farms of Secaucus, New Jersey, roll into these streets at that time. Shortly after the trucks have made their pick-ups, if no people are stirring, the rats appear and search for dropped scraps; they seem to pop out of the air.

The rats of New York are quicker-witted than those on farms, and they can outthink any man who has not made a study of their habits. Even so, they spend most of their lives in a state of extreme anxiety, the black rats dreading the brown and both species dreading human beings. Away from their nests, they are usually on the edge of hysteria. They will severely bite babies (there was an epidemic of this a year or so ago in a row of tenements in the Wallabout neighborhood in Brooklyn), and they will bite sleeping adults, but ordinarily they flee from people. If hemmed in, and sometimes if too suddenly come upon, they will attack. They fight savagely and blindly, in the manner of mad dogs; they bare their teeth and leap about every which way, snarling and snapping and clawing the air. A full-grown black rat, when desperate, can jump three feet horizontally and make a vertical leap of two feet two inches, and a brown rat is nearly as spry. They are greatly feared by firemen. One of the hazards of fighting a fire in a junk shop or in an old warehouse is the crazed rats. It is dangerous to poke at them. They are able to run right up a cane or a broomstick and inflict deep, gashlike bites on their assailant's hands. A month or so ago, in broad daylight, on the street in front of a riding academy on the West Side, a stableboy tried to kill a rat with a mop; it darted up the mop handle and tore the thumbnail off the boy's left hand. This happening was unusual chiefly in that the rat was foraging in the open in the daytime. As a rule, New York rats are nocturnal. They rove in the streets in many neighborhoods, but only after the sun has set. They steal along as quietly as spooks in the shadows close to the building line, or in the gutters, peering this way and that, sniffing, quivering, conscious every moment of all that is going on around them. They are least cautious in the two or three hours before dawn, and they are encountered most often by milkmen, night watchmen, scrubwomen, policemen, and other people who are regularly abroad in those hours. The average person rarely sees one. When he does, it is a disquieting experience. Anyone who has been confronted by a rat in the bleakness of a Manhattan dawn and has seen it whirl and slink away, its claws rasping against the pavement, thereafter understands fully why this beast has been for centuries a symbol of the Judas and the stool pigeon, of soullessness in general. Veteran exterminators say that even they are unable to be calm around rats. "I've been in this business thirty-one years and I must've seen fifty thousand rats, but I've never got accustomed to the look of them," one elderly exterminator said recently. "Every time I see one my heart sinks and I get the belly flutters." In alcoholic wards the rat is the animal that most frequently appears in the visual hallucinations of patients with delirium tremens. In Ireland, in fact, the D.T.'s are often referred to as "seeing the rat."

There are three kinds of rats in the city—the black (*Rattus rattus rattus*), which is also known as the ship or the English rat; the Alexandrian (*Rattus rattus alexandrinus*), which is also known as the roof or the Egyptian rat; and the brown (*Rattus norvegicus*), which is also known as the house, gray, sewer, or Norway rat. In recent years they have been killed here in the approximate proportion of ninety brown to nine black and one Alexandrian. The brown is hostile to the other kinds; it usually attacks them on sight. It kills them by biting their throats or by clawing them to pieces, and, if hungry, it eats them. The behavior and some of the characteristics of the three kinds are dissimilar, but all are exceedingly destructive, all are hard to exterminate, all are monstrously procreative, all are badly flea-bitten, and all are able to carry a number of agonizing diseases. Among these diseases, in addition to the plague, are a form of typhus fever called Brill's disease, which is quite common in several ratty ports in the South; spirochetal jaundice, rat-bite fever, trichinosis, and tularemia. The plague is the worst. Human beings develop it in from two to five days after they have been bitten by a flea that has fed on a plague-infected rat. The onset is sudden, and the classic symptoms are complete exhaustion, mental confusion, and black, intensely painful swellings (called buboes) of the lymph glands in the groin and under the arms. The mortality is high. The rats of New York are all ridden with a flea, the *Xenopsylla cheopis*, which is by far the most frequent transmitting agent of the plague. Several surveys of the prevalence in the city of the *cheopis* have been made by Benjamin E. Holsendorf, a consultant on the staff of the Department of Health. Mr. Holsendorf, a close-mouthed, elderly Virginian, is a retired Passed Assistant Pharmacist in the Public Health Service and an international authority on the ratproofing of ships and buildings. He recently supervised the trapping of many thousands of rats in the area between Thirty-third Street and the bottom of Manhattan, and found that these rats had an average of eight *cheopis* fleas on them. "Some of these rats had three fleas, some had fifteen, and some had forty," Mr. Holsendorf says, "and one old rat had hundreds on him; his left hind leg was missing and he'd take a tumble every time he tried to scratch. However, the average was eight. None of these fleas were plague-infected, of course. I don't care to generalize about this, but I will say that if just one plague-infected rat got ashore from a ship at a New York dock and roamed for only a few hours among our local, uninfected rats, the resulting situation might be, to say the least, quite sinister."

Rats are almost as fecund as germs. In New York, under fair conditions, they bear from three to five times a year, in litters of from five to twenty-two. There is a record of seven litters in seven months from a single captured pair. The period of gestation is between twenty-one and twenty-five days. They grow rapidly and are able to breed when four months old. That is why they can take a mile when given an inch; a ship that leaves port with only a few rats in it is apt to come back with an army of them aboard. The span of life is between three and five years, although now and then one may live somewhat longer; a rat at four is older than a man at ninety. Exterminators refer to old rats as Moby Dicks. "Rats that survive to the age of four are the wisest and the most cynical beasts on earth," one exterminator says. "A trap means nothing to them, no matter how skillfully set. They just kick it around until it snaps; then they eat the bait. And they can detect poisoned bait a yard off. I believe some of them can read. If you get a few Moby Dicks in your house, there are just two things you can do: you can wait for them to die, or you can burn your house down and start all over again." In fighting the rat, exterminating companies use a wide variety of traps, gases, and poisons. There are about three hundred of these companies in the city, ranging in size from hole-in-the-wall, boss-and-a-helper outfits to corporations with whole floors in midtown office buildings, large laboratories, and staffs of carefully trained employees, many of whom have scientific degrees. One of the largest is the Guarantee Exterminating Company ("America's Pied Piper"), at 500 Fifth Avenue. Among its clients are hospitals, steamship lines, railroad terminals, department stores, office buildings, hotels, and apartment houses. Its head is E.R. Jennings, a second-generation exterminator; his father started the business in Chicago, in 1888. Mr. Jennings says that the most effective rat traps are the old-fashioned snap or break-back ones and a thing called the glueboard.

"We swear by the glueboard," he says. "It's simply a composition shingle smeared on one side with a thick, strong, black glue. We developed this glue twenty-five years ago and it's probably the stickiest stuff known to man. It has been widely copied in the trade and is used all over. The shingle is pliable. It can be laid flat on the floor or bent around a pipe. We place them on rat runs—the paths rats customarily travel on—and that's where skill comes in; you have to be an expert to locate the rat runs. We lay bait around the boards. If any part of the animal touches a board, he's done for. When he tries to pull away, he gets himself firmly caught in the glue. The more he struggles, the more firmly he's stuck. Next morning the rat, glueboard and all, is picked up with tongs and burned. We used to bait with ground beef, canned salmon, and cheese, but when rationing came in we did some experimenting with many other foods and discovered, to our great surprise, that peanut butter is an extremely effective rat bait. Rats have to be trapped, poisoned, or gassed. Cats are worthless. They can handle mice, and do, but an adult brown rat will rip the hide off any cat. Ferrets aren't used against rats in New York any more, but exterminators in Philadelphia have to always keep a pair on hand. Some of the old families down there insist on that method. Personally, I like a ferret about as much as I like a rat.

"Insects, particularly the cockroach and the bedbug, are the No. 1 exterminating problem in New York. Rats come next. Then mice. Perhaps I shouldn't tell this, but most good exterminators despise rat jobs because they know that exterminating by itself is ineffective. You can kill all the rats in a building on a Monday and come back on a Wednesday and find it crawling with them. The only way rats can be kept out is to ratproof the building from sub-basement to skylight. It's an architectural problem; you have to build them out. Killing them off periodically is a waste of time; it's like taking aspirin for a cancer. We refuse to take a rat job unless the owner or tenant promises to stop up every hole and crack through which rats can get entrance and seal up or eliminate any spaces inside the building in which they can nest. That may sound like cutting our own throats, but don't worry: insects are here to stay and we'll always have more work than we can do. Rats are on the increase right now, especially the black rat. The other day I saw some blacks in an 'L' station in uptown Manhattan. Use to, you'd find them only on the waterfront. People don't have time to attend to rats with a war on. After the war, we'll pick up the slack. Twenty-five years ago there were easily two rats for every human in the city. They gradually decreased to half that, for many reasons. Better sanitary conditions in general is one reason. Fewer horses and fewer stables is another. The improved packaging of foods helped a lot. An increase in the power of the Department of Health is an important reason. Nowadays, if a health inspector finds rat tracks in a grocery or a restaurant, all he has to do is issue a warning; if things aren't cleaned up in a hurry, he can slap on a violation and make it stick. The most important reason, however, is the modern construction of buildings and the widespread use of concrete. It's almost impossible for a rat to get inside some of the newer apartment houses and office buildings in the city. If he gets in, there's no place for him to hide and breed. Take the Empire

State Building, which I know intimately. There's never been a rat in it, not a single, solitary one."

None of the rats in New York are indigenous to this country. The black rat has been here longest. Its homeland is India. It spread to Europe in the Middle Ages along trade routes, and historians are quite sure that it was brought to America by the first ships that moored here. It is found in every seaport in the United States, and inland chiefly in the Gulf States. It has bluish-black fur, a pointed nose, and big ears. It is cleaner and not as fierce as the brown rat but more suspicious and harder to trap. It is an acrobatic beast. It can rapidly climb a drapery, a perpendicular drain or steam-heat pipe, an elevator cable, or a telephone or electric wire. It can gnaw a hole in a ceiling while clinging to an electric wire. It can run fleetly on a taut wire, or on a rope whether slack or taut. It uses its tail, which is slightly longer than its body, to maintain balance. It nests in attics, ceilings, and hollow walls, and in the superstructures of piers, away from its enemy, the ground-loving brown rat. Not all piers are infested; a few of the newer ones, which are largely of concrete, have none at all. It keeps close to the waterfront, and until recently was rarely come across in the interior of the city. Whenever possible, it goes aboard ships to live. While docked here, all ships are required to keep three-foot metal discs, called rat guards, set on their hawsers and mooring cables. These guards sometimes get out of whack—a strong wind may tilt them, for example—and then a black or an Alexandrian can easily clamber over them. Occasionally a rat will walk right up or down a gangplank. It is almost impossible to keep a ship entirely free of them. Some famous ships are notoriously ratty. One beautiful liner—it was in the round-the-world cruise service before the war—once came in with two hundred and fifty aboard. Public Health Service officials look upon a medium-sized ship with twenty as excessively infested. The record for New York Harbor is held by a freighter that came in from an Oriental port with six hundred, all blacks and Alexandrians. The black and the Alexandrian belong to the same species, their appearance and habits are alike, and the untrained eye cannot tell them apart. The Alexandrian is frequently found on ships from Mediterranean ports. It is a native of Egypt, and no one seems to know, even approximately, when it first appeared in this country. It has never been able to get more than a toehold in New York, but it is abundant in some Southern and Gulf ports.

The brown rat, the *R. norvegicus*, originated somewhere in Central Asia, began to migrate westward early in the eighteenth century, and reached England around 1730. Most authorities believe that it got to this country during the Revolutionary War. From ports all along the coast it went inland, hot on the heels of the early settlers, and now it thrives in every community and on practically every farm in the United States. Its spread was slowest in the high and dry regions of the West; it didn't reach Wyoming until 1919 and Montana until 1923. It has a blunt nose, small ears, and feverish, evil, acutely intelligent eyes. Its fur is most often a grimy brown, but it may vary from a pepper-and-salt gray to nearly black. Partial albinos occasionally show up; the tame white rat, which is used as a laboratory animal and sometimes kept as a pet, is a sport derived from the brown.

In addition to being the most numerous, the brown rat is the dirtiest, the fiercest, and the biggest. "The untrained observer," a Public Health Service doctor remarked not long ago, "invariably spreads his hands wide apart when reporting the size of a rat he has seen, indicating that it was somewhat smaller than a stud horse but a whole lot bigger than a bulldog. They are big enough, God protect us, without exaggerating." The average length of adult brown rats is a foot and five inches, including the tail, which is seven inches. The average weight is three-quarters of a pound. Once in a while a much heavier one is trapped. One that weighed a pound and a half and measured a foot and eight and a half inches overall was recently clubbed to death in a Manhattan brewery; brewery and distillery rats feed on mash and many become obese and clumsy. Some exterminators have maintained for years that the biggest rats in the country, perhaps in the world, are found in New York, Jersey City, Washington, and San Francisco, but biologists believe that this is just a notion, that they don't get any bigger in one city than they do in another. The black and the Alexandrian are about two-thirds the size of the brown.

The brown rat is distributed all over the five boroughs. It customarily nests at or below street level—under floors, in rubbishy basements, and in burrows. There are many brownstones and red-bricks, as well as many commercial structures, in the city that have basements or sub-basements with dirt floors; these places are rat heavens. The brown rat can burrow into the hardest soil, even tightly packed clay, and it can tunnel through the kind of cheap mortar that is made of sand and lime. To get from one basement to another, it tunnels under party walls; slum-clearance workers frequently uncover a network of rat tunnels that link all the tenements in a block. Like the magpie, it steals and hoards small gadgets and coins. In nest chambers in a system of tunnels under a Chelsea tenement, workers recently found an empty lipstick tube, a religious medal, a skate key, a celluloid teething ring, a belt buckle, a shoehorn, several books of matches in which all the match heads had been eaten off, a penny, a dime, and three quarters. Paper money is sometimes found. When the Civic Repertory Theatre was torn down, a nest constructed solely of dollar bills, seventeen in all, was discovered in a burrow. Exterminators believe that most fires of undetermined origin in the city are started by rats. "They are the worst firebugs in creation," one says. "They set some fires by gnawing the insulation off electric wiring, but their passion for match eating is what causes the most damage. They often use highly inflammable material in building nests. For example, the majority of the nests in the neighborhood of a big garage will invariably be built of oily cotton rags. Let a rat bring some matches into such a nest, particularly one that's right beneath a wooden floor, and let him ignite a match while gnawing on it, and a few minutes later here come the fire wagons."

The brown rat is as supple as rubber and it can squeeze and contort itself through openings half its size. It has strong jaws and long, curved incisors with sharp cutting edges. It can gnaw a notch big enough to accommodate its body in an oak plank, a slate shingle, or a sun-dried brick. Attracted by the sound of running water, it will gnaw into lead pipe. It cannot climb as skillfully as the black and the Alexandrian, it cannot jump as far, and it is not as fleet, but it is, for its size, a remarkable swimmer. A Harbor Police launch once came upon three brown rats, undoubtedly from New Jersey, in the middle of the Hudson; in an hour and twenty-five minutes, swimming against the wind in tossing water, they reached the pilings of one of the Barclay Street ferry slips, where the policemen shot them. The brown rat is an omnivorous scavenger, and it doesn't seem to care at all whether its food is fresh or spoiled. It will eat soap, oil paints, shoe leather, the bone of a bone-handled knife, the glue in a book binding, and the rubber in the insulation of telephone and electric wires. It can go for days without food, and it can obtain sufficient water by licking condensed moisture off metallic surfaces. All rats are vandals, but the brown is the most ruthless. It destroys far more than it actually consumes. Instead of completely eating a few potatoes, it takes a bite or two out of dozens. It will methodically ruin all the apples and pears in a grocery in a night, gnawing on a few and then cutting into the others for the seeds. To get a small quantity of nesting material, it will cut great quantities of garments, rugs, upholstery, and books to tatters. In a big warehouse, it goes berserk. In a few hours a herd will rip holes in hundreds of sacks of flour, grain, coffee, and other foodstuffs, spilling and fouling the contents and making a wholesale mess. It sometimes seems that only deep hatred of the human race could cause the rat to be so destructive. Every January, the biologists of the Fish and Wildlife Service of the Department of the Interior get together and make an estimate of the amount of damage done during the past year by rats. Their estimate for the country in 1943 was two hundred million dollars.

In live-poultry markets a lust for blood seems to take hold of the brown rat. One night, in the old Gansevoort wholesale-poultry market, alongside the Hudson in Greenwich Village, a burrow of them bit the throats of three hundred and twenty-five broilers and ate less than a dozen. Before the Gansevoort market was abandoned, in 1942, the rats practically had charge of it. In three sheds, four thousand were trapped. They nested in the drawers of desks and leaped out, snarling, when the drawers were pulled open. Exterminators have occasionally been perplexed at finding eggshells and even unbroken eggs in brown-rat burrows under poultry markets and butter-and-egg warehouses. Irving Billig, president of the Biocerta Corporation, which makes pest poisons, at 303 Fifth Avenue, claims that he found out not long ago how the rats transport these eggs. Now and then Mr. Billig takes on a big exterminating job. The city once hired him to quell the rats in Central Park and in the dumps on Riker's Island. For a hobby, he hides in food establishments at night and studies the feeding habits of rats. "I'll swear to this," he says. "One night, in the warehouse of a grocery chain, I saw some egg-stealing rats at work. They worked in pairs. A small rat would straddle an egg and clutch it in his four paws. When he got a good grip on it, he'd roll over on his back. Then a bigger rat would grab him by the tail and drag him across the floor to a hole in the baseboard, a hole leading to a burrow. The big rat would slowly back into the hole, pulling the small one, the one with the egg, in after him." In an East River slaughterhouse, Mr. Billig once witnessed another example of the ingenuity of the *norvegicus*. "I'll swear to this, also," he says. "This place had a bad problem and I was called in to study it. I hid in a room where there were some sides of beef hung on hooks, about three feet clear of the floor. Around eleven P.M. the rats started wriggling in. In fifteen minutes there were around two hundred in the room. They began jumping for the beeves, but they couldn't reach them. Presently they congregated under one beef and formed a sort of pyramid with their bodies. The pyramid was high enough for one rat to jump up on the beef. He gnawed it loose from the hook, it tumbled to the floor, and the two hundred rats went to work on it." After telling about this, Mr. Billig shudders and says, "A sight like that leaves a mark on a man. If the rats come out of their holes by the millions some night and take over City Hall and start running the city, I won't be the least bit surprised. A few more world wars, a couple of epidemics of the bubonic plague, and the Machine Age'll be done for; it'll turn into the Rat Age."

So far, in the United States, the plague has been only a menace. From 1898 to 1923, 10,822,331 deaths caused by the plague were recorded in India alone; in the United States, in this period, there were fewer than three hundred deaths. The plague first occurred in this country in 1900, in the Chinatown of San Francisco. It is generally believed that the bacteria were brought in by a herd of infected rats that climbed to the docks from an old ship in the Far Eastern trade. This epidemic killed a hundred and thirteen people and lasted until the end of 1903. The plague broke out again in 1907, a year after the earthquake.

In the same year there was an epidemic in Seattle. There have been two epidemics in New Orleans—one in 1914 and one in 1919 and 1920—and there was one in Los Angeles in 1924 and 1925. Since then there have been only sporadic cases. However, there is a vast and ominous reservoir of plague infection in the wild rodents of the West. During the first epidemic in San Francisco, many rats fled the city and infected field rodents, chiefly ground squirrels, in the suburbs. In 1934, thirty years later, Public Health Service biologists turned up the fact that the plague had slowly spread among burrowing animals—ground squirrels, prairie dogs, chipmunks, and others—as far east as New Mexico and Wyoming. Late last year it appeared fifty miles inside the western border of North Dakota. Public Health Service officials say that there is no reason to assume that the infection will not infiltrate into rodents of the Great Plains, cross the Mississippi, and show up in the East. Most of the diseased rodents inhabit thinly settled sections and come in contact with human beings infrequently. Even so, every year several people, usually hunters, are bitten by infected rodent fleas and come down with the plague. Epidemiologists are greatly disturbed by the situation, particularly because there is an ever-present possibility that a few infected rodents may stray from rural areas and transfer the disease to town and city rats, settling an old score. If the disease gets loose among city rats, epidemics among human beings will probably follow.

There has never been an outbreak of the plague in New York. There have, however, been two narrow escapes. In 1900, plague-infected rats were found in ships in the harbor of New York, as well as in the harbors of San Francisco and Port Townsend,

Washington. They got ashore only in San Francisco, causing the first Black Death epidemic in North America. Plague rats were found in New York Harbor for the second time early in January of last year. Among themselves, health officials have already got in the habit of referring to this discovery as "the Wyoming affair." The history of the Wyoming affair was told to me the other day by Dr. Robert Olesen, medical director of the New York Quarantine Station of the Public Health Service, whose office is in an old, red-brick building overlooking The Narrows, in Rosebank, on Staten Island.

"I suppose there can be no harm in telling about it now," Dr. Olesen said. "First, it's necessary to explain how we inspect ships. Every ship in foreign trade that comes into the harbor is boarded by a party made up of a customs officer, an immigration officer, a plant-quarantine man from the Department of Agriculture, a Public Health doctor, and a sanitary inspector, whose main job is to determine the degree of rat infestation aboard. While the doctor is examining the crew and passengers for quarantinable diseases, the sanitary inspector goes through the ship looking for rat gnawings, tracks, droppings, nests, and for the presence of rat odor. An experienced inspector can smell rats. He pays particular attention to ships that have touched at plague ports. There are quite a few of these ports right now; Suez had an outbreak the other day and was put on the list. After he's made his search, he reports to the doctor, who orders a fumigation if things look bad. If infestation is slight and if the ship comes from a clean port, the doctor probably won't insist on a fumigation. I won't give you any wartime figures, but in one peacetime month, for example, we inspected five hundred and sixty ships, found that a hundred and thirty-two were infested to some degree, and fumigated twenty-four, recovering eight hundred and ten rats. Ships make rapid turnarounds nowadays, and it often happens that the time required for a fumigation will cause a ship to miss a convoy.

"We are short-handed, and most of our fumigating is done by a group of twenty-two Coast Guardsmen. They were assigned to us early in the war and we trained them to make rat inspections and fumigations. We use hydrocyanic gas, which has a pleasant, peach-blossom smell and is one of the most lethal of poisons. An infested ship is anchored and a fumigation party of four or five Coast Guardsmen goes aboard. First, they send the entire crew ashore, carefully checking them off one by one. Then one of the Coast Guardsmen goes through the ship, shouting, banging on bulkheads with a wrench, and making as much racket as possible. He shouts, 'Danger! Fumigation! Poison gas!' Then the Coast Guardsmen put on gas masks and toss some tear-gas bombs into the holds. That's to fetch out any stowaways who might be aboard. During the first months we used hydrocyanic, we killed a number of stowaways. A few weeks ago, in the hold of a South American freighter, the tear gas brought out eight weeping stowaways who had been hiding in an empty water tank. Two fellows in the crew had smuggled them aboard in Buenos Aires and had been feeding them. These fellows had kept their mouths shut and gone ashore, leaving the stowaways to be killed, for all they cared. When the Coast Guardsmen are satisfied a ship is empty of humans, they seal the holds and cabins and open cans of hydrocyanic, liberating the gas. They even fumigate the lifeboats; rats often hide in them. After a certain number of hours—ten for a medium-sized ship—the holds are opened and aired out, and the Coast Guardsmen go below and search for dead rats. The rats are dropped in oil-paper bags and brought to a laboratory in the basement here. They are combed for fleas. The fleas are pounded in a mortar, put into a solution, and injected into guinea pigs. Then each rat is autopsied and examined for signs of plague. Then bits of spleens and livers are snipped out, pooled, and pounded up. They are also put into a solution and injected into guinea pigs. If the fleas or the rats are infected, the pigs sicken and die. We began this work in 1921, and for twenty-two years we injected hundreds of generations of pigs with the fleas and spleens of rats from practically every port in the world without turning up a single Black Death germ. We didn't want to find any, to be sure, but there *were* days when we couldn't help but look upon our work as routine and futile.

"Now then, late in the evening of January 10, 1943, the French steamship Wyoming arrived from Casablanca, Africa, with a miscellaneous cargo, chiefly wine, tobacco, and vegetable seeds. A big convoy came in that evening, sixty or seventy ships, and we didn't get to the Wyoming until next day. Casablanca was on the plague list at that time; there had been an outbreak in December, shortly before the Wyoming sailed. The crew was carefully examined. No sign of illness. Then the captain brought out a deratization certificate stating that the ship had recently been fumigated and was free of rats; this certificate later turned out to be worthless. She was allowed to dock at Pier 34, Brooklyn, where she discharged some bags of mail. Next day she proceeded to Pier 84, Hudson River, and began discharging her cargo. Some rats were seen in her by longshoremen, and on January 13th we went over her and found evidence of infestation. She was allowed to continue unloading. On January 18th we fumigated her at her dock and found twenty rats. We combed and autopsied the rats, and inoculated a guinea pig. Four days later the pig sickened and died. An autopsy indicated plague infection and cultures from its heart blood showed an oval organism which had all the characteristics of *Pasteurella pestis*. We made a broth of tissue from this pig and inoculated a second pig. It sickened and died. It was the Black Death, no doubt about it. We had found it in the harbor for the first time in forty-three years.

"In the meantime, the Wyoming had moved from the Hudson to Pier 25, Staten Island, for repairs. On January 29th we went aboard her, removed all excess dunnage and gear to the decks, and ripped open all the enclosed spaces in the holds; we were afraid the hydrocyanic hadn't penetrated to these spaces. Then we refumigated. Twelve more dead rats were found. On the same day we got in touch with Dr. Stebbins, the Commissioner of Health for the city, and told him about the situation. We were greatly apprehensive. The Wyoming had touched at piers in rat-infested sections in three boroughs and there was, of course, a distinct possibility that infected rats had got ashore and were at that moment wandering around the waterfront, coming in contact with local rats and exchanging fleas. Mr. Holsendorf, the Health Department's rat consultant, quickly got together some crews of trappers and they began setting break-back traps on the Brooklyn pier, the Manhattan pier, and the Staten Island pier, and in buildings in the vicinity of each pier. The trapping was done unobtrusively; we were afraid a newspaper might learn of the matter and start a plague scare. Early in February the first batch of rats was sent for autopsies to the laboratory of the Willard Parker Hospital, an institution for contagious diseases, at the foot of East Fifteenth Street. We waited for the report with considerable anxiety. It was negative on every rat, and we began to breathe easier. Mr. Holsendorf and his crews trapped from the end of January to the middle of May and the reports continued to come in negative. At the end of May we concluded that no Wyoming rats had got ashore, and that the city was safe."

"How many rats did you find on the Wyoming the next time it came in," I asked.

"The Wyoming's number was up," Dr. Olesen said. "Shortly after the second fumigation she went back to sea. Two days out, on her way to Casablanca, she was torpedoed and sunk by a German submarine."

MR. HULOT

Lillian Ross

1954

THE FRENCH comedian Jacques Tati, whom we make
no bones about calling one of the funniest men alive,
was in town briefly for the opening of his movie, "Mr. Hulot's
Holiday." As was the case with his previous movie success,
"Jour de Fête," M. Tati is not only the star of the picture
but also its author and director. We called on this great
benefactor of humanity one warm afternoon recently and
found him perplexed in the extreme by the air-conditioning
of his hotel suite. He had on a blue-and-white striped sports
shirt and a heavy topcoat. "My first experience of your
winter-in-summer machines," he said in admirable English,
fingering his topcoat and shivering. "I do not yet understand
the principle. You take off your coat when you go outside and
you put on your coat when you come inside. *Bien!* But where
is the gain?" M. Tati is well over two yards tall and looks
taller. He has broad shoulders, long arms, and big hands,
and wears an expression of perpetual pleased surprise. No
sooner had we sat down than he volunteered to show us a
snapshot of his two children—Sophie, who is seven, and
Pierre, who is five. "They are simple and honest," he said
with a father's pride.

While Tati and his wife were in New York, their children stayed at Tati's father's house in Saint-Germain-en-Laye, a suburb of Paris. Tati was born a few miles from there, in Le Pecq, in 1908. His real name is Jacques Tati-scheff, and if he liked, he could call himself a count. His grandfather, Count Dimitri Tatischeff, an attaché of the Russian Embassy in Paris, married a Frenchwoman. On Tati's maternal side, his grandmother was Italian and his grandfather was Dutch. This man, van Hoof by name, ran a picture-framing shop in Paris and numbered among his customers Toulouse-Lautrec and van Gogh. On more than one occasion, van Gogh offered to pay his bill with some of his paintings, but canny old van Hoof held out for cash. Tati's father took over the business, and Tati, at sixteen, was sent to a college of arts and engineering to prepare him for a prosperous picture-framing future. After a year's fumbling with more mathematics than he knew what to do with, Tati gave up college, and his father bundled him off to London, to serve as an apprentice to an English framer. He boarded with a family whose son, also seventeen, had a passion for Rugby, and in six months Tati learned much English, much Rugby, and very little picture framing. "Rugby is not a gentle game," he told us. "Sometimes the players hurt each other quite badly, and afterward they wish to be friendly again, so they have dinner together and try to make one another laugh. I used to imitate the way Rugby players look during a game. Everyone would laugh at me, and I was encouraged to start imitating people playing tennis and other sports. My friends said, 'Why not go into the music halls?' I went back to Paris and told my father I wanted to quit picture framing and do imitations. You can imagine his anger. He said at last that I could do as I pleased but he wouldn't give me a sou."

Young Tati's specialty was so peculiar that not an impresario in Paris would look at him. "For years, I was broke," Tati said. "I slept every night in a different place. I sat in cafés and talked with friends, and when I needed to eat, I would go to a certain cabaret and imitate a drunken waiter who is constantly making mistakes. For an evening of supposedly drunken waiting, I would be given my dinner and fifty francs. It was the happiest and most free time I have ever known." Tati got his big break in 1934, when a friend arranged for him to appear on a program at the Ritz with Chevalier and Mistinguett. "I was so frightened that though I was supposed to go on first, I couldn't stand or talk," Tati said. "I hid in a corner backstage and the show started without me. When it was over and the people were leaving, the manager of the show saw me hiding in the corner. He ran out on the stage and shouted that one of the entertainers had been forgotten. Then he introduced me. The people returned to their seats and I had to go on. The next thing I knew, I heard them laughing. I could not imagine that they were laughing at me. I looked around for the entertainer they were laughing at. No one else was onstage. It had to be me. Soon they were applauding and shouting, and the manager was shaking my hand. Then came the impresarios, and I was playing in music halls and circuses all over Europe."

This was Tati's first visit to the United States. He was scheduled to play at the Radio City Music Hall in 1939 but wound up in the French infantry instead. He attended several baseball games in the course of his visit and plans to add a baseball pantomime to his sports act. It took him a year and a half to make "Jour de Fête" and as long to make "Mr. Hulot's Holiday," and he is only just beginning to think about a new movie. His favorite comedian is an English music-hall performer named Little Tich, whom he saw when he was seven, The comedian who makes him laugh most is the late W.C. Fields. He admires Chaplin, but for the most part Chaplin doesn't make him laugh. "Chaplin is full of ideas," Tati said. "I am so busy watching the working out of his beautiful ideas that I never find time to laugh."

REMEMBERING MR. SHAWN

Ved Mehta

1998

M Y BOOK, entitled "Walking the Indian Streets," was to be published in July. As the time approached, a lot of excitement arose. The publicity woman at Little, Brown rang to say that the editor of the *Times Book Review*—whose name, as it happened, was Francis Brown—had called her himself to say that the *Times* was sending a photographer to Cambridge to take pictures of me at Eliot House. "The scuttlebutt is that the *Times Book Review* is going to do a big picture spread about you with a big review of the book," she said. "We couldn't have asked for a better break. Perhaps they'll follow it up with an article on both your book and Dom's." (The two books were to be published at about the same time.) The photographer, accompanied by the publicity woman, spent the better part of an afternoon with me at Harvard. I started dreaming about pictures of me in the *Times Book Review* and about fame in Harvard Square.

A fortnight or so later, Weekes called to say that the idea of the big picture spread had been shelved. "We smell a rat," he said.

When a copy of the review came, I knew why. The review, by Herbert L. Matthews, was so devastating that I wanted to go to bed and never get up. Matthews wrote:

Ved Mehta plays an extraordinary trick on his prospective readers and on anyone who does not know about him or has not read his previous book, "Face to Face." Mr. Mehta, a Punjabi Hindu, now 25 years old, has been completely blind since the age of 3. He has written this book about his return to India after ten years' absence as if he had normal vision.

His publishers carefully play the game, saying nothing on the jacket blurb to indicate that the author is blind....

Mr. Mehta is doing in this book what he does in life. He asks no quarter and he lives, in so far as it is humanly possible, as if he could see. Knowing he is blind, we can only regard this work as an astonishing tour de force.

Mr. Mehta has learned to minimize his handicap amazingly, but it naturally remains a severe handicap. The author has tried to do the impossible.

Anyone reading the book simply as an account of India today by a young Hindu in possession of all his faculties will get an entertaining and touching work with flashes of deep insight.... Here are a few examples to show how the author confuses the reader:

"I find the newspapers and magazines too grim," he writes after getting to Delhi, "and search them for theater criticism."

Or this at the end of the book: "I open my journal and begin thumbing through my impressions of the summer in India."...

Knowing that Mr. Mehta is blind, one presumes that someone read the newspapers to him, that he has some method of keeping a journal he can read back.... The reader who does not know is simply—although harmlessly, to be sure—fooled.

The point of all this is that Ved Mehta handicaps himself doubly in "Walking the Indian Streets." He cannot help his blindness and has, indeed, turned it by a miracle of will power and courage into something resembling an asset, but he could not hope to write a book about India as if he were not blind.

He has done so, and it would be unfair to say that, even taken at its face value, this book is a failure.

Matthews had, perhaps unwittingly, tried to take the bread from my mouth. He seemed to be condemning me to be a blind writer, in which case I could write only about blindness, and that field, as far as I was concerned, was as barren as the Gobi Desert. I wanted to compete on equal terms with writers who could see, but the *Times Book Review* was such a powerful influence in publishing generally that I feared that, if I continued to write as though I could see, no publisher, and certainly no magazine, would publish me. Letters of commiseration about the review poured in, confirming my drastic interpretation. One of the letters was from Norman Cousins:

August 31, 1960

My dear Ved:

I bled when I first read the Matthews review, for it represented the essential defeat of everything you have been trying to do in life. In a curious sense, Matthews resented the fact that you were not asking for a privileged review which you could have had shamelessly by skillful exploitation of your blindness.

The shame, of course, is that Matthews doesn't know you personally. For then he would know that you live without handicap and that to claim one would be to feign one. Your achievement in life is that you have freed other people from their obligation to you. They can love you or despise you because of your goodness or your venality; they don't have to see you through special perspectives. And you are the same toward them.

It would be fatuous of me to tell you that you shouldn't feel hurt. A man would have to be an armadillo not to be hurt by it. But what I can do is to emphasize the fact that Matthews was not reviewing the book; he was reviewing philosophical factors that basically were apart from the book. In this sense, he was unwittingly paying tribute to it, for readers will be intrigued rather than offended by the point Matthews lamely tries to make.

If all goes well I hope to see you next week.

Affectionately,

Norman

Matthews's main point was: How dare a blind person write as if he could see? Isn't writing in that way dishonest? That was a matter that had preoccupied me for years. I had discussed the subject with Frederick Mulhauser and W.T., or Will, Jones, two professors at Pomona whom I respected and to whom I was close.

Mulhauser had happened to be in London once while I was at Oxford, and I had gone to see him over tea at a flat he was renting there. He was thoughtful and wise, and was physically well put together. He generally favored a tweed jacket with leather patches on the elbows and shirts with narrow stripes, and in the setting of Southern California he came across as the archetypal English professor. He was one of the best-loved teachers at the college.

"What plans do you have for writing more books?" he asked, pouring me a cup of tea. He had read a first, incomplete draft of "Face to Face," and eventually his wife, Margaret, had read the proofs of the book.

"I have not given the subject much thought," I said, and I added, as a conversational gambit, a little in the manner of a child who wants to get the attention of a beloved elder, "But if wishes were horses I would write many books in many genres—autobiographical books, journalistic books, fictional books, and travel books, besides scholarly history." Though I said this half-mischievously, I went on, in a tone so serious that I myself was surprised by it, "But I don't want to write like a blind writer. I feel I have written everything I know about blindness in 'Face to Face.' I feel I have done with the subject. I want to be free to write—to put it boldly—as if I could see."

Mulhauser stood up and started pacing vigorously, as he used to do when I was having a conference with him and had said something dumb and he was trying to work out how to set me straight without saying something crushing. An extremely energetic man, he had a touch of the athlete about him. Now he stopped and stared out of the window. "You talk differently from the way you used to talk at Pomona," he said, twiddling the string on the windowshade.

"I know," I said. "Oxford has strange effects on people."

"Shades of 'Zuleika Dobson' and 'Brideshead Revisited,'" he said. He himself had never gone to Oxford—he had attended Wooster College, in Ohio, and then Yale—but I got the impression that he wished he had. For some time, he had been working on the correspondence of the poet Arthur Hugh Clough, who had been a Scholar at Balliol. I'd always thought that there was a mismatch between the professor and the poet, for Mulhauser was optimistic, an amiable man who was perfectly at peace in the pleasant climate and amiable surroundings of Pomona, while Clough had continually been bedevilled by spiritual agitation and religious doubts, had generally had a dark outlook, and had died at forty-two. As for me, outwardly I was cheerful, like Mulhauser, but inwardly I identified with Clough.

I then pursued the subject of blindness, rather like a gambler who has put a substantial amount in the ante and can't draw back from the gaming table; at the same time, I felt that I had never been more cautious. "The fact is that I don't want to write as a handicapped writer," I told Mulhauser. "I feel that I am no more a blind writer than, at the risk of using exalted examples, Milton was a blind poet or Beethoven was a deaf composer. I want my work, however scanty or indifferent, to be judged purely on what is written, rather as I respond to 'Paradise Lost' or the Ninth Symphony. Nor do I want to write like an Indian writer. I feel that I am no more Indian than Conrad was Polish, or Nabokov is Russian, or Beckett is Irish. This is not to say that I don't feel sad about not belonging to a national tradition. Indeed, I am sure that, except for a few notable exceptions, all the really great writers do belong to one. Dante, Shakespeare, Voltaire, Tolstoy, Goethe, Melville, Yeats—all of them are inseparable from their national traditions. But, of course, as an Indian living in England and America and writing in English—my fourth language—there is no way I can lay claim to any national tradition."

Mulhauser returned to his chair and picked up his cup of tea.

"I would, of course, have to pass muster as an expatriate writer," I went on. "But I feel that my doing so will depend on my command of the English tongue and, of course, on my talent. In any case, it will have nothing to do with my blindness."

"'The Wound and the Bow,'" he said, abstractedly.

I didn't quite catch the literary reference, but I thought that he was saying something complimentary. I felt a rush of love for him. Without exactly realizing it, I made every teacher I loved into my father—into an almost god-like figure. Teachers I didn't like I hated passionately, as though they belonged to the Devil's party. For me, as for most people with romantic temperaments, there was no middle ground. I said, almost to myself, "But how am I to write as if I could see—convincingly, honestly, and naturally? To be blind and to want to do that is rather like trying to square the circle." The image was a favorite of one of my Oxford tutors.

"I sympathize with the impulse, but I think it is highly impractical," Mulhauser said thoughtfully.

I was taken aback. It was one thing for me to have reservations, quite another thing for my college professor to have them. Though I couldn't forget that Mulhauser was one of the most benevolent people I had ever met, I now told myself that perhaps he was not the best judge of my "impulse." He had settled for a comfortable life in a small college town when, given his considerable abilities, he might have aspired to something more adventurous and challenging.

"Maybe so," I said. "But I'm determined to try."

"How do you plan to go about it?" he asked kindly.

"Just the way I go about the business of living," I said, metaphorically thinking on my feet. "I live among the sighted.

I dress, I eat, I walk with the sensibilities of the sighted in mind. I hear the talk of the sighted from morning to night. My whole inner life is made up of visual assumptions. My unconscious must contain a whole reservoir of visual images and references. After all, I could see until I was almost four."

"I can understand that in fiction you can invent visual details, but in other kinds of writing you will have to describe the actual way people look and what they wear," he said. "How will you do that?"

I was stumped, and felt so frustrated that I almost had a murderous impulse against my beloved professor for throwing a realistic difficulty in my path.

"There are so many visual details about how things look that I just pick up by diligent use of my four senses," I finally said. "How could it be otherwise, when people are constantly talking in images—'It's a bright day,' 'What a pretty blue dress she has on' …"

I broke off. I felt tired.

"The subject of what visual images you have in your head and how you assimilate them from one day to the next would be worthy of book in itself," Mulhauser said. "And perhaps only you could write it. Writers do best when they exploit their special gifts, and your special gift may be to explore the universe of the blind."

"As I've told you, I feel I have done that in 'Face to Face.'"

"That's what you think now. But as you develop as a writer you will also develop as a person, and you'll find you have more to say about the subject and greater skills with which to say it."

The English tea, I had been brought up to think, was an occasion for chit-chat, not for talking about unpleasant or embarrassing matters. Among the reserved English, I had become as reticent as they were, and would certainly never have dreamed of getting into such a personal conversation, especially over tea. Mulhauser had brought out my confiding, American self, I realized, yet I wondered how I had come to bring up the subject. The only books I had ever hoped to write were scholarly ones. The fact that I was blind might be relevant to the method of my research but not to its results. I recalled that I had recently attended some lectures by Richard Pares, a historian I greatly admired. He was so enfeebled by paralysis that someone had to stand next to him and turn the pages of his lecture scripts, yet when people discussed his lectures after they were collected in book form, or wrote about his other books, it no more occurred to them to mention his physical infirmities than to mention, for instance, the youthful looks of Hugh Trevor-Roper when they were discussing his works.

"But I wish to be free of blindness—free of all the baggage that goes with it!" I cried.

Mulhauser apparently sensed the rising tide of my frustration, for he made no reply.

*   *   *

In 1988, when Mr. Shawn was no longer at *The New Yorker*, I asked him during one of our lunches if he had ever had any second thoughts about my writing as if I could see. While he was the editor, he had published my articles in that vein for twenty-seven years.

"No, I didn't," he said without a moment's hesitation. "Your writing seemed totally convincing and natural to me."

"How did you feel when people said that it was totally dishonest?"

"I didn't worry about it, since it worked."

To complicate matters, after I had written in that vein for more than twenty years I started writing like the blind person that I was. I brought up that subject and asked him how he had felt when, as it were, I switched horses in midstream. "I don't think that any other editor would have allowed me to write in both ways," I remarked.

"That was O.K.," he said. "The writing, whichever way you did it, was completely convincing. I felt that whatever you wanted to do, as long as it worked, was O.K."

The simplicity of his answer was stunning. In my years as a writer, I had seen many editors of books and magazines come and go. Each one had typed me as a blind writer or an Indian writer, for instance, and had been interested in my writing on only one or the other of those subjects. In contrast, Mr. Shawn, without having been given a word of preparation or explanation, had jumped in with me in my writing projects, each more outlandish and improbable than the last, as if he were my Siamese twin, who would have to accompany me wherever I went, even to the ends of the earth.

* * *

Of all the people I knew at *The New Yorker* who were eccentric, none was more captivatingly so than St. Clair McKelway. He had come to *The New Yorker* in 1933, at the age of twenty-eight, and was around right up to his death, at the age of seventy-four, in 1980. The son of a prominent Southern family, which numbered notable journalists among its members (a great-uncle of his, also named St. Clair McKelway, had been the editor of the Brooklyn *Eagle*, and from 1946 to 1963 his brother, Benjamin Mosby McKelway, was the editor of the Washington *Star*), he was an impressive figure in the office and on New York streets, for he had the air of a patrician about him.

In Ross's day, when the office was small, McKelway did some of everything—hiring people, coming up with ideas for articles, encouraging newcomers, and editing their copy—and for three years, from 1936 to 1939, he functioned as Ross's managing editor, or "jesus" (a corruption of "genius"): a sort of messiah that Ross was always searching for, to bring order to the chaotic office. As a jesus, McKelway is remembered for splitting *The New Yorker's* editorial workings into two distinct divisions: one, called fiction, which encompassed not only short stories but humor, poetry, and memoirs; and the other, first called journalism but later fact when the term journalism proved too narrow to accommodate the wide range of creative nonfiction material that the magazine soon started publishing. Prior to this reorganization, editors had shuttled back and forth between different kinds of pieces, but afterward they concentrated on pieces within their own fields of expertise. Indeed, those divisions, together with the art department, became fixtures of the magazine.

McKelway is also remembered as a great spotter of talent. He brought in many of the writers—Joe Liebling, Joel Mitchell, John Bainbridge, and Philip Hamburger, to name a few—who during the war years developed a form of reporting that distinguished *The New Yorker* and set it on its course of profound writing done in a seamless narrative style. Nor was that all: it was McKelway who first recognized Mr. Shawn's gifts, when young William Shawn was a Talk reporter, still a little wet behind the ears. Around 1937, McKelway made him one of his two assistants—the other was the esteemed and much beloved editor Sanderson Vanderbilt—and so prepared the way for Mr. Shawn to succeed him as Ross's next, and last, jesus. Moreover, McKelway had a hand in some of the longest-remembered Profiles to appear in Ross's *New Yorker*. He wrote a dissection, in no fewer than six parts, of the gossip columnist Walter Winchell; collaborated with Liebling on a sendup of the Harlem evangelist known as Father Divine; and was a valuable researcher for Wolcott Gibbs's classic examination of Henry Luce and *Time*. On top of that, McKelway wrote and published in *The New Yorker* not only amusing pieces—about impostors and outlaws, among others—but also remarkable short stories, some of them set in the Orient, where he had spent five years before coming to the magazine. But what he will perhaps be most remembered for are his wild narratives about himself, which, as far as I know, have no parallel in the history of letters.

One narrative tells how during the Second World War, when he was serving as a lieutenant colonel in the United States Army Air Forces in Guam, he took it into his head that the illustrious Admiral Chester W. Nimitz was a traitor, and how he then set about exposing him by sending a radiogram to the Pentagon. The idea of the admiral's treachery was a vast misinterpretation of events by McKelway, and General Curtis E. Lemay eventually had to apologize to the admiral in person on behalf of the Army Air Forces. McKelway ended up, as usual, in what Ross used to call "the bughouse." Another narrative tells how during a vacation in his ancestral Scotland in the summer of 1959 he imagined that he had stumbled upon a Russian plot to kidnap President Eisenhower, Queen Elizabeth, and the Duke of Edinburgh. Fancying himself an instrument of a counterplot run by British and American secret agents, he started chasing after any cars whose license plates happened to bear the initials of some of his *New Yorker* colleagues. What prompted these pieces were experiences he had had during periodic nervous breakdowns, but his talent was such that when he recovered he was able to write about his bizarre experiences with humor and grace, rather in the manner of a sane doctor observing the antics of an insane patient. "I have pretty much come to the conclusion that I have a great many heads," he asserted in one piece. "I've counted and identified twelve separate and distinct heads, or identities, that I know I possess." Mr. Shawn, who wrote many anonymous obituaries of staff members which appeared in *The New Yorker*, characterized him at his death in this way:

> McKelway saw events, people, facts — what is ordinarily regarded as reality—through his own particular prism. He must have known that the reality other people accepted was coarse, cruel, and painful, so he avoided it and devised an alternative reality—one that was bearable to him and was a source of endless pleasure to

his colleagues and his readers. He was no moralist. The behavior of nearly all people, including rascals and criminals, and plainly including him, came through to him as inherently funny. From time to time, he entered what was technically a manic phase but what he experienced as anything from "feeling good" to boundless euphoria.

McKelway became so used to his breakdowns that as soon as he felt one coming on he would check himself into a psychiatric hospital. Sometimes he was gone for months at a stretch. Whenever he reappeared, he seemed rested and cheerful and full of plans for catching up with all the things he had missed out on But the process wasn't as easy as it sounds. I remember that once a fellow-patient of his at the hospital was Robert Lowell, who was probably the only established American poet never to have appeared in *The New Yorker*, and whom the magazine would have very much liked to publish. At the hospital, Lowell, himself suffering from a nervous breakdown, wrote four lines of what were mainly gibberish and showed them to McKelway, and McKelway accepted them on the spot, as if he were the editor. In due course, he presented them as a done deal to the real editor, whereupon Mr. Shawn was faced with the unenviable task of rejecting Lowell, and doing so in such a way that the poet would not feel snubbed.

McKelway once told me that if he had had his choice he would have lived right in the office when he was not in the hospital, because the office was where his "real life" went on every day. The jacket copy of his book "The Edinburgh Caper," expanding on his Scotland article, noted that his "birthplace is rumored to have been a corridor near the watercooler in *The New Yorker* offices." In all the years I knew McKelway, he never had an apartment of his own but lived in rundown residential hotels within walking distance of the office. I remember that once he was determined to upgrade his accommodations, but the place he chose was the Iroquois Hotel, just opposite the Forty-fourth Street entrance of our building. He rented by the month an inexpensive room that had a steam pipe running right through the middle of it, which left floor space for little more than a single bed and a couple of chairs. Although he was glad that it was already carpeted and that it would not require any new furniture, he was dismayed to learn that he was responsible for his own bed linens. At just about that time, he happened to meet a friend of mine named Marguerite Lamkin, a divorcée with a charming Southern accent, and he immediately asked her if she would go on a shopping expedition with him. (By then, he had been married and divorced four times. Although he had such a way with women that he was said to be friends with all his ex-wives, he seemed to think that they knew him too well for him to ask them to go shopping for bed linens with him.) Marguerite was a great fan of his writings and readily agreed, and they spent an afternoon getting the bed linens and a few sundries for his room. By the end of the expedition, McKelway had fallen in love with her, and he proposed marriage. An extremely civilized woman, she turned him down without making him feel bad, and afterward they remained good friends.

Most of the time I knew McKelway, he was single, and, like a number of us on the magazine who either were not married or had trouble staying married, he was at loose ends at meal-times. One could cadge breakfast on the run, and one could find people to lunch with, but in the evenings married people disappeared into their own nests. They might invite friends like McKelway once in a while for a family meal, but most of the time he was left to fend for himself. He couldn't cook and found little pleasure in sitting down to a lonely dinner.

On the same side of Forty-third Street as *The New Yorker* offices was the Century, a men's club for writers, artists, and amateurs of the arts which served in the evenings as a water-ing hole for many bachelors and widowers. (It was so close to the office that when I was put up for the club I almost missed becoming a member because, on being asked by a worthy at my interview why I wanted to join, I failed to give an earnest answer, and said flippantly, "It'd make a great canteen.") Every evening during the week, members gathered at six o'clock for drinks at the Round Table, on the second floor, and at seven-thirty they went up for dinner at the Long Table, on the third floor. The evening atmosphere was very much that of a Balzac boarding house. The group might contract or expand, but essentially it stayed the same, for its core came month after month, year after year, and, in doing so, became increasingly set in ôdd habits and quirky ways. Ned Perkins, a retired Yankee lawyer, who was one of the oldest members of the club, was convinced that Arthur, the waiter who got the drinks from the bar for everyone, was half deaf. At the Round Table, Ned would ring the bell furiously and shout out his order for a drink, even though Arthur knew exactly what he had every evening and had already assembled the makings on his tray—a shot glass of freshly squeezed lemon juice, a little baking soda, and water, along with a shot of Jack Daniels. Lewis Galantière, a rather quarrelsome French-American man of letters, seemed never to leave the club until he had complained to the manager about something—stale bread, hard macaroons, unripe cheese. Jo Mielziner, the Broadway set designer, who was ordinarily a mild-mannered man, was always getting into a hot dispute with Galantière about who was going to pay for the taxi ride home to the Dakota, where they both had apartments. (The rest of the members simply split the fare when they shared a taxi.) There was Dr. Stewart (no one called him by his first name, Harold), a gentleman from the South, who was always so cold that he if he could have he would have worn his overcoat to the Round Table. Charles Saltzman, a partner in Goldman, Sachs, who had been a general in the Second World War, was sure to lose his cool if someone came up and greeted him as General, for he insisted that such titles were appropriate only for professional soldiers, and he was not one. Hobey Weekes, an elegant bachelor and born clubman, was known to drink his way through the day—beginning at the Princeton Club, going on to the Coffeehouse, and ending up at the Century—without his storytelling faculties being in the least impaired. A few times, he invited McKelway as a guest, and McKelway took to the life of the Round Table and the Long Table and immediately became eager to join the club. Those who knew of his turbulent nature were a little wary of putting him up for membership, since there was no telling what capers he might get up to while covering the short distance from the Iroquois or *The New Yorker* to the Century. Still, with his eccentric talent, easy charm, and courtly demeanor, he was a born Centurion He was duly proposed and quickly elected. For some months, he was happier than I had ever known him. But, as he later said, "every apple has a worm in it, and the club is no exception."

McKelway was a member for four years, from 1961 to 1965. He would arrive at the club at eleven in the morning and drink well into the evening, oblivious of the sure fact that at the end of the month there would be a reckoning in the form of a hefty bill. He was now carried by this member, now rescued by that. Every so often, he got a bit of money from *The New Yorker* or from a publisher and made a payment, but he could never catch up with his debts, and they kept on ballooning. He was warned that practically the only way a member could be expelled was by not paying his bills, and he was put on notice several times. He always pointed out that he would not have got into trouble if the club had required him to pay cash for whatever he ate or drank. The club tried to accommodate him, but in the end taking cash from only one member proved a nuisance for the bookkeeper. Anyway, the combination of his debts and the sight of him drunkenly stumbling down the grand staircase finally proved enough to get him ousted from the club.

Like many single people, McKelway used to get especially depressed during the holidays. He wished he were a minor Rip van Winkle, and could sleep through Christmas and wake up in the New Year. One winter, he hit upon what he thought was a marvellous way of getting through Christmas Day. He equipped himself with an impressive-looking briefcase, stuffed it with newspapers, donned a three-piece suit, as was his wont, and boarded a train for Albany. He got a table in the dining car and ordered an elaborate meal. Just as he had expected, the waiters were extremely deferential: they took him to be an important politician, whose business was so urgent that, Christmas or no, he had to travel to the state capital. In Albany, he got off the train and killed some time in the men's room. Then he boarded a train back to New York, feeling sure that he would get the same deferential treatment from a new set of waiters. He marched into the dining ear. To his horror, the same staff was on duty and recognized him. His Christmas Day was spoiled, because he was sure that its members had guessed his ruse. He had always been mesmerized by impostors, since he himself was at the mercy of a number of identities at any given moment.

Another time, when McKelway was in his manic phase but was on the verge of tipping into a depression and a psychiatric hospital, he took a fancy to a young Englishwoman, Kennedy Fraser, who was a writer at the magazine. She was only a third his age, but he was smitten by her and proposed to her. She laughed the proposal off, thinking it a sweet compliment and nothing more. Thereafter, he started scribbling meaningless words on the walls of the eighteenth floor. (It was a habit he shared with at least one other *New Yorker* writer, James Thurber, who went in for doodling on his office walls as he became totally blind.) Kennedy's rejection only made McKelway more obsessed with her, and one night he persuaded the police that she had been murdered. He must have told them a plausible story, because he arrived at her doorstep in the middle of the night with a posse of half a dozen policemen. When she opened the door, she was stunned by the crazy lengths that McKelway had gone to.

The next morning, when Mr. Shawn was apprised of this mad intrusion, he advised Kennedy not to discuss the matter with anyone and to stay away from the eighteenth floor for a time. Soon McKelway was back in the hospital, and Kennedy, shaken up, was back among us.

Mac's fourth, and last, wife, to whom "The Edinburgh Caper" was dedicated, was Maeve Brennan, a diminutive, red-haired Irishwoman, whom he married in 1954, when she was about thirty-seven. The marriage lasted only a few years. At the time I knew her, she had an office on the twentieth floor. She wrote short book reviews and also a series of Comment pieces, which were published as "communications from our friend the long-winded lady." The central irony of these Comment pieces was that they were vignettes—minutely observed impressions of how the city felt, looked, and sounded at a given moment. What she was best known for, however, were beautifully written *New Yorker* short stories, generally set in her native Ireland; they were collected in two volumes, "In and Out of Never-Never Land" (1969) and "Christmas Eve" (1974). Temperamentally a gypsy, she was drawn to run-down neighborhoods and to transients, and she camped out in a series of small hotels near the office. She was paid well for her work, but she was incapable of holding on to money. When she had it, it seemed to slip through her fingers, as if there were no tomorrow. Mr. Shawn often rescued her from going hungry and having nowhere to lay her head by seeing to it that, if she wanted to, she could go to a place in the city where she would have food and shelter.

Sometime in the early nineteen-eighties, Maeve began to haunt the nineteenth floor like a waif. Imagining that she was destitute, she moved into the office, did cooking in her cubicle on the floor above, and slept on a daybed in the nineteenth-floor ladies' room. The women on the nineteenth floor accommodated her behavior, even though it could sometimes turn violent, as if that were the fate of writers. Whenever we brought up the subject of her erratic behavior with Mr. Shawn, he would say, "She's a beautiful writer," and quickly walk away. He seemed to be at a loss to know how to handle her.

One morning, after Maeve had been living in the office for several months, we heard that she had thrown a chair through the top part of Greenstein's office door, which was opaque glass. "It's a cry for treatment," one colleague said to me, and Mr. Shawn and Greenstein finally entered her in a hospital. She was in and out of hospitals for the next decade, and died in 1993, at the age of seventy-six. In her last years, she was often seen on East Forty-fourth Street, a block or so away from the office, sitting on the sidewalk amid shopping bags and discarded papers.

Maeve seemed unaware of what was happening to her. In contrast, McKelway was an expert at knowing when a breakdown was coming. One morning in the nineteen-seventies, however, when he was hailing a taxi in Boston, he failed to catch the telltale signs. He stepped into the cab, leaned back in his seat in a princely fashion, and said, "Twenty-five West Forty-third Street, please."

The driver turned around and gave him a sharp glance. "That's in New York, Mac," he said.

"I know," McKelway said irritably, as if his intelligence were being questioned. As usual, he was wearing a finely tailored three-piece suit, and the driver decided to take him at his word.

"O.K., if that's what you want, Mac," he said, and put down his flag. "You know I'll have to come back without a ride, so you'll have to pay double what's on the meter."

"Of course," McKelway said dreamily. He thrust his hands in his pockets and sat back for the ride to the office.

Four or five hours later, the taxi pulled up in front of 25 West Forty-third Street, with several hundred dollars run up on the meter.

McKelway got out, thanked the driver grandly, as if he were speaking to his private chauffeur, and started to walk into the building.

The driver threw a fit. He leaped out of the taxi and chased McKelway up to the eighteenth floor, bellowing that if he didn't get his fare there would be murder to pay. The receptionist was terrified and called Mr. Shawn, and he came running down from his office, with Greenstein close behind. The two of them calmed the driver by assuring him that he would be paid, and then they ushered an oblivious McKelway out of the reception area. It was late afternoon, and the banks were closed, but somehow they scrounged up the cash, and the driver was paid.

McKelway later told me that if the driver had not called him Mac, his nickname, an alarm would have gone off in his head, and he would have realized what he was doing.

THE DAYS OF DUVEEN

S.M. Behrman

1951

WHEN JOSEPH DUVEEN, the most spectacular art dealer of all time, travelled from one to another of his three galleries, in Paris, New York, and London, his business, including a certain amount of his stock in trade, travelled with him. His business was highly personal, and during his absence his establishments dozed. They jumped to attention only upon the kinetic arrival of the Master. Early in life, Duveen—who became Lord Duveen of Millbank before he died in 1939, at the age of sixty-nine—noticed that Europe had plenty of art and America had plenty of money, and his entire astonishing career was the product of that simple observation. Beginning in 1886, when he was seventeen, he was perpetually journeying between Europe, where he stocked up, and America, where he sold. In later years, his annual itinerary was relatively fixed: At the end of May, he would leave New York for London, where he spent June and July; then he would go to Paris for a week or two; from there he would go to Vittel, a health resort in the Vosges Mountains, where he took a three-week cure; from Vittel he would return to Paris for another fortnight; after that, he would go back to London; sometime in September, he would set sail for New York, where he stayed through the winter and early spring.

Occasionally, Duveen departed from his routine to help out a valuable customer. If, say, he was in Paris and Andrew Mellon or Jules Bache was coming there, he would considerately remain a bit longer than usual, to assist Mellon or Bache with his education in art. Although, according to some authorities, especially those in his native England, Duveen's knowledge of art was conspicuously exceeded by his enthusiasm for it, he was regarded by most of his wealthy American clients as little less than omniscient. "To the Caliph I may be dirt, but to dirt I am the Caliph!" says Hajj the beggar in Edward Knoblock's "Kismet." Hajj's estimate of his social position approximated Duveen's standing as a scholar. To his major pupils, Duveen extended extracurricular courtesies. He permitted Bache to store supplies of his favorite cigars in the vaults of the Duveen establishments in London and Paris. One day, as Bache was leaving his hotel in Paris for his boat train, he realized that he didn't have enough cigars to last him for the Atlantic crossing. He made a quick detour to Duveen's to replenish. Duveen was not in Paris, and Bache was greeted by Bertram Boggis, then Duveen's chief assistant and today one of the heads of the firm of Duveen Brothers. While Bache was waiting for the cigars to appear, Boggis showed him a Van Dyck and told him Duveen had earmarked it for him. Bache was so entranced with the picture that he bought it on the spot and almost forgot about the cigars; he finally went off to the train with both. There was no charge for storing the cigars, but the Van Dyck cost him two hundred and seventy-five thousand dollars.

Probably never before had a merchant brought to such exquisite perfection the large-minded art of casting bread upon the waters. There was almost nothing Duveen wouldn't do for his important clients. Immensely rich Americans, shy and suspicious of casual contacts because of their wealth, often didn't know where to go or what to do with themselves when they were abroad. Duveen provided entrée to the great country homes of the nobility; the coincidence that their noble owners often had ancestral portraits to sell did not deter Duveen. He also wangled hotel accommodations and passage on sold-out ships. He got his clients houses, or he provided architects to build them houses, and then saw to it that the architects planned the interiors with wall space that demanded plenty of pictures. He even selected brides or bridegrooms for some of his clients, and presided over the weddings with avuncular benevolence. These selections had to meet the same refined standard that governed his choice of houses for his clients—a potential receptivity to expensive art.

On immediate issues, Duveen was not a patient man. With choleric imperialism, he felt that the world must stop while he got what he wanted. He had a convulsive drive, a boundless and explosive fervor, especially for a picture he had just bought, and a reckless contempt for works of art handled by rival dealers. On one occasion, an extremely respectable High Church duke was considering a religious painting by an Old Master that Thomas Agnew & Sons, the distinguished English art firm, had offered him. He asked Duveen to look at it. "Very nice, my dear fellow, very nice," said Duveen. "But I suppose you are aware that those cherubs are homosexual." The painting went back to Agnew's. When, presently, through the tortuous channels of picture-dealing, it came into Duveen's possession, the cherubs, by some miraculous Duveen therapy, were restored to sexual normality. Similarly, in New York, a millionaire collector who was so undisciplined that he was thinking of buying a sixteenth-century Italian painting from another dealer asked Duveen to his mansion on Fifth Avenue to look at it. The prospective buyer watched Duveen's face closely and saw his nostrils quiver. "I sniff fresh paint," said Duveen sorrowfully. His remarks about other people's pictures sometimes resulted in lawsuits that lasted for years, cost him hundreds of thousands of dollars, and brought to the courts of London, New York, or Paris international convocations of experts to thrash things out.

It was one of the crosses Duveen had to bear that the temperaments of the men he dealt with in this country were the direct opposite of his own. The great American millionaires of the Duveen Era were slow-speaking and slow-thinking, cautious, secretive—in Duveen's eyes, maddeningly deliberate. Those other emperors, the emperors of oil and steel, of department stores and railroads and newspapers, of stocks and bonds, of utilities and banking houses, had trained themselves to talk slowly, pausing lengthily before each word and especially before each verb, in order to keep themselves from sliding over into the abyss of commitment. For a man like Duveen, who was congenitally unable to keep quiet, the necessity of dealing constantly with cryptic men like the elder J.P. Morgan and Henry Clay Frick and Mellon was ulcerating. He would read a letter from one of his important clients twenty times, pondering each evasively phrased sentence. "What does he mean by that?" he would ask his secretary. "Is he interested in the picture or isn't he?"

For a great many years, Duveen's secretary was an Englishman named H.W. Morgan. Some have said that Duveen hired him simply because his name was Morgan. It has even been suggested that Duveen made his secretary adopt the name, so that he could feel he was sending for Morgan instead of Morgan's sending for him. In any case, one of H.W. Morgan's duties was now and then to impersonate Mellon. The day before a scheduled interview with any of his important clients, Duveen would go to bed to map out the strategic possibilities. But before such an interview with Mellon, Duveen would, in addition to going to bed, rehearse with Morgan. Mellon was particularly hard to deal with, because he was supremely inscrutable. "Now, Morgan, you are Mellon," Duveen would say. "Now you go out and come in." Morgan would come in as Mellon, and Duveen would start peppering him with questions; Morgan would try to put himself into Mellon's inscrutable state of mind and answer without saying anything. The fact that Mellon's Pittsburgh speech was now strongly doused in Cockney did not impair the illusion for Duveen.

Duveen sometimes came home from a talk with Mellon so upset by Mellon's doubts that he had to go back to bed, this time to ponder the veiled issues. There were never any doubts in his own mind. Each picture he had to sell, each tapestry, each piece of sculpture was the greatest since the last one and until the next one. How could these men dawdle, thwart their itch to own these magnificent works, because of a mere matter of price? They could replace the money many times over, but they were acquiring the irreplaceable when they bought, simply by paying Duveen's price for it, a Duveen. (When a Titian or a Raphael or a Donatello passed from Duveen into the hands of Joseph E. Widener or Benjamin Altman or Samuel H. Kress, it became a Widener or an Altman or a Kress, but until then it was a Duveen.) Still, Duveen learned to bear this cross, and even to manipulate it a bit. While coping with their doubts, he solidified his own convictions, and then charged them extra for the time and trouble he had taken doing it. Making his clients conscious that whereas he had unique access to great art, his outlets for it were multiple, he watched their doubts about the prices of the art evolving into more acute doubts about whether he would let them buy it.

Whenever Duveen was in Paris or Vittel, he received daily reports from his galleries in New York and London—précis of the Callers' Books, telling what customers or nibblers had come in, what pictures they had looked at and for how long, what they had said, and so on. From other sources he got reports on any major collections being offered for sale, and photographs of their treasures. There were also reports from his "runners," the francs-tireurs he deployed all over Europe to hunt out noblemen on the verge of settling for solvency and a bit of loose change at the sacrifice of some of their family portraits. These reports might include the gossip of servants who had overheard the master saying to an important art dealer, as they savored the bouquet of an after-dinner brandy, that he might—in certain circumstances, he just might consider parting with the lovely titled Gainsborough lady smiling graciously down at them from over a mantel. Once Duveen had such a clue, he hastened to telescope the circumstances in which the Gainsborough-owner just might. Often the dealer who had enjoyed the brandy did not find himself in a position to enjoy the emolument that went with handling the Gainsborough. In negotiating with the heads of noble families, Duveen usually won hands down over other dealers; the brashness and impetuosity of his attack simply bowled the dukes and barons over. He didn't waste his time and theirs on art patter (he reserved that for his American clients); he talked prices, and big prices. He would say, "Greatest thing *I* ever saw! Will pay the biggest price *you* ever saw!" To this technique the dukes and barons responded warmly. They were familiar with it from their extensive experience in buying and selling horses.

In Paris, Duveen often got frantic letters from his comptroller in New York imploring him to stop buying. Duveen, who was never as elated by a sale as he was by a purchase, usually laid out over a million dollars on his annual trip abroad, and occasionally three or four times that sum. These immoderate disbursals of money paralleled the self-indulgence of Morgan. Frederick Lewis Allen, in his biography of Morgan, writes, "As for his purchases of art, they were made on such a scale that an annual worry at 23 Wall Street at the year end, when the books of the firm were balanced, was whether Morgan's personal balance in New York would be large enough to meet the debit balances accumulated through the year as a result of his habit of paying for works of art with checks drawn on the London or the Paris firm." Each man, his bookkeeper thought, spent too much on art.

Duveen's finances were a puzzle to his friends, his clients, his associates, and other art dealers. In July, 1930, when art dealers all over the world were gasping for money, he stupefied them by paying four and a half million dollars for the Gustave Dreyfus Collection. Bache, who was a close friend as well as a client, once said, "I think I understand Joe pretty well—his purchases and his sales methods. But I confess I am quite in the dark about his financing." Depression or no depression, it was Duveen's principle to pay the highest conceivable prices, and he usually succeeded in doing so. Adherence to this principle required finesse, sometimes even lack of finesse. A titled Englishwoman had a family portrait to sell. Duveen asked her what she wanted for it. Meekly, she mentioned eighteen thousand pounds. Duveen was indignant. "What?" he cried. "Eighteen thousand pounds for a picture of this quality? Ridiculous, my dear lady! Ridiculous!" He began to extol the virtues of the picture, as if he were selling it—as, indeed, he already was in his mind—instead of buying it. A kind of haggle in reverse ensued. Finally, the owner asked him what he thought the picture was worth. Duveen, who had already decided what he would charge some American customer—a price he could not conscientiously ask for a picture that had cost him a mere eighteen thousand pounds—shouted reproachfully at her, "My dear lady, the very least you should let that picture go for is twenty-five thousand pounds!" Swept off her feet by his enthusiasm, the lady capitulated.

Duveen had enormous respect for the prices he set on the objects he bought and sold. Often his clients tried, in various ways, to maneuver him into a position where he might relax his high standards, but he nearly always managed to keep them inviolate. There was an instance of this kind of maneuvering in 1934, which concerned three busts from the Dreyfus Collection—a Verrocchio, a Donatello, and a Desiderio da Settignano. Duveen offered this trio to John D. Rockefeller, Jr., for a million and a half dollars. Rockefeller felt that the price was rather high. Duveen, on the other hand, felt that, considering the quality of the busts, he was practically giving them away. He allowed Rockefeller, in writing, a year's option on the busts; they were to remain for a year in the Rockefeller mansion as non-paying guests. During that time, Duveen hoped, the attraction the chary host felt for his visitors would ripen into an emotion that was more intense. After several months, the attraction did ripen into affection, but not a million and a half dollars' worth, and Rockefeller wrote Duveen a letter with a counter-proposal. He had some tapestries for which he had paid a quarter of a million dollars. He proposed to send Duveen these tapestries, so that *he* could have a chance to become fond of *them*, and to buy the busts for a million dollars, throwing the tapestries in as lagniappe. As the depression was still on and most people were feeling the effects of it, Rockefeller thought, he said, that Duveen might welcome the million in cash. This letter threw Duveen into a flurry. It bothered him more than most letters he got from clients. His legal adviser told him that the counter-offer, unless immediately repudiated, might result in a cancellation of the option. Duveen sat down and wrote a letter himself. As for the tapestries, he told Rockefeller, he had some tapestries and didn't want any more. Moreover, he stated, he was not in the stock market, and therefore not in the least affected by the depression. He let fall a few phrases of sympathy for those who were; by his air of surprised incredulity at the existence of people who felt the depression, Duveen managed to convey the suggestion that if Rockefeller was in temporary financial difficulty, he, Duveen, was ready to come to his assistance. He appreciated Rockefeller's offer of a million dollars in cash, but he implied that, just as he already had some tapestries, he also already had a million dollars. Having dispatched the letter, Duveen, with his customary optimism, prophesied to his associates that Rockefeller would eventually buy the busts at his price. At Christmastime, with a week or so of the option still to go, Rockefeller told Duveen that his final decision was not to buy the busts, and asked Duveen to take them back. Again, Duveen was prepared to be generous, this time about the security of Rockefeller's dwelling. "Never mind," he said. "Keep them in your house. They're as safe there as they would be in mine." In all love affairs, there comes a moment when desire demands possession. For Rockefeller, this occurred on the day before the option expired. On the thirty-first of December, at the eleventh hour, he informed Duveen that he was buying the busts at a million and a half.

On his visits to Paris, Duveen often gazed admiringly at the building occupied by the Ministry of Marine, a beautiful production of the illustrious Jacques-Ange Gabriel, court architect to Louis XV. The noble façade executed by Gabriel stretches its lovely length to front an entire block along the Place de la Concorde. The Ministry consists of a tremendous central edifice, flanked by great wings. One day, in his lively imagination, Duveen snipped off and reduced in size one of Gabriel's wings and saw it transferred to New York. With his immense energy and drive, he set about materializing this snip at once. In 1911, he engaged a Philadelphia architect, Horace Trumbauer, and a Paris architect, Réné Sergent, to put up a five-story, thirty-room reproduction of Gabriel's wing at the corner of Fifth Avenue and Fifty-sixth Street, to serve as his gallery. Even the stone was French-imported from quarries near St. Quentin and Chassignelles. The total cost was a million dollars, but this was not too much for an establishment that was to house the Duveen treasures. The eight or ten big clients who would enter the building—the handful of men with whom Duveen did the major part of his business—to look at the garnered possessions of kings and emperors and high ecclesiastics were rulers, too, and must be provided with an environment that would tend to make them conscious of their right to inherit these possessions.

In Paris, Duveen always stayed at the Ritz. A permanent guest at this hotel, with whom Duveen had many encounters over the years, was Calouste S. Gulbenkian, the Armenian oil Croesus. Gulbenkian, who controls now, as he controlled then, a good deal of the oil in Iraq, is often said to be the richest man in Europe, and possibly in the world, and possesses one of the world's most valuable art collections. Of all his achievements, perhaps the most chic is that he several times outmaneuvered Duveen. One day, happening upon Duveen in one of the Ritz elevators, Gulbenkian told him that he knew of three fine English pictures for sale—a Reynolds, a Lawrence, and a Gainsborough. The owner wanted to sell them in a lot. Gulbenkian proposed that Duveen buy them and give him, as a reward for his tip, an option on any one of the three, with this proviso: Duveen was to put his own prices on them before Gulbenkian made his choice known, but the total price was not to exceed what Duveen had paid. Duveen bought the pictures and went about setting the individual prices. As he wanted from Gulbenkian a sum that would become the richest man in Europe, he pondered deeply before deciding which picture he thought Gulbenkian would choose. The finest, although the least dazzling, of the three was Gainsborough's "Portrait of Mrs. Lowndes-Stone." The showiest was the Lawrence. Duveen concluded that the Lawrence would have the greatest appeal to his client's Oriental taste. He put a Duveen price on the Lawrence, and therefore had to set reasonable figures for the two others. He overlooked the fact that Gulbenkian is a canny student of art as well as an Oriental. Gulbenkian took the Gainsborough. It was one of the few times anyone acquired a Duveen without paying a Duveen price for it.

Altogether, Duveen wasn't fortunate in his dealings with Gulbenkian. He tried hard, but he didn't meet with the success that favored him in his dealings with his American clients. Not only that, an effort Duveen made in 1921 to get a couple of Rembrandts for Gulbenkian led to an acrid lawsuit in which he found himself in the embarrassing position of having to testify against one of his best American clients, Joseph E. Widener, the celebrated horse and traction man. The paintings, "Portrait of a Gentleman with a Tall Hat and Gloves" and "Portrait of a Lady with an Ostrich-Feather Fan," were considered very good Rembrandts. The Russian Prince Felix Youssoupoff, the slayer of Rasputin, had inherited them. He left Russia for Paris rather hurriedly after the Revolution, but he managed to take the pictures with him. Soon, finding himself in need of cash, he proposed to Widener, whom he went to see in London, that he lend Widener the pictures in return for a loan of a hundred thousand pounds. Widener replied that he was not in the banking business; he would buy the pictures for a hundred thousand pounds, but he wouldn't lend a penny on them. Widener returned to New York, and after some weeks of negotiating by cables and letters, Youssoupoff signed a contract in which he agreed to sell Widener the pictures for a hundred thousand pounds, with the understanding that Widener would sell them back for the same sum, plus eight per cent annual interest, if on or before January 1, 1924 (and here Youssoupoff was expressing a nostalgia for the future), a restoration of the old regime in Russia made it possible for Youssoupoff again "to keep and personally enjoy these wonderful works of art." Just about this time, Gulbenkian indicated to Duveen a hankering for Rembrandts. Duveen took hold of Gulbenkian's wistfulness and turned it into an avid melancholy. "If you're interested in Rembrandts," he said, "you've just lost the two best in the world to Widener. He bought them both for a hundred thousand pounds, and each of them is worth that." Gulbenkian was indignant that a man of Rembrandt's talent should sell for less than he was worth; he was willing to give the artist his due. News of Gulbenkian's suddenly developed sense of equity was transmitted to Youssoupoff, who was delighted to hear that Rembrandt was coming into his own. On the strength of the two hundred thousand pounds that seemed about to accrue to the artist, Youssoupoff felt he was in a position to ask Widener to give his pictures back. This he did. Widener wanted to know what revolution had taken place that would enable the Prince to enjoy the pictures again. Youssoupoff said that it was none of his business. Widener said that an economic revolution had been stipulated in the contract, and that if Youssoupoff was going to be so reticent, he jolly well wasn't going to get the pictures. Youssoupoff's reply to this was to bring suit against Widener for the return of the pictures.

This lawsuit, which was heard in the New York Supreme Court in 1925, was something less than urbane. One of Widener's lawyers said of Youssoupoff that "any man who paints his face and blackens his eyes is a joke." Emory S. Buckner, one of Youssoupoff's lawyers, contended that the Prince had merely mortgaged the paintings to Widener for a hundred thousand pounds at eight per cent and another of the Prince's lawyers called Widener a "pawnbroker." Clarence J. Shearn, a third lawyer, declared that Widener was a sharp trader who had taken in a gentleman. With extraordinary reserve, he abstained from making even harsher allegations against Widener. "I could shout 'perjury' from the housetops," he said. "I could say that Widener is a thief, a perjurer, and a swindler. This is not necessary. He has drawn his own picture on the witness stand." Duveen, called in by the defense as a witness, gave the court a somewhat different picture of Widener. He testified that Widener had, in the past few years, bought six hundred thousand dollars' worth of art from him, and he, Duveen, had told him that the Widener name on his books was good enough for him. "You can pay when you want," he had said. Youssoupoff's lawyers, during their attempt to establish that Widener had taken advantage of Youssoupoff, countered by putting Duveen on the stand as a witness for the plaintiff. Duveen testified that he had once offered the Prince five hundred and fifty thousand dollars for the two Rembrandts and that the Prince had wanted a million. At the Prince's price, Duveen said, he himself could have made only ten per cent on whatever deal he might have effected. Sometimes, though, he said, he did sell at a very small profit, sometimes even at a loss. "I sold some art once to Mr. Widener for three hundred and fifty thousand dollars, and I sold to him losing the interest," he said. "That seems to be the usual way with people who deal with Mr. Widener," Shearn observed. There was an objection, and he withdrew the remark, but at least he had had the pleasure of making it. Later in his testimony, Duveen let it be known that his enthusiasm for the disputed Rembrandts had diminished; there were better ones, he said, than the Prince's pair. He mentioned one he himself had sold to Widener. After all, Youssoupoff's Rembrandts had never been Duveens.

Other unconventional vignettes were drawn at the trial. The art dealer Arthur J. Sulley, Widener's London agent, who had delivered the hundred thousand pounds to Youssoupoff in the form of two checks—one for forty-five thousand pounds and one for fifty-five thousand—testified that when the Prince came to his office to sign the contract and pick up the checks, he brought along several friends, who kept snatching at the checks before the contract was signed. Sulley had had to hold them over his head to keep the friends from grabbing them, he said. They told him they merely wanted to look at the checks. When Widener, who had written Youssoupoff asking him to keep the entire transaction secret, was asked why he had done that, he testified, "I didn't think it would be a good thing to have it known publicly that large sums of money were being spent for works of art at that time. I thought it might tend to foster a spirit of Bolshevism." This was one of the many occasions on which the millionaires of the era demonstrated that they thought it expedient for their conspicuous consumption to be kept inconspicuous.

Gulbenkian's name was brought into the suit early. Shearn stated that Gulbenkian, as a *beau geste*, had advanced money to Youssoupoff to buy the pictures back and that Youssoupoff, out of courtesy, had insisted on Gulbenkian's taking a lien on them. The defense, on the other hand, set out to prove that Gulbenkian wanted to get hold of the pictures for himself, not for Youssoupoff, that Youssoupoff was not trying to put himself in a position "to keep and personally enjoy" the pictures but simply trying to sell them for a higher price. The Prince tried to raise the dispute to a less tawdry plane. On the stand, he made it clear that he considered Gulbenkian's offer the fiscal equivalent of a new regime in Russia, and that he felt that Widener, in his insistence on a return of the Romanovs, was being technical. He went on to say that he came of a Russian family that had been worth half a billion dollars, and that, despite the Revolution, he owned a summer home in Geneva worth a hundred and seventy-five thousand dollars and a house in Paris worth forty-five thousand dollars. There was also an estate in Brittany worth seven hundred and fifty thousand dollars; his family had given it to the French government, but he was expecting to get it back any minute. Several days later, the Prince took the stand again and testified that he had forgotten to mention seventy thousand dollars' worth of jewelry in England and a New York bank account amounting to $62,250. One of Widener's lawyers said tartly, "By all this haziness and loss of memory, do you want to appear to the Court as being very simple?" "I do not want to appear to the Court," replied the Prince with manly modesty. "I want only to be myself as I am."

Widener, unnecessarily complicating matters for himself, mentioned the fact that Youssoupoff not only had signed the contract but also had sent him a cable confirming the closing of the deal. When Widener was asked to produce the cable, he couldn't find it. "I concede that the cable couldn't be found," Shearn said generously, "because it appears quite plain that such a cablegram was never sent." The Interstate Commerce Commission at that time required that the cable companies keep duplicates of cables for a year, but after the year was up, the companies destroyed them. "All anyone would have to do if they were impelled by a sinister motive," Shearn continued, "would be to wait a year and then testify as to the contents of a fictitious cable, the actual sending of which could never be traced, especially if the plaintiff in such a case were to bring along a host of retainers and secretaries to swear as to the contents of such an unproduced cablegram as against the emphatic denial that such a message was sent from the person who is alleged to have sent it." Goaded by these remarks, Widener sent several Pinkertons to Lynnewood Hall, his estate in Elkins Park, outside Philadelphia, where they ripped pillowcases open and peered into the secret compartments of antique escritoires, but the missing cable did not turn up. Nevertheless, Widener won the case. The Court decided that his contract with Youssoupoff amounted to a sale, and that if Gulbenkian were permitted to lend the Prince the money to buy the pictures back, Gulbenkian would be the man "to keep and personally enjoy" them. A year before Widener's death, the Rembrandts went to the National Gallery, in Washington, where they now hang. Months after the suit was over, the missing cablegram fell out of an old studbook in the Widener living room.

When Duveen was in London, he stayed at Claridge's, and his suite there, like his accommodations at all points on his itinerary, was transformed into a small-scale art gallery. He had infallible taste in decoration—even his detractors admit that—and he arranged the paintings, sculptures, and objets d'art he travelled with so that his clients and friends could visit him in a proper setting, and possibly take home some of the furnishings. He was never without a favorite picture (invariably the last one he had bought), and he kept it beside him on an easel whenever he dined in his suite and took it along to his bedroom when he retired. At Claridge's, titled ladies from all over Europe, and merely rich ones from America, would drop in to see him. With his long succession of lady clients—the first one he attracted, when he was fairly young, was the remarkable Arabella Huntington, the wife of, consecutively, Collis P. Huntington and his nephew H.E. Huntington—Duveen seems to have had the relationship Disraeli had with Queen Victoria; he gave them the exciting sense of being engaged with him in momentous creative enterprises. The ladies felt that he and they were fellow-epicures at the groaning banquet table of culture.

One of Duveen's closest London friends in the days between the two World Wars was Lord D'Abernon, the British Ambassador to Germany during the early twenties. Lord D'Abernon used to describe Duveen as an exhilarating companion. It was his interesting theory that Duveen's laugh, which was famous, was a copy of the infectious laugh of a well-known British architect; Duveen's partiality for architects started early. Everyone agrees that his enthusiasm was irrepressible, and that he engaged in a kind of buffoonery that was irresistible. Most of his friends were, like D'Abernon, older men, and they enjoyed his company partly because he made them feel young. Duveen was even able to rejuvenate some of his pictures. Once, in the late afternoon, he was standing before a picture he had sold to Mellon, expatiating enthusiastically on its wonders to the new owner. A beam from the setting sun suddenly reached through a window and bathed the picture in a lovely light. It was the kind of collaboration Duveen expected from all parts of the universe, animate and inanimate. When his dithyramb had subsided, Mellon said sadly, "Ah, yes. The pictures always look better when you are here."

In London, Duveen occasionally, and uncharacteristically, devoted himself to the artistic tutoring of a non-buyer who was not even a potential buyer. For a period, with the tenderness of a master for a pupil whose aesthetic perceptions were virginal, Duveen piloted Ramsay MacDonald, then an M.P., around the London galleries. This had the look of a disinterested favor, and it was one, for MacDonald came from a social stratum that did not indulge in picture-buying. But even Duveen's altruism proved to be profitable. MacDonald became Prime Minister in 1929, and shortly afterward Duveen was appointed to the board of the National Gallery, a distinction that had never before been conferred on an art dealer and that caused a scandal and a rumpus. Was it decorous for a man on the selling end of art to be on the buying end of a publicly supported institution? Neville Chamberlain, who became Prime Minister in 1937, didn't believe it was, and he revoked the appointment. This deposition shadowed the last years of Duveen's life. Earlier, however, MacDonald and Duveen had a good time sitting next to each other at board meetings of the National Gallery, and in 1933 the grateful pupil brought Duveen the apple of the peerage. At a birthday dinner for MacDonald, given by Duveen at his beautiful house in New York, at Ninety-first Street and Madison Avenue, a few years before, the visiting Prime Minister had announced, "I think I know what Sir Joseph's ambition is. If it's the last act of my life, I shall get it for him." MacDonald personally canvassed the heads of all the art museums in England, asking them to petition the King for Duveen's elevation to the peerage. Duveen had been knighted in 1919; he had been made a baronet in 1927; and now, in 1933, he was made a baron. Very often, Englishmen elevated to the peerage have commemorated their home town in their titles, as Disraeli did Beaconsfield. But Duveen, who had no settled home for a long time except for the house on Madison Avenue, chose to commemorate the section of London known as Millbank, because that is where the Tate Gallery, to which he had made numerous gifts, is situated. So he became Lord Duveen of Millbank.

Each time Duveen arrived in New York from London, there were fanfares of publicity for him and his most recent fabulous purchases. The "Twenty Years Ago Today" column of the *Herald Tribune*, which provides a capsule immortality for those judicious enough to have exerted themselves two decades before, has been studded for some time now with Duveen tidbits, such as:

February 19, 1926.

Sir Joseph Duveen, the art dealer, has bought the Wachtmeister Rembrandt for $410,000, one of the highest prices ever paid for a Rembrandt, and is bringing it to New York. The painting, which is called "Portrait of a Young Man," was sold by Count Carl Wachtmeister and it has been in the possession of his family for 200 years.

July 18, 1927.

Sir Joseph Duveen, international art dealer, bought in London yesterday the entire collection of 120 Italian old masters belonging to Robert H Benson. It will be brought intact to New York. The purchase price was $3,000.000.

January 7, 1929.

LONDON: Andrew W. Mellon, Secretary of the Treasury of the United States, has purchased [from Duveen] for $970,000 Raphael's "Madonna," known as the "Cowper Madonna." The painting bears Raphael's signature and the date "1508."

Once, Duveen brought back Gainsborough's "The Blue Boy," which he had already sold, in Paris, to Mr. and Mrs. H.E. Huntington; another time, he brought back Lawrence's "Pinkie," the portrait of a girl who sat for Lawrence when she was twelve, in the last year of her life, and whose brother became the father of Elizabeth Barrett. There were tearful farewells for both these eminent children when they left their native heath, and jubilant welcomes when they arrived in their adopted land. The circumstances attending Duveen's purchase of "Pinkie," in 1926, illustrate his tenacity in the fight he made to establish his preëminence among the art dealers of the world. His chief rival in this country was the venerable firm of Knoedler. When Duveen was starting out, Knoedler had arrangements with Mellon and several other big collectors to make all their art purchases for them, on a fixed commission. From the beginning, Duveen felt that his educational mission was twofold—to teach millionaire American collectors what the great works of art were, and to teach them that they could get those works of art only through him. To establish this *sine qua non* required considerable daring and a lot of money. When it was announced that "Pinkie" was to be sold at auction at Christie's, in London, a partner in Knoedler's came to Duveen, who was then in London himself, with the suggestion that they buy it jointly. Knoedler's, he said, had a client he was sure would take it. Duveen suspected that the motive for this friendly overture was to keep him from forcing the price up for the prospective buyer, and he politely declined. The Knoedler man said that no one could outbid his client. Duveen said that no one could keep him from buying "Pinkie." On the eve of the sale, Duveen went to Paris, leaving behind him an unlimited bid with the manager of Christie's. In Paris, he awaited the result, with increasing nervousness. On the day of the sale, he informed his friends that he was buying a great picture, that he had once sold it himself for a hundred thousand dollars, and that, as a rich bidder was interested, the price might go to two hundred thousand. That evening, he learned that he had paid three hundred and seventy-seven thousand dollars for "Pinkie." When he recovered from the shock, he brought the young lady to New York and gave her a lavish reception at his Ministry of Marine. While she was being ogled by an invited throng, Duveen telephoned Mellon, in Washington (he had known all along who his rival's rich client was), and offered her to him for adoption. Mellon said that he had indeed been trying to get her but that Duveen had paid an outrageous price for her and he wasn't interested. Duveen admitted that the price he had paid was steep, but he repeated his cardinal dictum: "When you pay high for the priceless, you're getting it cheap." Another saying of his, endlessly repeated to his American clients, was "You can get all the pictures you want at fifty thousand dollars apiece that's easy. But to get pictures at a quarter of a million apiece— that wants doing!" Duveen now repeated this to Mellon, too. Mellon, having heard all this before, was still not interested. Duveen then told Mellon that "Pinkie" was being offered to him as a courtesy, because a man of his taste was worthy of her, but that if he thought her price too high, it was all right, because he had another prospective purchaser. Mellon was skeptical, and he was still not interested. The next morning, Duveen telephoned H.E. Huntington, at San Marino, the Huntington mansion near Pasadena. The mansion is today a public art gallery and library and there "Pinkie" now hangs.

This demonstration to Mellon of the *sine-qua-non* principle was worth all Duveen's trouble. Mellon did not make the same mistake again. When, shortly afterward, the Romney "Portrait of

Mrs. Davenport" was put up for auction at Christie's, Knoedler's once more suggested to Duveen that he go shares with them, and once more Duveen refused. To get revenge, Knoedler's kept bidding until the picture cost Duveen over three hundred thousand dollars, the highest price ever paid for a Romney. Duveen was less vindictive than they were; despite Mellon's earlier lapse, Duveen offered him the Romney, and Mellon immediately bought it.

In his five decades of selling in this country, Duveen, by amazing energy and audacity, transformed the American taste in art. The masterpieces he brought here have fetched up in a number of museums that, simply because they contain these masterpieces, rank among the greatest in the world. He not only educated the small group of collectors who were his clients but created a public for the finest works of the masters of painting. "Twenty-five years from now," Lincoln Kirstein wrote in the *New Republic* in 1949, "art historians... may investigate the ledgers of Duveen, as today they do the Medici." The phenomenon of Duveen was without precedent. In the eighteenth century, Englishmen making the Grand Tour bought either from the heads of impoverished families or directly from the artists, as, three hundred years before, Francis I bought from Leonardo da Vinci. Generally speaking, the nineteenth-century collectors of all nations operated on the same basis. There had never before been anyone like Duveen, the exalted middleman, and he practically monopolized his field. Ninety-five of the hundred and fifteen pictures, exclusive of American portraits, in the Mellon

Collection, which is now in the National Gallery, in Washington, came to Mellon through Duveen. Of the seven hundred paintings in the Kress Collection, also in the National Gallery, more than a hundred and fifty were supplied by him, and these are the finest. It has been stated by the eminent American art scholar Dr. Alfred M. Frankfurter that except for the English collections that were put together in the eighteenth and nineteenth centuries, this country has the largest aggregation of Italian pictures outside Italy. Of these, according to Dr. Frankfurter, seventy-five per cent of the best came here through Duveen.

When the twentieth century began, the American millionaires were collecting mainly Barbizons, or "sweet French" pictures, and English "story" pictures. They owned the originals of the Rosa Bonheur prints that one can remember from the parlors of one's youth—pastoral scenes, with groups of morose cattle. Those pictures are now consigned to the basements of the few big private houses that still exist or the basements of museums that no longer have the effrontery to hang them. Troyons, Ziems, Meissoniers, Bouguereaus, Fromentins, and Henners crowded the interstices of the mother-of-pearl grandeur of the living rooms of the American rich, and their owners dickered among themselves for them. When Charles Yerkes, the Chicago traction magnate, died in 1905, Frederick Lewis Allen says in "The Lords of Creation," "his canvas by Troyon, 'Coming from the Market,' had already appreciated forty thousand dollars in value since its purchase." Duveen changed all that. He made the Barbizons practically worthless by beguiling their luckless owners into a longing to possess earlier masterpieces, which he had begun buying before most of his American clients had so much as heard the artists' names. Duveen made the names familiar, and compelled a reverence for them because he extracted such overwhelming prices for them. Of the Barbizon school, only Corot and Millet now have any financial rating, and that has greatly declined. A Corot that in its day brought fifty thousand dollars can be bought now for ten or fifteen thousand, and Millet is even worse off.

Although the French painter Bouguereau represented the kind of art that Duveen was eager to displace, he was flexible enough to make use of him in order to bring the education of the Duveen clientele up to his level. A highly visible nude by the French master was used by Duveen as an infinitely renewable bait to bring the customers who successively owned it sensibly to rest in the fields in which Duveen specialized. This Bouguereau travelled to and from Duveen's, serving—a silent emissary—to start many collections. Clients enrolled in Duveen's course of study would buy the Bouguereau, stare at it for some time, get faintly tired of it, and then, as they heard of rarer and subtler and more expensive works, grow rather ashamed of it. They would send it back, and Duveen would replace it with something a little more refined. Back and forth the Bouguereau went. Sometimes, Duveen amused himself by using it for a different purpose—to cure potential customers who had succumbed to the virus of the ultramodern. Some collectors who had started with painters like Picasso and Braque grew hungry for a flesh-and-blood curve after a while, and presently found themselves with the travelling Bouguereau. Duveen sent it to them for a breather, and afterward they went the way of the group that had started with the Bouguereau.

Duveen has been called by one of his friends "a lovable buc-caneer." Whether he was or not, he forced American collectors to accumulate great things, infused them with a fierce pride in collecting, and finally got their collections into museums, making it possible for the American people to see a large share of the world's most beautiful art without having to go abroad. He did it by dazzling the collectors with visions of an Elysium through which they would stroll hand in hand with the illustrious artists of the past, and by making other dealers emulate him. His rivals could no longer sell their old line of goods, and the result was that he elevated their taste as well as that of his customers. An eminent English art dealer whose family has been in the business for five generations and who could never endure Duveen says, nevertheless, that with Duveen's death an enormously vital force went out of the trade. The dealers are still living off the collectors he made, or off their descendants. Duveen had a cavalier attitude toward prospective clients, and there was a certain majesty about it. He ignored Detroit for years after it became rich. Then its newly made millionaires came to him, and they were delighted to be asked to dine at Lord Duveen's. Once, when he was told that Edsel Ford was buying pictures, and was asked why he didn't pay some attention to him, he said, "He's not ready for me yet. Let him go on buying. Someday he'll be big enough for me."

When Duveen entered the American art market, he was barging into a narrow field and one that was dominated by long-established dealers. Duveen not only barged into this field but soon preëmpted it, although, for the most part, his American clients didn't especially care for him. "Why should they like me?" he once asked one of his attorneys rhetorically

"I am an outsider. Why do they trade with me? Because they've got to. Because I've got what they can't get anywhere else." The daughter of one client, who competed with Duveen in a long contest for her widowed father's attention and ultimately lost out, tells, in a voice still weary with frustration, how Duveen managed to elude her even when she was sure she had him in a corner. Once, her father had asked several friends to their home to inspect some of his latest acquisitions from Duveen. Among the guests, in addition to Duveen himself, was a distinguished art connoisseur. She showed the connoisseur, a French count, around the gallery in which her father housed his collection of paintings. The count was full of admiration for them until he came to a Dürer that Duveen had sold her father for four hundred and fifty thousand dollars. Then the expert's face darkened. His hostess urged him to explain what was bothering him. He looked around, spotted his host and Duveen at a distance, and whispered, "I'm terribly sorry, but I don't think this Dürer is the real thing." To his horror, his companion triumphantly summoned her father and Duveen. "Count X—— thinks that this Dürer is not genuine!" she cried as they approached. The host turned a stricken countenance to Duveen. Duveen's famous laugh pealed out. "Now, isn't that amusing?" he said to his client. "That's really very amusing indeed. Do you know, my dear fellow, that some of the greatest experts in the world, some of the very greatest experts in the world, actually think that this Dürer is not genuine?" Duveen had reversed the normal order of things. Somehow, the expert who was present, as well as all the experts who were not present, became reduced in rank, discredited, pulverized to fatuousness.

On another occasion, the beleaguered daughter, with Duveen and her father, was inspecting a house that Duveen had chosen for them, and that they eventually bought. She said it was too big—it had eighteen servant's rooms—and running it would be a terrible chore for her. "But Joe thinks it's beautiful," her father said. A few days later, the three of them, now accompanied by Duveen's aide Boggis, were looking at the house again. Duveen enlarged on its potentialities, then abruptly looked at his watch. "No more time today," he said, firmly but not unkindly. "What about tomorrow, Joe?" the humble millionaire wanted to know. Again Duveen's famous laugh rang out. He turned to Boggis. "What am I doing tomorrow, Boggis?" he asked. Boggis knew. "Tomorrow, Lord Duveen, you have an appointment in Washington with Mr. Mellon," he said. Against this there was no argument. The client automatically accepted his lesser place in the Duveen hierarchy, grateful for the blessings he had received that day.

Sir Osbert Sitwell has an interesting theory about Duveen— that he was a master exploiter of his own *gaffes*. He expounds it in one volume of his memoirs, "Left Hand, Right Hand!":

Since the following anecdote often appears in the press, I had better recount it myself, correctly. In later years, and especially in 1926, when I visited New York, I used to see a certain amount of Lord—then Sir Joseph—Duveen, and several times went to his house there. The following summer I met him at the opening day of some exhibition in the Leicester Galleries, and he rushed up to me, and said, "Oh, my dear Mr. Lytton Strachey, I am so glad to see you again."

Lytton and I were not much alike, for I was tall, fair, clean-shaven, and certainly by no means thin, whereas he was bone-thin and angular, as well as tall, and bearded, with something of the reflective air of a pelican. In fact, no two people could have resembled each other less. Consequently, I telegraphed to him: "Delighted to inform you that I have this morning been mistaken for you by Sir Joseph Duveen. Osbert." Lytton telegraphed back: "One can only say again how utterly duveen. Lytton." [The "again" was a reference to a celebrated remark made by the late Belle da Costa Greene, director of the Pierpont Morgan Library, when she was first shown through the art collection in Jules Bache's Fifth Avenue house: "How utterly duveen!"] Sir Joseph, with his expert amiability, which resembled that of a clownish tumbler on the music-hall stage, heard of these telegrams and subsequently always referred to them at some moment of any luncheon or dinner party at which he and I happened both to be present, appealing to me to "tell the story about Strachey." Being a remarkably astute man in most directions, I think that, in this different from most people, he enjoyed having the stupid side of his character emphasized; it constituted a disguise for his cleverness, a kind of fancy dress.... After the story had been related, he used to add, "Of course I knew Osbert Sitwell. I love his books. He's written about my country." At first this statement rather surprised me, until I comprehended that by it he meant Scarborough and the district round, which are said to figure in my novel "Before the Bombardment."

Sir Osbert's surprise at Duveen's reference to his "country" was due to the fact that Duveen was so seldom in England. Indeed, he was sometimes assumed to be an American, he was here so much. (It was only in America that he was always taken for an Englishman.) To counteract this notion, Duveen, who was actually a native of Yorkshire, bought a country home in Kent. He rarely visited it, however. In his New York gallery, Duveen was a stickler for keeping up the correct English tone. The members of his staff, in the words of a former associate, were invariably "dressed like Englishmen—cutaways and striped trousers." The censorship of the staff was linguistic as well as sartorial. You could drop an "h" there with impunity, but under no circumstances pick up an Americanism. One day, a Duveen employee, throwing caution to the winds, said, "O.K." Duveen was severe. This was unbecoming in an English establishment, a colonial branch of the House of Lords, engaged in the business of purveying Duveens. After that, Duveen was yessed in English.

Duveen looked like a conservative English businessman. He was of middle height, stocky build, and ruddy, almost apoplectic coloring. He had clear, penetrating gray eyes and a cropped mustache. He exuded opulence. He sometimes played golf or went to the theatre, but only halfheartedly; he was interested in practically nothing except his business. He never carried more than a little cash; money in small amounts was something he didn't understand. His valet decided what he would need for incidentals and provided him with it. When he dressed Duveen, he would put in his pocket a few bills to enable him to get about. Once, when the valet was ill, Duveen said that he, too, would have to take to his bed, because there was no one to give him cash for taxi fare. Duveen was meek toward his valet, but in general he was imperious. He had the Oriental habit of clapping his hands when he wanted people; an acquaintance who visited the British Museum with him recalls that Duveen clapped his hands even in that august institution, and that the attendants came running. After becoming a peer, he was proud of being a member of the House of Lords and would occasionally drop in there, to prove that he could. Politics meant little to him, but when he wanted to terminate an interview, he would suddenly remember that he had a political side. "Sorry, old man, but I've got to go to the Lords," he would say. "Important measure coming up." Like some of his clients, he seldom read anything. (It has been suggested that a number of his American clients gobbled up his wares with such avidity because they could thus indulge in expensive contemplation without making the painful effort of reading.) But if a book said something about a picture Duveen was interested in, he was eager to see it. His impetuosity was sometimes extreme. Once, when the custodian of an immensely valuable collection of books on art he kept in the Ministry of Marine brought him a rare volume he wanted, he seized it and tore out of it the pages he was after, to free himself from the encumbrance of irrelevant text.

The favored art critics who were permitted to use Duveen's library say that in his time it was in some respects superior to the Metropolitan's and Frick's. One critic, looking up an item in another rare volume, found an irate crisscross of pencil marks over the passage he was after, and, scribbled in the margin, the words "Nonsense! It's by Donatello!" Shocked by this vandalism, he took the book to the librarian, who said calmly, "Oh,

Joe's been at it again." Duveen's habit of editing by mutilation impaired the pleasure of students using the library. To books that weren't in his library Duveen was flamboyantly indiffer-ent. Once, on the witness stand, opposing counsel asked him if he was familiar with Ruskin's "The Stones of Venice." "Of course I've heard of the picture, but I've never actually seen it," he answered. When his error was later pointed out to him, he laughed and said he'd *always* thought Ruskin was a painter, and not a very good one, at that.

Duveen was more interested in the theatre than books. His favorite play, which he thought illustrated a great moral lesson, was an English comedy, "A Pair of Spectacles," adapted from the French by Sydney Grundy, and first produced in London in 1890. It was about a kindly and gentle man who gets into all sorts of trouble because, as he starts out from his house one morning, he picks up the wrong pair of spectacles, and thereafter finds himself becoming mean and distrustful. Duveen said that this play showed how necessary it was to look at life through the right glasses, and that it was his function to furnish his clients with the right glasses for looking at works of art. He joked about it, but he believed it. At the theatre, his appreciation of a funny line was sometimes given audible expression five minutes after the rest of the audience had got the point. He didn't mind at all impersonating the guileless and traditional British Blimp; speaking of himself, he often repeated the formula for giving an Englishman a happy old age: tell him a joke in his youth. He had a fondness for basic humor. A friend, chiding him about his persistent litigiousness, made the mistake of telling a "darky" story—the one about the colored man arrested for stealing chickens who, when confronted by irrefutable evidence, said to the magistrate, "If it's all the same to you, Jedge, let's forget the whole business!" Duveen made the friend repeat it whenever they met. Perhaps, in the steam bath of litigation in which Duveen was immersed all his life, the number of occasions on which his own attitude toward the judge approximated the colored man's made him such an enthusiastic audience for this story.

Certain men are endowed with the faculty of concentrating on their own affairs to the exclusion of what's going on elsewhere in the cosmos. Duveen was that kind of man, and the kind of man who, if he met you out walking, would take you along with him, no matter where you were bound or how urgent it was for you to get there. One day, walking along Central Park West, he ran into the art dealer Felix Wildenstein, who was going the other way, bent on what was, to him, an important errand. Duveen, with his infectious friendliness, linked his arm through Wildenstein's and suggested that they go for a walk in the Park. Wildenstein explained that he was hurrying to keep an appointment, but they were presently walking in the Park. Duveen turned the conversation to queries and interesting speculations about his own personality, in which he took a detached but lively interest. "What do people think about me?" he asked. "What are they saying about me?" Wildenstein quoted a slightly derogatory opinion a friend had expressed; he had to have some revenge for being so abruptly swept off his course. Duveen was not upset by the derogatory opinion. "That's all right," he said, as if a favorable opinion *would* have upset him, "but does he think I am a great man?"

Duveen's New York home was filled with rare and lovely things. To an illustrious Englishman invited to a dinner party there, Duveen said, as they sat down, "For you, I'm bringing out the Sèvres!" During dinner, the Englishman overheard Duveen say to another guest, "How do you like this Sèvres? I haven't used it since Ramsay MacDonald dined here." Duveen seemed to make a point of showing his multimillionaire clients that he lived better than they did. Over a period of many years, he dined once a week at Frick's house when he was in New York. One evening, he remarked to his host that the silverware at the table was not quite in keeping with the many Duveen items in the house. Frick asked Duveen what he should have. The work of the greatest of English silversmiths, Duveen replied, and explained that this master was Paul De Lameric, who had practiced his craft in the eighteenth century; each of De Lamerie's creations was a museum piece, and Frick ought to have only De Lamerie silver in his home. Frick asked his uncompromising guest if he could supply a De Lamerie service. It wouldn't be easy, said Duveen, and it would take time, but he would be willing to accept the commission. After some years, he succeeded in making it possible for Frick to invite him to dinner with a feeling of perfect security.

Duveen's clients, as their friendship with him ripened, saw their homes become almost as exquisite as his. A new house that Frick built in 1913 at Seventieth Street and Fifth Avenue was, in the end, thanks to Duveen's choice of its architect and decoration, a jewel of such loveliness that Duveen could have lived in it himself. Duveen chose the firm of Carrère & Hastings as the architects, and his friend the late Sir Charles Allom, who had been knighted by King George V for doing *his* place, as the decorator. The collaboration between Duveen and Allom was comprehensive; Duveen indicated to Allom what precious objects he had in mind for the house and Allom devised places in which to put them. It was Duveen who supplied the paintings for the magnificent Fragonard and Boucher Rooms, to mention only the most famous of the pleasances that have attracted many visitors to the house, now the Frick Museum. By the time it was done, the place was beautiful, and Duveen, when he went to dinner for the first time, was—except when he contemplated the silverware, which hadn't yet been replaced—thoroughly at ease.

On one occasion, Duveen found it necessary to subject Frick to the same kind of benevolent but firm discipline to which he later subjected Mellon; that is, to teach him that no great picture was to be obtained except through Duveen. At dinner on a night in 1916, Duveen noticed in his host an air at once abstracted and expectant. Duveen was adept at following the nuances of his clients' moods, reaching out antennae to probe their hidden thoughts. He knew there was something in the wind, because Frick, always laconic, on this occasion faded out completely. He finally drew from his client and host the fact that he was on the trail of a really great picture, the name of which he refused to disclose. Duveen went home and pondered. To allow Frick to buy a great picture through anyone else was unthinkable. He cabled his office in London and inquired whether anybody there knew of an outstanding picture that was for sale. Through the underground of the trade, Duveen found out in a few days that Sir Audley Dallas Neeld, whose home, Grittleton House, was in Wiltshire, was about to sell Gainsborough's "Mall in St. James's

Park" to Knoedler's. Obviously, this was the picture Frick had in mind. Knoedler's had an even bigger in with Frick than it had with Mellon; Charles Carstairs, one of the heads of Knoedler's and a man of great charm, was an intimate friend of Frick's. Duveen immediately cabled his English agent exact instructions. He believed that Knoedler's man, sure the Gainsborough was in the bag, would be in no hurry to consummate the deal. Duveen told his agent to take the first train next morning to Wiltshire, tell Sir Audley that he was prepared to outbid everyone else for the picture, and offer him a binder of a thousand pounds to prove it. Duveen got the Gainsborough for three hundred thousand dollars. The next time he dined with Frick, he found his host depressed. "I've lost that picture," Frick told Duveen. "I was on the trail of a very great painting—Gainsborough's 'Mall in St. James's Park.'" "Why, Mr. Frick," Duveen said, "I bought that picture. When you want a great picture, you must come to me, because, you know, I get the first chance at all of them. You shall have the Gainsborough. Moreover, you shall have it for exactly what I paid for it." In the first joy of acquisition, Frick was ecstatically grateful, not stopping to think that Sir Audley would probably have sold the picture to Knoedler's for so much less that Knoedler's price with a profit would have been lower than Duveen's without one. Duveen charged the lost profit off to pedagogy. When he brought the Gainsborough to Frick, he pointed to it triumphantly and laughed his infectious laugh. "Now, Mr. Frick," he said magnanimously, "you can send it to Knoedler's to be framed."

ART TALKER

Calvin Tomkins

1977

A FIERY REDHEAD with the speed of light, a cloud of
blue chiffon, and a hearty "This lecture is about a very
good-looking man with rather thin legs who was born just under
five hundred years ago and had ideas about hospitality which
most of us would find it hard to put into practice"—who but
Rosamond Bernier, talking about François I of France, on a
recent Wednesday evening at the Metropolitan Museum of Art?
We are not alone in thinking Mme. Bernier the most stylish art
talker around. A recent lecture series in the Met's Grace Rainey
Rogers Auditorium was sold out two months in advance. Her
invigoratingly literate television interviews with Philip Johnson,
the architect, on CBS-TV's "Camera Three" made the three
Sunday mornings when they were shown astonishingly bear-
able for a much larger audience. Could we catch up with this
scintillating creature (who has been married since 1975 to John
Russell, the *Times's* equally scintillating art critic) and importune
her with a few questions? We could and we did.

"Imagine being paid to talk!" Mme. Bernier said to us over
lunch in a midtown French restaurant the other day. "I've been a
listener all my professional life, and here I am talking everybody's
head off." Mme. Bernier's lecturing self, it seems, rose quite

recently from the ashes of her former, publishing-and-writing self. After twenty-odd very busy years in Paris, where she and her ex-husband, Georges Bernier, founded the magazine *L'Œil* in 1955 and made it into one of the century's best art journals, she was, as she put it, left "absolutely flat" when, in 1969, she lost both Bernier and *L'Œil* through divorce. "All at once, I had nothing to do," she said. "I just cried all day." Friends did what they could to cheer her up, but nothing really helped until Michael Mahoney, an art historian, persuaded her to give fourteen lectures on modern art to his students at Trinity College in Hartford in the fall of 1970. "I was terrified at the start, but it worked," she said. "I'm probably the only person you know who hasn't been psychoanalyzed. Those lectures literally saved my life."

Mme. Bernier, who was born in Philadelphia but grew up mostly in London, approached her subject from the point of view of an active participant. Having arrived in Paris in 1946 as European feature editor for the American *Vogue*, she followed her natural bent toward art by becoming a close friend of virtually all the important European artists of the period. Picasso took to her because she spoke fluent Spanish as well as French, and she was the first to see and report on his postwar paintings. Matisse saw to it that she wrote the first article on the chapel he was designing in Vence. Miró, Braque, Max Ernst, and many other artists gave her exclusive interviews and became lifelong Bernier-philes, and from 1955 on they all took a personal interest in the development of *L'Œil*. In her lectures at Trinity, she was careful to avoid the "famous-men-who-have-breathed-on-me" sort of gossip, but her close connection with the Paris art scene, her memory for the telling detail, and her own infectious delight in recapturing the atmosphere of the period made for a wonderfully vivid presentation.

The Hartford success led to an invitation from Rice University, in Houston, where she spent a month in 1971 as a guest of John and Dominique de Menil. "Roberto Rossellini was staying with them, too, and we became great friends," she told us. "What a talker! He would sit down at the breakfast table and say, '*Pascal n'avait pas raison*,' or something similar, and we'd be off on that for an hour." The Metropolitan Museum heard about her Rice lectures and signed her up for the fall of 1971, and she has been in demand ever since, from places as far apart as Paris (where she has lectured at the Grand Palais on the painters of the School of Paris) and Yakima, Washington (where she spoke last spring on contemporary French painting).

As one could gather from her Metropolitan lectures on "Four Royal Collectors" (François I, Charles I, Queen Christina of Sweden, and Catherine the Great), Mme. Bernier does not limit herself to modern art. *L'Œil's* slogan was "*Tous les arts, tous les pays, tous les temps*," and Mme. Bernier, who draws upon her years with the magazine for most of her lecture ideas and much of her material, now has more than thirty lectures in her quiver. But whether she is discussing the French Renaissance under François I, the Paris of Paul Poiret, or the effect on art of writers such as Baudelaire, Mallarmé, Apollinaire, and Proust, she manages to bring to her subject what sounds like firsthand knowledge. "I'm not a scholar or an art historian," she told us. "As a matter of fact, I've never gone to lectures—once, I went to hear Erwin Panofsky, but that's about it. I've always loved books and magazines, and playing around with images, and to me making a lecture is just like making a book. I started projecting two slides simultaneously, side by side, because that's like having an open book with facing pages. And I love making the juxtapositions between images, tying things together, without a lot of big blocks of talk. That keeps things moving, and it keeps people amused. I think it's important to be amused, don't you? I must say, after one of my early lectures at the Met I overheard one woman in the audience say to another, 'Well, she's obviously slept with Léger. I wonder what she'll have to say next week about Braque.' Actually, I never slept with any of them, worse luck. But I'm enjoying it all very much. In fact, I've recently had two of the biggest thrills of my life. The first was dancing the Charleston and the Black Bottom with Merce Cunningham, at the Whitney Museum dinner for Sandy Calder. Merce Cunningham! And later John Cage told me that Merce had said he enjoyed it. The second was flying across the country for a lecture, getting off the plane, and seeing a huge sign in red lights that read 'Welcome to Yakima Rosamond Bernier.'"

THE EVENTS IN MAY

A PARIS NOTEBOOK PART I

Mavis Gallant

1968

MAY 3

PHOTOGRAPHS, in newspapers, of students in front of the Sorbonne. Members of Occident, an extreme-right-wing student group, waiting in the street to beat up Nanterre *enragés,* start fighting with police when they see *enragés* arrested.

MAY 4

H.T. caught in traffic jam around Saint-Germain-Saint-Michel in midst of student disorders. Says this is "different"—they all seem very young. He sees a barricade made of parked cars they have moved away from the curb. Is very impatient—hates disorder.

Talk with M.B. She saw the police charge, outside the Balzar Brasserie. Says their apartment full of tear gas—they live on the fifth floor! Wouldn't let her daughter talk on telephone in sight of windows. Police think nothing of throwing grenades into houses. Doubt if they could throw one up to fifth floor. Says gas makes it impossible to sleep at night.

Crowds, traffic jams. See a crowd. I feel the mixture of tension and curiosity that is always the signal of something happening, and I hear shouting and see police cars. I duck into Saint-Germain Métro. I hate these things. See more pictures in papers, and accounts, surprising, of how the students, far from fleeing, "regroup and charge."

MAY 6

In the night, hear that familiar wave of sound, as during the crisis in 1958. Get dressed, go out as far as Carrefour Raspail. All confusion. Students do not run—it is not 1958, after all. Attack in a kind of frenzy that seems insane. The courage of these kids! Don't get too near. See what is obviously innocent bystander hit on the ear by a policeman. Decide not to tell anyone, as friends would have fit. All night, shouts, cries, harsh slogans chanted, police cars, ambulances, cars going up and down my one-way street, running feet. I open a shutter and see that I am the only person on the street at a window. Are they scared, or respectable, or what? Scared of police, or of students?

MAY 7

Dined at the B.s', Quai Saint-Michel. No one takes a car now—not safe to park in the area. Students are marching all over Paris: "*Libérez nos camarades!*"—meaning those who were sentenced by a monkey court on Sunday. From the B.s' living room you see Seine, sunset, expanse of quais, very few cars, scarcely any traffic, many police. Christine (fifteen) says, "But is my *duty* to be out there with the students." Nothing doing. However, I notice she does not eat her dinner with us. Has it by herself in the kitchen. Almost seems like the heart of the matter—not with the adults, not with the kids. In Métro, find I have tears in my eyes. Astonished. Think: I must be tired— working too much? See everyone is dabbing and sniffling. It is tear gas that has seeped down. By Saint-Placide it is almost unbearable, prickling under the lids, but so funny to see us all weeping that I begin to laugh.

Out of the Métro, Rue de Rennes a wall of people. The end of the student march. They have been all over Paris. Quiet, grave, in rows straight across the road, linking arms, holding hands. Boys and girls. I find their grave young faces extremely moving. Perfect discipline, a quiet crowd. They are packed all the way up the street to the ruined Montparnasse Station—I can't see the end of them. They hold the banners of the C.N.R.S. (National Scientific Research Center) and a banner reading, "LES PROFESSEURS DE NANTERRE CONTRE LA RÉPRESSION." Behind a red flag, a tight cluster of non-identified, other than by the meaning of the flag. Ask if I can cross the street. Boy parts the rows so I can get through; girls begin chanting at me, "*Avec nous! Avec nous!*" Slogans start up, swell, recede as if the slogans themselves were tired: "*Li-bé-rez nos ca-ma-rades. Fi-ga-ro fa-sciste.*" Marchers look exhausted. The police bar their route up near the Hôtel Lutetia. Sometimes the marchers have to move back, the word is passed along: "*Reculez doucement!*" A number of good citizens of our neighborhood watch without commenting and without letting their faces show how they feel. A little girl, about four feet nine, collects from everyone "for the wounded." Notice that the non-identified lot behind the red flag give freely, the watchers around me a little less. At midnight, the news; someone has parked a minute car on the edge of the crowd with a portable radio on the roof. Touching narcissicism of the young; a silence, so that they can hear the radio talk about *them*. When the announcer describes where we are—the Rue de Rennes—and says that there are about fifteen thousand left out of the thirty thousand who were earlier on the Champs-Élysées, a satisfied little ripple is almost visible. Something to do with looks exchanged. But then he says, "The police are simply hoping they will, finally, be tired and go home," and a new slogan is shouted, quite indignantly: "*Nous sommes pas fatigués!*" This is a good one—three beats repeated twice—and goes on quite a long time. But they are tired. They have, in fact, been sitting down in the roadway. They remind me of children who keep insisting they are not sleepy when in reality they are virtually asleep on the carpet. This seems to me the end. Unlikely that they will press on for the release of their *camarades*.

MAY 10

Walked from Île Saint-Louis to top of Boul' Mich'. Light evening. The bridges are guarded by C.R.S. (Compagnies Républicaines de Sécurité)—riot police, under the Ministry of the Interior. Self-conscious as one walks by (they, not I). Middle-aged men, professionals. "*Laissez passer la dame,*" etc. They must know they are hated now. They may wonder why. One fastening the other's helmet chin strap, as if going to a party. I mistake their grenade-throwers for guns, and I think: If they have these guns, they must intend to use them. Place Saint-Michel. I am part of a stupid, respectable-looking small crowd staring—just dumbly staring—at the spectacle of massed power on the bridge. Up the Boul' Mich'. Crowds, feeling of tension. Street dirtier than usual, and it is never very clean. Still has that feeling of a Cairo bazaar. Side streets leading to Sorbonne and Latin Quarter blocked by more police, and I have that feeling of helpless anger I had earlier today. The Sorbonne is empty, and it is kept empty by a lot of ignorant gumshoes. The last stand of the illiterate. Difference between now and early afternoon is that the students are back from their mass meeting in Denfert-Rochereau and—shifting, excited, sullen, angry, determined—they want to get by those large, armed men and back to *their* Latin Quarter. Electric, uneasy, but oddly gay. Yes, it is like a holiday in a village, with the whole town out on the square.

Home, turn on news. Suddenly wonder about Barbara, who was at Denfert-Rochereau. She turned up at her family's apartment between ten and eleven tonight with some hairy youth and said, "*Maman, je voudrais la permission de passer la nuit au Quartier Latin—il y a des barricades.*" She is seventeen. Nice kid, came all the way home, knew they'd be worried. Parents handled it beautifully—said they hadn't eaten, took both kids to a restaurant. Barbara, *pure et dure*, said, "How can I eat in a restaurant while my *camarades* are out there, etc.?" Call their apartment and am told that parents have persuaded boy to spend night at their place, and, without actually forbidding anything, have kept both kids out of it. Z. tells me this in low voice. Boy is sleeping in living room. Both kids worn out, upset.

MAY 11

Listened to nightmare news half the night. Around two o'clock, when the C.R.S. were "regrouped and ordered to charge," I said to no one, "Oh no! No!" I've never seen barricades "charged," but once you have seen any kind of police charge in Paris you never forget it. They charge on the double—they seem invincible. How brave these kids are now! Until now I'd never seen them do anything but run. Finally fell asleep, thought I had dreamed it, but on the eight-o'clock news (Europe I) the speaker said, "Have you slept well? Because this is what went on in your city last night," and told.

The ripped streets around the Luxembourg Station. People who live around here seem dazed. Stand there looking dazed. Paving torn up. The Rue Royer-Collard, where I used to live, looks bombed. Burned cars—ugly, gray-black. These are small cars, the kind you can lift and push around easily. Not the cars of the rich. It's said that even the car owners haven't complained, because they had watched the police charge from their windows. Armed men, and unarmed children. I used to think that the young in France were all little aged men. Oh! We all feel sick. Rumor of two deaths, one a student, one a C.R.S. Rumor that a student had his throat cut "against a window at 24 Rue Gay-Lussac"—so a tract (already!) informs. They say it was the police incendiary grenades, and not the students, that set the cars on fire, but it was probably both. A friend of H.'s who lost his car found tracts still stuffed in it, half charred, used as kindling. Rumor that police beat the wounded with clubs, that people hid them (the students) and looked after them, and that police went into private homes. When the police threw the first tear-gas bombs, everyone in the houses nearby threw out basins of water to keep the gas close to the ground.

Shopkeeper saying, "I sold nothing all day. I gave water away, without charge. That's all the business I did." Feeling of slight, unpleasant pressure. I don't like it. Shopkeepers "encouraged" (by whom?) to proclaim, with signs, publicly, their "solidarity" with the students. Well, they did have their shops wrecked, and shopkeepers have no solidarity with anyone. Anyway, I don't like it. Too much like post-Occupation.

Am told that a Belgian tourist bus stopped, a father and son descended, son stood on remains of barricade with a stone in each hand while father took his picture. Then they got back in the bus. Didn't see this, but saw plenty of people taking pictures. Last thing I'd want to photograph. Curious tendency—men and boys pick up these paving stones, weigh them, make as if to throw them. See themselves as heroes. Am embarrassed by elderly professors suddenly on the side of students. If they thought these reforms were essential, why the hell didn't they do something about it before the kids were driven to use paving stones? Maurice Duverger, professor of political science—gray crewcut on TV, romanticism of barricades. Wanted to say, "Come off it, *vieux père*."

Voice of the people: Wife of a Garde Mobile (paramilitary police, the Gardes Mobiles belong to the Army) lives in my *quartier*. Much surrounded. Very simple, plain creature. Says, "When my husband came in this morning, he told me that the barricades were manned by North Africans aged forty and fifty. That was why the police had to be so rough." This is *believed*.

Indignant housewives. "Send them back to North Africa!" I have a queer feeling this is going to be blamed on foreigners— I mean the new proles, the Spanish and Portuguese. And, of course, the North Africans are good for everything.

Evening. The Boul' Mich' still smells of tear gas. Last night like a year ago. One's eyes sting and smart under the lids, the inner corners swell. Aimless youths wander up and down under the trees and street lights. No cars. It is a pleasant evening, and this aimless walking up and down (curious onlookers on the sidewalks, young people in the roadway) is like a *corso* in a Mediterranean town.

Gardes Mobiles and the C.R.S. here now are big, tough middle-aged men. Their black cars and their armored grey cars have brought them from Marseille and from Bordeaux—we recognize the license plates. Stout, oddly relaxed, they stand around and about the intersection of the Boul' Mich' and the Boulevard Saint-Germain, both of which are thronged with a holiday sort of sightseeing crowd. I can't believe these young people are students. I think the students were last night, on the barricades. These boys simply don't resemble the kids I saw last night. They look like suburban working-class boys on any Saturday night—like the boys we called *blousons noirs* in the nineteen-fifties. H.T. says I am mistaken. Anyway, they form an untidy knot, spread out, begin to walk up the Boulevard Saint-Germain. The police stand still, and those kids going up and down the road, restless, moving, more and more of them, remind me of waves on a rock. The police just in themselves seem to be a sort of provocation, and for the life of me I can't see why the police aren't taken right out of the Latin Quarter at once. Finally, a compact crowd crosses the Boulevard Saint-Germain singing the "Marseillaise" and giving the cops the Nazi salute. The police laugh. These are obviously a fresh lot. If they had been around last night, they wouldn't be laughing.

The police: The police involved in last night's debacle had been brought in from Brittany, where Breton nationalists had been staging a strike. They travelled all night. From the morning, when they arrived—from their breakfast time, say—they were given no more food. They stood from noon until two o'clock in the morning without one scrap of food—they stood, they didn't sit down—and they watched the barricades going up, knowing they were going to have to demolish them and the kids behind them. At around two in the morning, they were given the order to charge. They had been given clubs to hit with and gas bombs to throw. What were they supposed to do? Boy who lives in my building tells me a story that sounds like a dream. How the people who lived on those streets showered the students with *saucissons* and chocolate and brought them coffee (not the police!). How some of the students actually began to talk to the police. Not arguing—discussing. Talking (he says seriously) about their problems and, dear God, the structure of society. The C.R.S were just people, and not all of them middle-aged, some of them only boys. At around two, their order came: Regroup, get back in your lines, put on your helmets, and charge. He says it was unreal, dreamlike—the tear gas, the armed men with those great round shields, the beatings, but they were the same men.

Talk with young Barbara. "The German students are being deported," she tells me. "But we need them here—they are organized, they can tell us what to do. *Oui, nous avons besoin des allemands."* Her mother, who spent the war years in a concentration camp, says nothing. I feel as if I were watching two screens simultaneously.

De Gaulle still invisible. Says nothing.

MAY 13

On the Boulevard du Montparnasse, not a traffic policeman in sight. Students (I suppose they are) direct traffic. From about the Rue de Montparnasse on, considerable crowd collected on pavements. Reach intersection Saint-Michel-Montparnasse a little after five: Marchers pouring by, red flags, black flags. On a pole near me are a poster sign for the Gothic exhibition at the Louvre and a French flag. Demonstrator, young man, shinnies up, rips off the flag, lets it drop. I burst out, *"Ce n'est pas élégant!"* Am given some funny looks, but no one answers. Man in crowd picks flag up off the pavement, hangs it over the poster. In the middle of the road, small island for pedestrians. Make my way over to traffic island between a wave of Anarchists and a ripple of North Vietnam supporters. Stand on step of traffic island, which means standing with one foot in front of the other, heel to toe, and hang on to *borne* with arm straight back from the shoulder. Remain in this position, with only minor shifts, until a quarter to nine. I can see straight down the Boulevard Saint-Michel. Nothing but people, a river running uphill. Red flags, black flags, flag of old Spanish Republic, flags I can't identify. Mixture of students and workers. O.R.T.F. (Office de Radiodiffusion-Télévision Française, the state-owned radio-TV organization), led by the critic Max-Pol Fouchet, who gets a hand. Hospital personnel, lawyers (small group), film stars—recognize Jean-Pierre Cassel, Michel Piccoli. Recognize film directors—all the New Wave, except for those still in Cannes. Helicopter overhead, the same helicopter that hovers over all demonstrations, making a count. I am joined by a nurse from Pitié Hospital. Tells me she is on night duty but wanted to see this anyway. Confirms rumor that one student had a hand amputated, denies rumor about "secret" deaths (i.e., student deaths kept secret under police pressure)—says impossible to camouflage a death in a hospital. Tells me one or two things about police. Confirms what I'd heard, but she is a calm girl and does not add imaginary trimmings. Truth quite enough. Yes, they continued to beat the wounded who were lying on stretchers. True that they would not let anyone be taken to hospital until they had checked that person's identity, no matter how serious the injury. We are joined by a *lycée* professor, woman of about forty, who has marched as far as Denfert-Rochereau and come back as a spectator. She holds a sign on a stick—"À BAS LA RÉPRESSION POLICIÈRE," in rather wobbly capitals. Holds stick upside down and leans on it. Says she had been a Gaullist all her life until last Friday. Are joined by young man with a beard; young girl whose political vocabulary is C.P. but ordinary vocabulary just rather slangy (could be a salesgirl in a small store); boy who dropped out of Anarchist group; another boy, who stands for about three hours repeating "*Camarades, hôpital*," so that they won't sing or chant slogans, because we are in a hospital zone. From about half past five until a quarter to nine, waves of people flood up the boulevard. The Anarchist has a small radio; we learn that as the head of the cortege is dispersing at the Place Denfert-Rochereau, thousands of marchers still are waiting at the Place de la République. The students have had a longer walk—they started from the Gare de l'Est. The tone of the demonstration is one of great dignity. The union people are used to marching—one can see that. I loathe slogans; I hate shouting; I am most suspicious of a man wearing a raincoat who walks with his hands in his pockets and who whispers slogans out of the corner of his mouth to a brigade of students; but it is impossible not to understand that this is very serious. A whole factory marches by, men in dark suits at the head, workers straggling along, large sign: "NOS PATRONS SONT AVEC NOUS." Also read "BON ANNIVERSAIRE"—this for de Gaulle. The thirteenth of May was the day he took over ten years ago. He isn't mentioned much. The police come in for it, which is to be expected. That is what the demonstration is probably about. The helicopter has relayed news to the radio, and now we are told something staggering: the count is about three million. The population of Greater Paris is about eight and a half million, so common sense tells one this is luna-tic. Nevertheless, we—the little group standing on the traffic island—are caught in a collective fantasy. It is as if everyone in the world had been marching up the boulevard and parting at the traffic island, which is to say at our feet. We hear the roar of slogans and the "Internationale," but because of the young man and his tireless "*Camarades, hôpital*" we are here on our little island in a silent sea. We are up, they are down; we are noisy, they are quiet. Why couldn't three million people surge up the hill? The bearded boy turns to me and says, "We are seeing something historic, aren't we?" He looks dazed. The girl with the impressive vocabulary begins telling everyone, "*Vous êtes trois millions!*" The marchers seem to think it quite natural. It can't be. I touch one of them on the arm, and say, "The radio says you are three million." "It's a ridiculous figure," he answers. "What's the population of the city?" *Merci, Monsieur.* I see familiar faces, and the sight adds to the slightly feverish quality of the afternoon. Julie B., surrounded by what must be the best-looking boys in the School of Medicine, rushes up and kisses me. She is looking for her sister, who is marching with the film technicians. Barbara marching behind the banner of Lycée Saint-Louis. Lovely girl. I recognize all the children, but where are the parents? A parents' association seems to have no more than about fifty behind its banner. They are all home listening to the radio and worrying. Wouldn't they worry less if they were here? Perhaps it's none of their business, as a great deal of it is none of mine? But I'm not French and these aren't my children. The small group with me begin to quarrel. Two of the boys say they were on the barricades last Friday. They are, already, Old Veterans. All they need is the beret. One says, "What a glorious sight it is to see the paving stones pulled out of the road!" "That is simply folklore," says the little Communist girl severely. "What is important is …" And she tells them. The Party disapproves of barricades and Cuban confusion. Wages, shorter hours of work … This bores the two boys. The *lycée* professor joins in. She is about to tell her entire political history, which began only last Friday but can be stretched when the boy with the radio says, "The police have fired on students on the Boulevard Raspail!" He steps into the sea, still flowing on either side of our island, and I hear him telling people that two students, he thinks, have been wounded or killed. I beg the bearded one to make him stop; finally, backed by the professor, I say something sharp about spreading rumors, and tell him that if he turns this into a riot they will lose everything they have achieved, etc., which works. Curious movement of a crowd when a rumor moves through it. Something quick, like a boxer feinting. Mendès France goes by, looking exhausted, pale gray, as if he could scarcely imagine the next few feet of road. They say he is ill. Curious business with the radio: We, on our island, are convinced we are seeing some sort of spontaneous generation, a mixture of people who have never marched together before. But the radio tells us that at Denfert-Rochereau, the destination, they are already quarrelling among themselves—the unions and the students. And while that is going on, part of the cortege is still waiting in the Place de la République to begin the march. The end of it, just before nine, is a chain of students, about forty across, holding hands. I am convinced I have seen something remarkable.

D.C., medical student who lives in my building, tells me that when the students came to the houses of people (on the Boulevard Saint-Michel) who had taken them indoors on Friday, given them something to eat, or simply protected them from the police, the cortege called in cadence "*Mer-ci! Mer-ci!*" and that the people watching on their balconies were in tears. Didn't see this. Where I was, two little girls stood on a third-floor balcony piping, "*Vive les étudiants! À bas les C.R.S.!*" This got a laugh and a hand. The little monkeys were careful about their timing. They'd wait about ten mintues before starting again.

H.T. saw the cortege taking off from the Place de la République. He wants to know why there was no delegation of people whose cars were burned last Friday night. "Instead of a banner or a flag, they could have carried a piece of burned metal." Not a bad idea. I imagine a banner reading, "ET NOUS AUTRES?"

MAY 14

Yesterday, at the big *manif'*, the woman professor kept looking at me coyly, with her head to one side, and speaking to me as if I were a plucky child recovering from brain fever in a Russian novel. Turned out she thought I was an Algerian, and that was her way of showing she wasn't racist. Brief flash of what it must be like on the receiving end of liberal kindness. The awful sugar. Lesson and warning. TV apparently gave a very low figure—a hundred and seventy thousand or so. Weren't they there? E. annoyed and irritated when I said the *manif'* had the same chemical makeup as the Resistance—workers, intellectuals, the left, and the young. She kept saying, "This isn't a war." Everyone enjoyed the general strike so much that no one has gone back to work, from the sound of it.

MAY 15

Decided to put the car in a garage somewhere and forget about it. All garages full—I suppose a lot of other people want their cars off the streets. I finally put it in Rue de Vaugirard for a wash, and simply don't go back.

Rumors: First there were two dead, then three. A doctor came and spoke to the students at the Lycée Saint-Louis and told them that there had been two dead among the students but that the bodies had been smuggled out of the hospital by the police. Who is this doctor? *Was* he a doctor? I find this story impossible to believe. You would need the complicity of the students' families, for one thing, and why would they co-operate? Someone from the students' union, in an interview over Europe I, spoke of six deaths. The reporter, quite rightly, said, in effect, "I am a newsman and until you give me the names of the dead there are none." The student leader said, "Police pressure on families."

MAY 16

Catherine, E.'s elder daughter, says the story now is that there were seven dead. Their bodies are supposed to have been thrown in the Seine by the police. Only to rise again a few miles downstream? For the kind of complicity this requires among police, doctors, and even parents you would need a truly Fascist state that had been in power a long, long time. Until I know the names, I shan't believe it. The one death that was mentioned of a C.R.S. was never referred to again. We never learned his name. He was hit with a paving stone dropped from a roof. Cohn-Bendit on TV. Intelligent, cunning, devious, has the memory of everything he has ever read; impertinent; good, rapid speaker; wraps up his opponents (a trio of middle-aged newsmen). He has the ruthlessness of someone unable to put himself in another's place. Pompidou then speaks for what seems no more than two minutes. We look at each other and say, "Is that all?"

MAY 17

Dinner with C.R. and Z. and H.T. and young Barbara. C.R. says, "I want only one thing—*la paix dans le pays que j'habite*." Z. tells me that last night Barbara went to her room saying, "I haven't the least desire to discuss the student situation with your friends." I gather they were fairly gloom-and-doom. We all wish de G. had not gone to Rumania (his Rumanian trip is virtually all that the TV news gives us; it is as if nothing were taking place in Paris, in a sense), and we wish he would come back. Only one of us—C.R.—expects much. The expression for de G. for years has been "*qui-vous-savez*." We lift glasses, H.T. says, "*À qui-vous-pensez*." Even anti-Gaullists are hoping for something. Funny—even among close friends, we don't say it. Ask Barbara what goes on at the Faculté des Sciences, where she attends meeting after meeting. She says, "We vote and vote and vote." Students don't know if there will be exams, what form they will take, if they will be put off this year or forever. Watching Barbara, I suddenly wonder if she has read her mother's books, if her mother's youth (concentration camp) can possibly have any meaning for her, and if she knows that her father was really quite remarkable in the last war.

MAY 18

Morning news nothing but a list of strikes. It is like watching a brick wall fall down.

A.J. scathing about the students' trying to "help" the workers. Tells me the student leader, the one aptly named Castro, said

something like "Poor workers, begin every morning at eight."
Had never heard of the 6 A.M. shift. A.J. walked to the Sorbonne
every day when a student, didn't drive a car. But nobody did
then—anyway, not here. Class walls virtually impossible for
me to understand. When workers are asked, in interviews,
what they think of the students, they invariably refer to them
as "our future bosses," and say they hope this experience will
make better *chefs* of them than their fathers have been. French
Revolution all for nothing?

Last night, when the cortege of students walked from
the Latin Quarter to Boulogne-Billancourt to bring aid and
comfort to striking Renault workers, it was first funny, then
sad. How could one not laugh at that presumptuous banner
about the handing over of the torch of resistance—"DES
MAINS FRAGILES DES ÉTUDIANTS"? This to a working class
in battle for thirty years. Thought of the Seizième, and kids
straggling through behind a red flag. Wonder if people
fainted, or went on rushing away for the weekend and saw
the cortege as a mild traffic jam? But then how could one
not feel their disappointment when the C.P., anxious to keep
its children from playing with nasty children who use foul
language, locked them out? Daughter's purity was protected
and the rejected suitor walked once around the block singing
the "Internationale."

The occupied Sorbonne is "Paris by Night"—something to
visit after dinner. *Quartier* crowded, cars triple-parked. Outside
the École des Chartes, an arrow points: "*Sorbonne par là.*" Afraid
of being invaded. Bright, cold night. This autumn coldness
(the heat has been turned on in my apartment) adds to the

unreality. Squeeze into the courtyard with difficulty—steady flow of people in and out. In the vast forecourt, a long table piled with Mao's red book, selling at one franc twenty. Cheap banners with Mao, Lenin, and so on, and Stalin. So shocked to see Stalin that H.T., Z., and I stare. Girl behind the counter not French, could be Mexican. We ask, "Why Stalin?" She hesitates, has been asked this before, says in a parrot's voice, "We are prepared to admit his errors, but he was a revolutionary, too." Then so was Hitler. H.T. steers Z. and me away before polemic develops. China-tendency paraphernalia trashy, tawdry, cheap, and I remember, as so often, A.S. saying, "It is the ugliness that attracts them." Z. is upset because of Stalin, trembling. Walls plastered with Peking-style papers and posters, including quotations from *Harpo* Marx. Throngs of every kind of person you might see in any Paris restaurant, just wandering. Sandwiches. Someone sleeping on a bench in a dark corridor with his face to the wall. Hairy discussion groups sitting on the floor. In the large amphitheatre, packed to the very ceiling, the light (dim, brownish, as in East Berlin, for instance, but this must be the normal Sorbonne level) produces Goya faces—little blobs of paint in dimness. A "worker from Renault" has the microphone. Seems to be telling his life story. Key words bring boos or applause. I am reminded of meetings to promote the Second Front in the last war—meetings that consisted of phrases repeated and repeated until they produced an automatic reaction, but lost all meaning for N. and me. Intent young faces, tense, listening. Near me, a middle-aged man answers, says something difficult to understand, and there is an ugly movement of hatred: "*Tu veux qu'on te cogne sur la gueule?*" This bothers me as Stalin bothers Z., and I push my way out. Have the feeling that people are releasing emotions, and not saying what they think. That idiot cheering at key words—no, it is not good enough. But this is only the scum on the pond. Upstairs, notices on closed doors read, "Tourists Keep Out," and I can only hope something other than "*Je te cogne sur la gueule*" is being said.

Everything tatty, a folklore now—China, Cuba, Godard's films. Our tatty era. I see Jean-Pierre, Jacques H.'s friend, looking pleased and superior, as if this were the aim of the revolution. As if this were all he wanted. I remember the luncheon I had with him, and his suddenly saying, "Too many foreigners in France—they should all be helping construct Socialism in their own countries, if they happen to be Polish, for instance," and my suddenly thinking: Why, you are just a mean little bourgeois after all!

In the milling courtyard at midnight, from a lighted window, someone calls, "*Camarades!* The *camarades* from Turin need ten thousand francs [about twenty dollars; nobody speaks in new francs] to get home with. Bring the money to Room No. X." "Watch the stampede," says H.T. He is disturbed at the filth of the place. "They have been given their university now to do as they like with, and this is all they can do—*parler et pisser.*" Drive to Montparnasse. Just behind the Odéon, we see Jean-Louis Barrault on the pavement with a couple of young friends. Z., particularly enraged by his behavior, rolls the window down, leans out, and says, "*Êtes-vous un homme, Jean-Louis Barrault? Non!*" Is revenged for Stalin. She minds because he jumped on the train after it left the station.

MAY 19

Rain and cold. Can't sleep, get dressed—loden, boots, umbrella—walk as far as the end of the street. Sleeping houses. Rain reminds me of Menton and the drenched garden in midwinter. It is cold. I realize that we are in a dream condition here, in France, and that I am frightened for these children who would be angry at being called children. It is the dream feeling of the weekend when President Kennedy was killed. Not a sound anywhere. De Gaulle back from Rumania last night. Even I hope for something from him. This is the second time since *les événements* began that I have had this claustrophobic feeling in the middle of the night and had to go out—though the first time it was to see what the shouting was about at Rennes-Raspail....

In daylight, the above seems absurd. Still cool, with a cold wind. From the Rotonde, before lunch, see thirteen armored police cars creeping by. Three young men at the next table lift beer glasses in ironic salute. One of the unfortunate police actually waves back. Probably the first friendly gesture they've seen since May 3rd. *Journal du Dimanche* is out; vast post-Mass First Communion crowd takes newsstand by storm. Everyone nervous, expectant, waiting for de G. to speak. M.L. says she has seen a kind of Sunday-morning shopping that seems to her unusual, and thinks it must be the beginning of hoarding.

Rumors: Paris is surrounded by tanks. Bruno Coquatrix has closed the Olympia Music Hall and put it "at the service of the movement." Rumor that banner in front of Opéra reads, "AT THE SERVICE OF THE PEOPLE." Rumor of definite connection between Cohn-Bendit and C.I.A.

As soon as the news of de G.'s only remark on the situation (*"La réforme, oui; la chienlit, non"*) comes over the radio, the phone starts ringing. Nobody knows what it means. Look it up in Larousse, find it means "carnival mask." But if read as pronounced it is very ugly. Suzanne B. rings up, says that her brother says it is a filthy expression. On my way out, at eight o'clock, find *Journal du Dimanche* out with a new front page, with the word very large. Look it up in E.'s Littré, and find it is, indeed, three words, exactly as it sounds.

MAY 20

The big *manifestation* a week ago today seems like an hour ago. Every day a Sunday now. Today a new Sunday—no mail, no papers, no trains, no Métro, garbage not collected. Banks to vote a strike. H.T. very kindly turns up with a hundred dollars in case of bank strikes. No one but H. would think of this. Find that everyone is shocked and upset over the *"chienlit"* bit. Notice in conversations a deep feeling of resentment: "We have been waiting for him to speak, and he dismisses us with this." Wonder why my street so silent. Turns out the hotel training school across the street is on strike. Usually the kids' power bikes roar down the street early every morning. Today, phone rings all morning. Even friends who live within walking distance compare news. Have you got any money? Have you been to a bank? New popular term for money: *"du liquide."* Morning news almost entirely taken up with *"chienlit."* Announcers read definition out of dictionary and give page number of dictionary. Everyone sounds outraged.

Today's rumors: Red flags on naval ships in Marseille. Cohn-Bendit secretly engaged to daughter of one of de Gaulle's ministers. Cohn-Bendit getting revenge on society because both parents gassed in camps. (Utter rubbish. He is only twenty-three, has a ten-year-old sister! It is true that his parents have died, but since 1958.) Cohn-Bendit "protected" by someone "close to de G." His police residence permit is delivered to his door by special messenger. Someone I know knows someone "high up" on the special committee that discusses the case of unwanted foreigners. When C.-B.'s name came up, this committee was told C.-B. was not to be touched—and so on and on. A red-hot-Gaullist friend harps on C.-B.'s being "foreign," says, "How would you, a Canadian, feel if some foreigner went to Canada and tried to interfere?" I say, "Some foreigner did." Point missed, so I say, "It was some Mexican or other, I think."

Live with the transistor, carry it from room to room. News not so much a list of strikes as a list of things still functioning: gas, electricity, water. Bitterly cold day. The concierge has turned the heat on "for as long as the oil lasts." Why should there be an oil shortage? De G. meets with heads of Army, security, police. Dockers on strike. This time, I do hear on the morning news, "Red flags on naval ships." Not followed up. Noise of traffic jams reaches down the quiet street and into the flat. Concierge's husband, a striking postman, who once told me he thought strikes never went far enough, pads about pretending to dust door handles.

Walking up the Rue de Rennes, I saw what seemed to be a fleeing population. They had packed whatever could be stuffed into a few cases and sacks. The half-destroyed old Montparnasse railway station looks bombed, and they seemed to be turning their backs on some catastrophe no one could stop to describe. Suitcases, pushcarts, cardboard boxes full of—yes, it is food. Monday is closing day for most shops, but the Monoprix is always open, and so is its basement supermarket, and the shops along the Rue Littré have Monday opening. So that is the catastrophe. The Monoprix has gone on strike—the ground floor is empty, in darkness. Downstairs, the *directeur* and *directrice* are alone with hoarders. These are a solid lava stream, unmoving, or barely, stretching back up the broad stairs and out into the street and around the corner. From another door, left open for them, they come out, one at a time, with sugar, rice, noodles, flour, oil, cornflakes (!), and those great drums of detergent. Potatoes. No conversation in the lava stream. Have never observed a crowd so silent. Young man distributing anti-student tracts: "Unite, unite, and save the country." I dare him to hand tracts into that crowd. He wanders off. A few doors later, a similar queue at the bank, not as long, mostly men. Won't join it—they all make me sick now. Down Rue Littré. In front of greengrocer's, see an American sight—a woman loading a car with groceries. Out of the ordinary here, where virtually no one has a deep freeze, the refrigerator is really not all that common, and it is the custom to shop for each meal, everything fresh, small quantities. She has a crate of oranges, another of potatoes, a case of about twelve bottles of oil, and I hear her saying to her little boy, "I told Mémé [Granny] to get some, too."

During the Suez crisis, everyone bought candles and salt. Candles for power failures, and salt because of an extraordinary rumor that it protects one from radioactivity. You were supposed to fill the tub with salt and water and pop the whole family in the tub and be saved. Not more preposterous than what I am seeing today. It is now about half past ten; the greengrocer's seems just about cleaned out. At the baker's, there is plenty of ordinary bread, but no one is buying that. Rush on the wrapped stuff, which keeps, on *biscottes*, and on pastry flour. Girl tells me they've sold one week's supply of wrapped bread in three hours. Don't buy anything, and decide I shall never eat again. Hate all Parisians until five minutes later, when the laundress who does the sheets offers to lend me money should I run short. Final stop for a newspaper. No hope: delivery strike. Only paper in sight is a gossip sheet with headline "QUEEN ELIZABETH HUMILIATES MICHÈLE MORGAN." Pictures of both ladies, and then, boxed: "Why Did the Queen Do It?" Shop owner turns out to be a revolutionary. Has pictures of police and students from last week's *Paris-Match* pinned up: "People must be made to see."

Discover most of my friends feel as I do—don't want to buy anything, don't want to eat, can't spend, don't care. Everyone compares notes on loss of appetite, disgust with hoarders, etc. No one gives two pins for the Vietnam peace conference—it might just as well be taking place in Sydney, Australia. Yet until May 3rd Vietnam was all we talked about.

When you aren't able to do anything (no transport, no money), you have no problems. You discover nothing was important after all. Very peaceful. You think, out of habit, I must do something about this or that, find you can't, and forget it. Live with the radio. Carry it everywhere in the flat. Bitterly cold. G.F. says, "We seem to be in a tunnel wondering what is at the other end."

MAY 22

Le Monde reports on a ripple of the Cultural Revolution: YOUNG JEWS OCCUPY THE ISRAELITE CONSISTORY. "Several dozens of young Jews" are in occupation and holding "a permanent general assembly." Their aim is to "contest the archaic and undemocratic structure of the present community.... They appeal to Jewish youth to join them." The item ends with this: "The telephone switchboard is in their hands. No incident has been reported." Professional football players now occupying *their* headquarters. Not quite sure what they are demanding.

Phone conversation with J. de T., who is "like a tiger in a cage." Can't get to the hospital in the morning and his patients can't get to him in the afternoon.

Gray, cold. Hear on all sides, "No sugar, no flour, no potatoes." Feel the change in people in the shops: those buying enormous quantities of anything sense the disapproval. Bank strike. How simple life becomes without mail, without money! Z. (ever the anxious one) says solemnly, of mail, "*Mais il y a des gens malades de qui on voudrait avoir des nouvelles.*"

The tyrant grandfather who made the whole house tremble is suddenly in a wheelchair. The grandchildren are edging the wheelchair toward the staircase, and the grandfather's favored children, who owe him something, or once said they did, are not lifting a finger. The rest of the family are in the parlor making conversation and waiting for the crash, and wondering what to do.

Sartre, speaking to students in the Sorbonne, says de G. destroyed the Resistance as a structure when he returned to power. A student says, "You are a good artist, M. Sartre, but a lousy politician."

Schools on strike. Anne-Marie does not know what to do with her little boy. She can't take him to work with her, and so she locks him up in the flat. Says, "He knows about never answering the door." Bitterly cold, with a cold wind. See a collection of fascinating old cookbooks, including an original Ali Baba (Curnonsky), but the shop is shut and looks barricaded. Hairdresser's empty. Something squalid, uneasy about a food shop closed because of hoarding. Primistère near the Boulevard du Montparnasse shut for lack of provisions. The customers broke into the shop storeroom and helped themselves, and finally the manager just shut the place altogether.

Cohn-Bendit inspires (in my friends) apprehension among the Jews, who are afraid he is attracting too much attention, and jealousy among the old Marxists: "*C'est de la blague! Il n'a aucune idéologie!*" There is also, though not among the young, "*Qu'est-ce que c'est que cet étranger?*" When I answer, "Régis Debray," I am told, "That was different."

No papers, no magazines, no plays, no good music. (France-Musique plays pop and syrup all day; all three FM stations have the same program now, like the music you hear in a cocktail lounge in a hotel in America.) No telegrams, no mail, no *biscottes*, no sugar. I chase nothing except newspapers, and the only strike I dread is electricity: It is like the blood stopping. They will save that until the end.

Occident has wrecked the Conservatoire, Rue Madrid. Now, why that particular place?

TV wavy, like a window blind rippling. Receive explanation of which I don't understand a word. Something about factories' not using all the power they are supposed to. "*Les secteurs sont disjoints.*" Turn my mind off, snap back in time to say, "Thank you *very* much. Now I understand." Debate on the motion of censure. Blah-blah-blah. Like something out of the Fourth Republic. Feeling of something new fading in debates, rhetoric, talk of referendum. "Thank God the Communist Party has taken this movement over!" This from A.J.—meaning they are sensible men who like a quiet Sunday. Taxi strike. In the well-to-do suburbs, the lawn-and-private-school belt, they are stealing gas from each other's cars.

Barbara is strike picket at her *lycée*. Her mother says nothing. "At her age, I would have been the same." But she worries. The evening Barbara went to that big demonstration at Denfert-Rochereau, I saw her father's face: "*Donc, elle est là? Elle est là aussi?*" I can imagine what he was thinking: She will lose an eye, she will be trampled, she will be beaten by the police. But they have brought her up to think for herself (best parents I know), and if they seemed inconsistent now she would never respect them again.

"*Les copains ont fait une gaffe,*" a student said. They have indeed. When they were renaming all the amphitheatres in the Sorbonne, one of the first they changed was Jean Cavaillès. Resistance hero, shot at forty-one. Never heard of him, I guess. It must seem so far away! A nineteen-year-old doesn't know de G. was voted (and how overwhelmingly) into power in 1958. Thinks he took over with some kind of Army march on Paris. I say, "Ask your mother and father. They probably voted him in." Mother, there, says nothing.

H.T. says Stalin's picture gone from the Sorbonne.

G.'s Russian friend at the Sorbonne every day, wild with enthusiasm. Is reminded of Petrograd when friend was on the barricades, at the age of seventeen. "Now we know the age of my friend," says G. Rich with my five hundred francs, offer money to G., who offers even more back to me. Tiny, red-haired wife of *marchand de couleurs* (hardware) on Rue du Cherche-Midi says if I run out I am to come to her, and Jacqueline, who has plenty of responsibilities of her own, calls up to see if I am all right. As in a city under siege.

Gray, rain, cold. Think of people walking miles and miles to work and wondering what is going to happen next. Radio says, "Still milk, bread, electricity, gas, water." That is what adds to the unreality. Suppose that in any city—in Montreal, say—everyone heard on the morning news, "You still have gas, light, and so forth," wouldn't everyone panic? Rush out and buy sugar because the man forgot to say "You still have sugar"? You would think it was the siege of Leningrad and we were all eating rats.

Everyone disgusted with the way the movement has taken a political turn, and with the debate. In every conversation: "When will it end?" (Meaning the strikes.) F.W. tells me that a C.G.T. (Confédération Générale du Travail, the Communist-led labor union) official told the U.N.E.F. (Union Nationale des Étudiants de France, the students' union) that the unions could hold out four months. Still no vote in the Chamber, but the power is so clearly in the hands of the unions you wonder why the bother. Nobody cares.

Touching appeal on radio to the younger *lycée* students a few days ago. Some are eleven, twelve, thirteen. Tactful man from a parents' association. Said please don't parade around in the streets; the most useful thing you can do is go home at once and explain to your parents the meaning of the movement.

Cold drizzle. Walk to Right Bank with M.L., who has to get to her bank. Less traffic than usual—the department stores on strike, for one thing. And yesterday's traffic jams (three hours to cross the Concorde; some drivers simply abandoned their cars) may have kept people at home. Probably faster to walk. Every second shop closed. It is like Monday closing. In front of the Chamber, little queue under umbrellas. Think of utter misery of people walking home tonight in this cold and wet. M.L.'s bank the Royal Bank of Canada, on the Rue Scribe. Manager worried about "image" of Royal Bank and "bad publicity," because the bank mentioned by name in the *Daily Express*. Accused of not making any payments over two hundred dollars (something like that). Tell him that all the banks in Paris have limited payments and some not paying anything at all. Say to M.L., "Who cares about the Royal Bank and its image?" M.L. chides me, "You don't know what it is to have a head office." Look into Morgan Guaranty, on the Place Vendôme. Entirely empty. No queue. They say that Monday was frantic. Cash check with no trouble, so as to repay H.T. Every employee has an opinion—all very lively. Food shops probably have their normal quota of food, but to us they look overstuffed. Some kind of collective hallucination must be at work. We are *already* so installed in the abnormal, have so quickly settled into it, that anything usual seems suspect, peculiar. Delivery trucks all over the streets, replacing stocks after the hoarding rush.

The D.s are revolutionary! My most conservative friends! Gilles is "reforming" his engineering school "night and day," Hugues is all for the students, and his mother is furious because his father's ministry is not taking advantage of the situation to go on strike. "Not that we want the Communists," she says, "but de G. must go." She sounds as if she had just stepped off a barricade. In the last election, they voted so far to the right that I lost sight of them—they slipped over the horizon. Husband not only won't strike but walks to his *ministère* every day. Tells me that steel industry will take longer to pick up than we think, that even after they agree to go back to work there will be a gap of about fourteen days before things roll. Wife interrupts: "Who cares about boring old steel production?" *Vive la révolution!* Says she doesn't mind walking—walked all the way to the Hôtel Druout for sale of antique furniture.

G.P. and A.J. have both let their books go. Feel it is futile. A.J. says that book doesn't fit into new world, that everything will be changed. How to tell? I live between typewriter and transistor, TV news (everything else seems trivial), telephone (rings like a machine gone mad).

The recording that tells the time over the telephone is on strike. No watch or clock owned by me has ever worked. Didn't realize how much I depended on *l'horloge parlante*. The concierges are on strike! Their instructions are to look after the garbage, "in the interests of salubrity," but "not to answer questions or give any more information." Our concierge probably can't read. Works harder than ever, polishing mirrors and the glass doors, Gauloise hanging on lower lip, and gives information of all kinds. Her cat, M. Pussy (pronounced "poosy"), neglected.

Spends his time having doors opened for him. No one can be bothered now. Victim of *les événements*.

A few days ago—whenever the last sunny day was, Sunday perhaps—two tall girls looking like New Zealanders (longish skirts, rolled woolen socks, gym shoes, and enormous packsacks) but with Irish accents asked the way to the Eiffel Tower. I said, "It's a long way to walk, and they may not let you up." "Why not?" "It's guarded by police." "Why?" I said, "You do sense there is something going on in Paris, don't you?" "Oh, yes. No buses." Off they went anyway, with two hundred pounds of worldly goods strapped to their shoulders.

Suddenly found it difficult to buy stockings. Everything shut or on strike. Magasins Réunis on Rue de Rennes open, across from striking Gaz de France and from striking Monoprix. It is like a dream—I am the only customer. After a few moments, other customers wander in to the cosmetics counter, but the place resembles a hangar.

Say that the student movement is not French, that it started in America. Receive skeptical smiles. Everyone knows U.S. students eat ice cream all day. (The same smiles that Anthony S. found so discouraging when he was teaching at the British Institute here. He would say that Samuel Johnson was important, for example. But everyone knew that only Charles Morgan and Lawrence Durrell were important.) Press on, explain about Columbia. No one has ever heard of Columbia. Give up.

J. de T. walks to hospital and back each day. About an hour and a half each way, I should imagine. Afternoons and evenings, some patients get to him. Says that the young—the disturbed young, that is, his patients—are "*traumatisés*" by the events, that the young move out of reality all too easily at the best of times. Bad phone connection; can't hear more. A psychiatrist friend of A.J.'s goes to the Odèon every day taking notes. Collective hysteria.

Bought weekly lottery tickets, discovered drawing put off "indefinitely." Pari-mutuel betting, the sacrosanct P.M.U., also out. There is talk of Mother's Day being put off, perhaps made a joint holiday with Father's Day in June. Astonished to discover the French do not know this is a commercial holiday. It is thought of as ancient and immutable, like Christmas. Florists protesting—all their potted plants are ready. Parents upset: "How can we explain it to our children?" Like the truth about Santa Claus. Bank on the Rue Littré closed. Frail young girl stands with her arm across the door. You can put money in, but you can't take any out. Radio Luxembourg partly replaces mail and breakdown of telephone. (Only kind of phone working is *l'automatique*.) Radio explains it will relay only important messages, between half past nine and midnight, every ten minutes, and that it is "not substituting for public services"; i.e., not interfering with strikers.

Schools on strike. Teachers out, students in—they are occupying. No provision was made for the boarding students at the *lycées*. Those who live outside Paris and who can't get home because of the transport strike are on their own. What if they have no money? The parents, who can't send them anything, must be frantic. The R.s have taken in a boy, a classmate of their daughter. Moody boy, sits and broods. Won't help around the place. Says at home he is paid if he helps.

Snake queues outside the banks. Empty grocery shelves (canned goods gone, mostly). No mineral water—very hard on mothers who need it for *biberons*. They can always boil the tap water, of course The fruit merchant puts down his iron shutter early—too much sold. Gas pumps now have a sign, "*Panne Sèche*," meaning dry as dry. It is what you say if your car runs out—"*J'ai une panne sèche*." Gas shortage caused by nothing but panic.

Weather cold, bitter. Motion of censure to be voted today. E. so opposed to hoarding she won't even buy a candle in case there is a power strike. All my smoker friends dread cigarette shortage. (Hasn't happened, but there is a run on *tabac-brun* cigarettes, such as Gauloises and Gitanes.) Revolutionary *élan*, the Barcelona feeling, fades in votes, debates, rumors of a referendum. Forty-eight-hour strike at Les Halles. Theatres on strike. No TV except for the news. Department stores closed. Friend with small children at home (schools out), husband going mad (can't get to work), no *liquide* (didn't get to a bank), says, "I keep going, make the same daily gestures."

Suddenly remember G. is coming to dinner and we are supposed to go to Censier (Sorbonne annex) for medical-psychiatric-all-out-discussion, which G. assures me is worth the walk. Forty-five-minute break between Pompidou's speech and the voting, rush out to shop for food. *Stupéfaction*: I am the only customer. The hoarders have spent all their money! Buy everything I need—strawberries, cream, etc. Buy roses. Florist upset over threat of change in Mother's Day. At the *charcutier's*, ask girl to hurry, want to see result of vote on TV. Large, stupid eyes. She says, "I heard something on the radio." Ask if she knows what is going on. She hesitates, and says, "Something sad? Bizarre?" Then says, "We did good business on Monday."

Dream image (but real) of middle-aged men shuffling up in alphabetical order to vote. Phone call from London. I watch the screen, I reassure. The London papers must be showing the streets here running with blood. Phone call from one of G.'s patients, or husband of one: G. will be late or perhaps not get here at all. Caught in traffic, still visiting patients in 18th, 19th Arrondissements. Brave G., in that *Deux-chevaux*, as ill as the patients, if they only knew. Call from New York. Tell B.M. I am probably going to medical thing at Censier, shall not go to demonstration tonight. He says, "I trust your common sense," hear his voice fade with "Take care." After I hang up, I hear the demonstration not far away, pull on boots, coat, leave note on door (though don't really expect G. now). Drizzly night. Carry umbrella. On Rue de Rennes, they sweep by, the young: really students—no "*éléments*," as they are called. At first, I don't know what I am hearing, it is so strange. Then it becomes clear; it is like rubbing frost away from a window. I hear them chanting, "*Nous sommes tous des juifs allemands.*" It is because of Cohn-Bendit, because that is how he is dismissed. They are answering their parents. This is France, they are French, I am not dreaming. *Nous sommes tous des juifs allemands.* It is really so unlucky to be either one here—imagine what it means to say one is both! It is the most important event, I think, since the beginning of this fantastic month of May, because it means a mutation in the French character: a generosity. For the first time, I hear a French voice go outside the boundaries of being French. I walk along beside them, on the pavement. Two boys from *Action Française*, a right-wing group, silently hold up banner reading, "NO RED FLAGS OVER THE SORBONNE." That is brave of them. They are only two. They simply stand there. But this crowd glances, just like that, and the slogan changes to "*On s'en fout des frontières*." Of course, there are only a few thousand of them, and they are excited, with that black flag and that red flag—perhaps they would say anything. They are still answering their parents—I feel that. We all sweep down the Boulevard Raspail. A woman shakes a red flag out of a window; the kids applaud. I am on the *terre-plein* with trees, in the middle of the boulevard, where the market is held twice a week; the kids are on the roadway. New slogans: "*De Gaulle en Suisse*" and "*De Gaulle chienlit*" (he asked for that one). Suddenly they begin that "hop-hop-hop" cry and start to run. It is a Korean (I think) *pas gymnastique*, stepping along fast with your knees very high. When it is done properly, it gives the walker great mobility; you can move a mass of people sharp left or right quite quickly, fluidly. It was with this step that about thirty thousand students swept over the Pont de la Concorde on May 7th; the C.R.S. were simply taken by surprise. They must have thought they were dreaming—imagine thousands of people suddenly saying "hop-hop-hop" and quite literally hopping over a bridge! But tonight the marchers don't know the *pas*; they simply run and scatter suddenly, up on the *terre-plein*, where I seem to be the only observer. People are watching the marchers, but on the left-hand pavement, separated from them by the southbound half of the Boulevard Raspail. I find this running frightening, always—the sound of it behind one. I stand behind a plane tree, and they scatter by on either side. Cross to left-hand pavement when all clear. Wonder about their parents (because this is a monologue, about being *juifs allemands*), and on the corner of the Rue de Sèvres am answered A nice-looking couple, well dressed, don't look stuffy, just puzzled "If *that's* what they want," the man says. He doesn't sound angry, just stunned, almost hurt: "*Si c'est ça qu'ils veulent—d'être des juifs allemands!*"

Unreal—lamplight, indigo sky, small bright leaves all over the trees, "*On s'en fout des frontières!*" Only a few thousand. Two? Three? I can't judge. But what a turning upside down and inside out of the French character! It seems to me more important than today's vote, of which I don't yet know the result. No one in my generation said it, and God knows *il y avait de quoi.* I am convinced this lot are better than we were. For one thing, they have never been frightened. Frightened in theory but not in fact. Cohn-Bendit born a refugee, but after the war. He doesn't *know.* He can imagine, as I could have imagined the 1914 war. Something else.

Negro says to me, "Where are they going?" In fact, he says, "*Où vont ces troupes?*" Tell him not to get close unless he is involved with the movement—could be dangerous. "What movement?" Too long to explain, and his French isn't good. We walk along together. Can't share my umbrella with him—he is miles tall. "Why are you going if it is dangerous?" I understand him to say. Tells me he has a passport. When we come to the first cordon of police up a side street (cordon of students holding hands in front of the police, to prevent other students from doing something stupid), I point to the police, and, when we are a little past them, make the gesture of being hit over the head, using my umbrella, implore him to leave—it would be foolish for him to be involved, understanding nothing. Understands, nods, does an about-face. I have finally realized we are going to the Palais Bourbon.

Kids don't look at police, sweep by them. "Hop-hop-hop" under the trees. Umbrellas. A few tourists. Grown man (American, from his hair) gives clenched-fist salute. Being funny? Only a month ago, I was still saying, "The young in France? Senile. Little old men." They have written on the walls of the Sorbonne, "*L'imagination prend le pouvoir.*" People find this irritating—pretentious. Why? It seems to me more important than their not having swept out the courtyard.

Girl rushes from side street to catch up, singing, out of breath, out of tune, the "Internationale." Long hair floating. Well dressed, good shoes, clothes too fragile for the night. That seems to be it. I go home. Radio says they've dispersed.

MAY 23

Now about nine million out. No strike pay in France. How long can they go on? C.G.T. now openly breaks with students. Fear that strikers will have some idea beyond and outside material demands, I suppose. The Communist Party seems like *Papa-Maman*, and the student movement like an interfering social worker. *Papa-Maman* explain to the children, "Think with your stomachs. We are the brains."

There were about five thousand kids last night—more than I'd imagined. The *heurts avec la police* took place in the Place Maubert and at several other points. *No* radio reporter mentions what I saw and heard—they merely say the students "expressed their contempt for Parliament." I have three different versions of what went on in the Place Maubert. E. tells me her daughter woke her up in the middle of the night, said the demonstrators were all toughs from the suburbs, setting fire to cars. H.T. says that it was a mixture of students and toughs, that they set fire to the garbage now all over the streets.

Mme. L. says, "Oh, I see you have stocked up on matches." Always have several boxes in the kitchen, and, anyway, these are taper matches someone brought me from Germany. Can see she is nervous about matches, so I give her a box. There is *no shortage of matches*. Everyone mad, afraid of something imaginary.

E. comes around. Her bank won't give her a *rond*. She won't accept more than a hundred new francs, though it won't go far with the hordes of young she seems to be feeding twice a day now. Says she dreads a cigarette shortage more than anything. "In my internment camp, I traded everything they gave me to eat for cigarettes." Tell her that in her place I would stock up—she has a choice of feeling guilty and sane or civic-minded and bonkers. What she wanted to hear. Give her an opaque shopping bag so no one will know, and off she goes.

Look at appointment book. Everything cancelled. What a relief I needn't go anywhere.

Red-haired German in the Select is mistaken for Cohn-Bendit and escorted (in car with German plates) by motorcycle cops to nearest police station. Is photographed from all angles. Comes back a hero.

H.T. describes non-stop discussion at Faculté des Sciences. Each laboratory to be on its own, a private soviet. "But where is the money to come from? They are dividing up a cake they haven't got." Discuss Cohn-Bendit's having said in Berlin that there were eleven dead. "He has signed his expulsion papers with that remark," says H.T. "He will never be allowed back."

We both think statement irresponsible. I am more and more suspicious of C.-B. What is all this publicity? It smells.

Taxi strike still on. Today like a Sunday. *Femme de ménage* says that the parties and receptions where she does work as cook and *serveuse*—is much in demand—are not cancelled; people come on foot. She informs me that Cohn-Bendit is financed "by Cuba and by the Americans." What Americans? "The F.B.I.," she says. Haven't heard about F.B.I. in such a long time that they almost sound like stodgy old relations.

E. tells me about the Musée de l'Homme ethnologists trying to occupy the apartment of the Minister of the Interior. They climbed over a trellis onto the Fouchet balcony. E.: "All they had to do was ring the bell at the front door and walk in." Then they cut the phone wires, but they cut the wrong wires, being intellectuals all the way, and Mme. Fouchet was on the phone to the police while they were still sawing away at the wrong thing. Police came and took them off to jail. All they succeeded in doing was frightening one of the Fouchet children into hysterics. I have the feeling that even in jail they were all saying to each other, "I haven't felt as young as this in thirty years."

The flight of the *beau monde*. The *gens du monde* have fled to Switzerland, to the Midi, to Germany, to Italy. With what gasoline? The J.D.s went without even waiting for de G. to speak.

Walked to Petit Palais in downpour. Hadn't realized *all* museums on strike. Wanted to see the Dead Sea Scrolls. Wonder if they are still there or if they have been taken back to Israel.

Around seven, meet D.M. in the Rotonde. Streets thick with police cars—reminds me of Algerian war. D. looking pretty, freshly washed golden hair. Waiter tells neighbor that Coca-Cola stocks will be gone in two days. Man says he doesn't care, but what about Pernod? Waiter says beer and bottled water will go next, upon which man looks grave. Garbage trucks go by manned by soldiers.

At home, turn on radio—riots on Boul' Mich', fires, "uncontrollable elements," student leaders trying to get them back to the Sorbonne. Turn it off, dash off to États-Généraux of the Photography School, around the corner on Rue de Vaugirard, to which G.F. has invited me. A state School of Photography and Cinematography. I've never been inside, but I know some of the students by sight from the café that is across the street from it and just up the street from me. The students are on strike and occupying the school—sleeping in—and they feel it is now or never if they are to reorganize the school from top to bottom. Their chance. They've invited the top photographers, technicians, photo editors, etc., in Paris, and about fifty have turned up, which is astonishing—no transport, after all. The school is desolate, filthy. A row of latrines in the courtyard. Go into what would be furnace and storerooms in, say, a small Protestant church in America, or in a very poor country school, and into the *salle de projection*. Church-basement feeling reinforced: filthy, splintered board floor; collection of hard little chairs that look as if fished out of a junkyard. Everything tacky, wretched, except for the lighting, which is modern but very ugly indeed. Meeting presided over by a pale boy who looks about fifteen. No more than eighteen or twenty students (this is photography only, not film, which has a larger student body), mostly sitting around walls and not saying much. Nothing abstract about the meeting; they want advice from the professionals. The professors sit at the back looking surly. One of them—large, in tweeds, looks like a boxer—takes the microphone and says something about the teaching profession's being dragged in the mud. Only one of the teachers sits with the students and the professionals. He stands up and tells us something I can hardly believe: There isn't a single photograph in the whole school. Not one. Not only is there no film library, there is nothing at all. When he wants to show his pupils the work of celebrated photographers ("some of you here right now"), he says, he has to "drag his class here and there across Paris to exhibitions"—when there are exhibitions. Until two years ago (I believe it has been a state school only two years; it was private before), there wasn't a book in the place. "I have managed to obtain a few books—very few," he says. So much for the school. No library, no pix. The professionals are unbelievable. Their one terror seems to be that these kids will grow up and become photographers. It reminds me of the Odéon (occupied by so-called Anarchists), where everyone gets up and tells his life story in a kind of permanent psychodrama. One after another, the professionals describe how (a) they went to school and learned nothing, or (b) they never went to school at all. One white-haired gent, who is in analysis, if one can judge by his vocabulary, stands up and implores these serious, exhausted, and extremely sympathetic kids to "explore their conscious and unconscious motivations—to see what subconscious needs and desires have impelled them to choose this profession" (where there is no room for them, he implies). Nice kid takes the microphone, says politely that they haven't time just now for self-analysis—that what they really want is help in turning a school everyone seems to agree is second-rate into something better. Picture editor of fashion magazine complains that when young people bring her their work they can't answer the question "Why do you want to be a photographer?" Kids look glum, don't reply. Another professional accuses them of all wanting to be "*des virtuoses*," tells them that they all want fast cars and four-star hotels, that they see themselves as stars. Here follows a flurry of testimonials, all from virtuosos: Why don't you become technicians? You can be just as happy in a laboratory. Kids completely crushed, it seems to me. Some want to be technicians, some don't, but they murmur this to each other. Only one student tries to explain: "*We* are in an inadequate school. You, the professionals, say we don't learn anything here—tell us what is wrong. Here is our program—look at it. Tell us what you think." What they encounter is the secret hostility and jealousy of the entrenched. They can expect very little. Around midnight, committees are formed. Man stands up and says, "It isn't up to us to help you. It's up to the young to supply their own cultural revolution." I hear a couple of kids calling him Frankenstein among themselves. I ask one of the kids why so few of them are here tonight. He is all beard and pipe; I know him by sight, as he seems to know me. "Some are on the Boul' Mich'," he says. "Some who live in the provinces left Paris just before the railway strike. They had to go home, as their parents weren't able to send them any money." He adds, "*Nous dépendons de nos parents*," which seems very touching—a paradox. "We get one or two hours' sleep a night," he adds. Only two of the professionals say anything concrete. One describes exactly how these schools function in Germany and Belgium, and speaks of the old Bauhaus, which in this locale is something like evoking Versailles to Eskimos. Another gives an account of the famous school at Vevey. Kids listen. They seem bewildered, disappointed. I don't wonder. They will have to act *in spite of* their elders. Unfortunately, these are the elders they will depend on for jobs. Leave meeting just after midnight. The students at this school have forgotten one problem—money. I would guess that after the strikes are settled there will be very little left over for film libraries, that the sullen-looking teachers will be back where they started. Hope, enthusiasm. Suddenly wish students at American colleges could see this place. Occupying a place like Columbia would seem like living in what that dumb photographer called a four-star hotel.

Group on pavement with transistor. My street deserted, lovely night. Perhaps spring arriving after all. *Le joli mai.* Windows open, lights, everyone listening to Radio Luxembourg or Europe I, the non-government stations. I recognize the voices now. Tell of fighting, fires, grenades, all only ten minutes' walk away. Not a sound here but radios. Want to go there, but my presence would be entirely useless. It could be Asia, from immediate evidence, but it isn't Asia—it is ten minutes' walk. All I would want to say is "Please stop." Listen to the radio much of the night. Around two, I realize I have forgotten to eat any dinner.

MAY 24

This morning, I had trouble remembering whether the news was real or I'd dreamed it. Last thing I heard (or dreamed) was "Small groups setting fire to trash in Les Halles." Shall never know, because the newsstands now on strike until Monday.

Europe I gives two versions of last night's fighting: the official one and its own. *Manifestations* all over France today—farmers, tonight the students again. The announcer says, "Today is going to be a long day."

Friend calls, says, "*Ce soir il y aura peut-être des morts. Quelque chose se prépare.*" I am offered a window in Boul' Mich' to see the fight. Turn it down. Talk with Jacques—ask him if National School of Oriental Languages had ever attempted any sort of reform before the students went into action. "*Vous me posez une question sérieuse?*" he says. Yes, they had, but the Ministry of Education never so much as acknowledged their letter. When they asked for more teachers, they were told that as they had asked for too much, they wouldn't be given anything. He was "out" last night—thinks that as his students are out fighting he ought to be with them. Tells me about material difficulties in his school. Like School of Photography and Cinematography, but more and worse.

Am astonished to see carpenters working outside barbershop on Rue du Cherche-Midi. Butcher's dark, gloomy, everyone nervous, curious atmosphere in the sense that everyone seemed to be trying to be nice to the butcher, in case of a shortage, and he, usually so pleasant, was being a little dictator, sneering. Yet there is *no* shortage of meat! They were all acting in an imaginary situation!

Femme de ménage comes in calling, "*Il y a de tout!*" Has found oil, potatoes, etc., in the market this morning. Says stocking still heavy—nothing left in the market by noon. No racing, no lottery, no papers, no garbage collection, Rue de l'Abbé-Grégoire like a city dump (shops). My street (no shops) perfectly clean.

Garbage indoors. Astonish man in shoe shop by buying shoes. I'm almost the first customer they've seen since May 11th. After telling about strikes, shortages, last night's fighting, and future prospects, radio breaks into "Bye Bye Blues."

H.T. dined with friends in the Latin Quarter last night, came out to a wall of flame. Girl with their party had to get home ("My mother will be frantic"), no phone. H. ties a handkerchief over the girl's face (tear gas) and they walk across Rue des Écoles between a burning barricade and the lined-up police. Leaves her at her door, walks back. Tells this as he might say, "I walked along the Seine." Have never seen him frightened at any time, but he does have an odd tendency (a European tendency, I'd say) to be aggressive with the police, and that could have been the only danger.

From Odéon Métro station onward, the Boulevard Saint-Germain has something desolate, ruined about it, as if swept by a very old war, a long time ago. Or like a poor and shabby street no one has time or money to keep clean. Grilles up from around the trees, stop signs and one-way signs lying in the gutter, traffic lights smashed. This odd look of seeming as if it had always been like that. Shops closed, or striking. Outside Hachette, a cardboard streamer hanging from the sixth floor to ground level with one word: "OCCUPATION." I knew that trees had been cut down and that it would shock me, but I had not expected to feel true grief. A lovely tree. They tried to burn it— the leaves are singed. Some of the leaves on the standing trees singed, too. We waited all winter for the leaves, and now they have tried to kill them. Great sections of Rue des Écoles torn up. Agitation around the Sorbonne. Don't go in. H.T., who loathes destruction, suddenly bursts out, "*Ils n'ont jamais connu la misère!*" He was a brilliant scholarship boy from a poorish family, has a reverence for universities, for learning, for the very stones of an old school. School was miraculous. As for the war ... I daren't answer (because it would be impertinent) that their not having known *la misère* and *la guerre* is the source of their nerve. Think of Canadians marked by the Depression, really affected by it. It made them ambitious but not daring, and certainly not strong. Can't say any of this. Remains of a barricade on Rue Saint-Jacques. These stones are larger, not paving stones, and, anyway, the street isn't torn up. H.T. interested, does rapid tour of immediate neighborhood. I stay there, watch as people pick up stones (several men do this; it seems to be irresistible), make as if to fling, imagine themselves on barricades. All say too heavy to throw. H.T. comes back, says these stones from a building site, obviously brought here by truck. That means the barricade was not, could not have been, "spontaneously" built by students. You need the time, the plan, the gas, the stones, and the truck. *Bon.* Place Maubert like one of those dumps that smolder all the time, with a low fire that you can smell for miles. Blackened garbage, singed trees, a burned car. Don't want to see more. Walk down the Seine. Keep turning my ankles—so many holes in the ground, and so many stray wood, stone, and iron *things*. Nothing has a shape or a name. Along the quai, walking grimly, with a purpose, five young men. Not students, not working-class boys. Helmets, long leather gauntlets, black wind-breakers, long, greasy hair under the helmets, faces that look like those faces the police assemble from descriptions given by several witnesses—the lumpy faces you see in a newspaper

over "The killer looks like this." Walk with their shoulders
hunched forward. One has a *nerf-de-boeuf*—one of those thin,
licoricelike blackjacks—at his waist. You can kill with it if you
know how. What used to be called *les blousons noirs* during the
nineteen-fifties, and then they just disappeared, and I used to tell
strangers, "There is little or no juvenile delinquency in France."
They seem to be about thirty. The same boys grown up?

The Place Saint-Michel still full of tear gas. Crossing to
the fountain, start to sneeze, eyelids smart, tears form. The
fountain is like the Cour des Miracles. A man of thirty or so,
sandy hair, sandy face, small, one of those one-color men (could
be albino but happens to be sand), stands beating with a stick
on the metal covering over the lights that light the fountain at
night. He beats the three-plus-two rhythm that used to mean
"*Al-gé rie fran-çaise*" but now stands for "*C-R-S S-S.*" He beats
and beats, he can't stop, he grins, he can't, can't stop, he stares
at the bridge across the Place (cars and police), he is without
any doubt a poor, sick rag of a man. You can't mistake the grin,
the repeated action (he could just as easily be sitting rocking),
and eyes that look *toward* but not *at*. On the rim of the fountain,
sitting, waiting, grinning, men like him. They wear the rather
shabby, nondescript suits you see on men in institutions, and
for a moment I have the unreal idea that they were being taken
from observation to a mental hospital and that their doctor
had to leave them there. One of them squawks over and over,
"Speech-speech-speech-speech." H.T. pulls me away: "Stop
staring at them! Can't you see?" "But they're mad!" "Yes.
They're attracted by the violence, the blood. They're waiting
for tonight, for something more to happen."

Cohn-Bendit at frontier, met by *sous-prefet*, escorted back to Germany. If he is paranoid (as someone who knows him swears), he must be in heaven. But paranoia is an easy rumor, too. At eight o'clock, de G. speaks. Stare at the screen after he has stopped. Feel again it is like the Kennedy weekend. De G. looks old; nagging childhood memory finally comes up as George Arliss, the actor. He looks like Arliss playing someone distraught, not attending. Is that all? Nothing more? Phone rings: "Did you ever?" "No, never." Only A.J. says, "Well, what else could he say?" Am confused by news—fighting in Lyon (the city) and at the Gare de Lyon. As the announcer predicted this morning, it has been a long day; it merges into another night of radio.

MAY 25

Cloudy, mild, oppressive. Can't remember which day today is. Listened to the radio until about 3 A.M., when the Minister of the Interior spoke of "*la pègre*" (gangsters) in the same breath as "*les anarchistes*." Inaccurate, unreal, unfair. Fell asleep and went on dreaming the news.

Ex-Army men astonished at the professional skill of barricade-builders, how quickly they get the barricades up, their choice of materials. Whose idea was it to cut down the beautiful trees everywhere, Right Bank and Left? *Students*'? Is it normal for students to carry power saws?

Seem to be about an inch from civil war, ripples spreading. I think of the education of French children: *Il faut que tu sois raisonnable*. But no one is reasonable. The students who set the Bourse on fire knew without hesitation where everything was kept, even ladders to enable them to get up on the roof. They threatened to burn the concierge's daughter alive. Students, who had never been inside a stock exchange in their lives before.

Law students active last night for the first time. Most conservative of *facultés*, they would have nothing to do with the *contestation*. Suddenly have become more than active — positively virulent. They were distinguished yesterday by their dress (they dress for a demonstration as if going somewhere for lunch—anyway, ties), by their rather snobby way of speaking, which they cultivate in order to annoy the plebs, and by their miniskirted girls. In action last night, among the most *enragés*.

Walk in morning rain to Luxembourg Gardens, on an impulse I cannot define. To see uninjured trees? Gates are shut, chained, and padlocked. Behind them the silent trees. Walk all the way around, past the Senate, past the occupied Odéon—its curb a hedge of spilled garbage. This is the fringe of the battleground: more and more spilled *ordures*, a blackened car still running, another car looking as if it had been kicked and punched. Something dreamlike about the locked secret garden: green on green, chestnut petals all over the filthy pavement; behind the iron-spike fence a Sisley in the rain, a Corot with the sun gone. A fountain jet still playing. The final unreality—three workmen and a small bright-orange jeeplike thing for transporting rakes and shovels. I believe—I do believe—they were about to sweep the paths and rake the gravel. Anyway, they were in working blues. A man shaking their hands through the grille fence. Traffic lights working. Turn away from the park, walk into broken glass, garbage, upturned road signs. Only one café open—curious brown light over the bar, men reading newspapers as if it were any Saturday. Pons patisserie closed, the café next to it smashed, I think—I look away. This is tear-gas country; the rain keeps the gas close to the ground, and there is no wind. In the middle of the Place, a hole like a bomb crater. People stand silently around it. Woman says to her mother (I think), "*Moi, je suis malade pour les arbres.*" Enormous truck on its side. Charred cars pushed half on each other, like the dead after an accident; the cars look like the *people* you see lying beside the highway after a smash, half sprawled over each other. Something indecent. Partly, not entirely, burned. Like lips drawn back from the teeth of the dead. It reminds me of that. One, a Gordini, stuffed with bags of garbage—to make it burn faster, I suppose. The garbage intact. I sneeze, cry, am blinded, stumble across the street and into the branches of a murdered tree lying across the pavement. I actually stumble into the leaves. Very strange, for it is not a place for grown people; you swing up into leaves as a child. Wreck of Dupont's (the café). Just wrecked. There are perhaps fifty of us, ten with cameras. We all stand weeping, red-eyed; we seem to be mourning the death of the square. Stunned, grieved. How quickly a street becomes mud and garbage! I cannot identify this new ground I am walking on. A pavement of mud, papers, tracts, clay, iron sheeting, piles of stones, bombs (they look like little tuna-fish tins), yet nothing is as definite as that. Weeping, remembering not to rub the eyes (a sort of prickly itching under the lids makes one want to scratch, but the most unpleasant feeling to me is the painful irritation at the inner corner of the eye, that little pink bit), turn down Rue Monsieur le Prince. This end of the street all steps and terraces. Part of the iron railings torn up. Barricade of paving stones. In rain, mud, we seem to be skirting a minor precipice. Only steps. I remember A.S., the first time he came out of Warsaw, saying, "You think you will win because you have prettier teacups, but the new young crave ugliness. It is the very ugliness, the material ugliness, that attracts them. You will see." Walking back along Rue de Vaugirard, see slogan on a wall: "LA CULTURE EST L'INVERSION DE LA VIE." Nuts.

Radio, after news of two deaths, one in Lyon, gives us "Douce France." Police cars as far as the eye can see crawl along Boulevard du Montparnasse. Apart from that, Paris as always, in a Sunday-Monday way. Day suddenly goes dark. At eleven-thirty, I turn all the lights on. Phone rings and rings— the tone of the day is disappointment over last night's speech. People were hoping for (1) a curfew to calm everyone down, and (2) garbage collection. This last seems to bother them most. They aren't used to dirty streets, as we are in English-speaking countries. The condition of Paris is sad but not startling to a North American. Concierges have been asked to put everything in large, stout bags distributed by the *mairies* and to keep it in the basements, not outside. Ours is stacked along the wall in the courtyard and looks for all the world like sacks of mail or potatoes or flour. Neat, battened down. Some streets are bad—streets with shops. One realizes now how well the streets are usually kept here—washed and sluiced and swept.

Lunch with A.J. Chez Josephine. First time I have been in a restaurant since the start of "the events." Only four tables besides our own—place usually so packed at lunchtime you need to book. Feel it is wartime and we are all black-marketeers. Man beside me looks like one, he really does, drinking very good Beaujolais with ice up to the top of the glass, fussing over his cheese. "*Menu de la révolution*," A.J. says sardonically. *Saucisson, pain, beurre, veau aux morilles, fraises au sucre*, etc. Mme. D., the owner's wife, "offers" two whacking glasses of *poire*. A.J. has brought two tins of Kitekat, picked up on the way. Cat is having a "*crise de désespoir*" and is tearing out all its own fur. Mme. D. takes this to heart, says Kitekat "too strong"—too many vitamins. I think this cat is some sort of refugee. Talk at next table really is black-market—how to get gas for your car at a pump marked by a red cross and reserved for people like G. You drive your car *in* the garage; you pretend you are having something repaired, looked at; the garage man (properly tipped) gives you the petrol in a jerry can, strictly illegal, this without being seen by the the the C.G.T. inspector who is there to watch that fair is fair. At another table, "the events" are discussed rather as Françoise Sagan is discussed in normal times. M.D. thinking of closing the restaurant. Can't get deliveries; no customers; no laundry, even—these are the last clean tablecloths. Lipp Brasserie using paper, plastic. A.J. very bitter about Cohn-Bendit. Sighs, says, "*Quel dommage, ce juif.*" "What?" "*Ce juif qui parle allemand.*" I tease, "And you a Catholic!" Yes, but Jewish all the same. I describe the students saying "*Nous sommes tous des juifs allemands.*" A.J. says, "If you had been here in the war, during the Occupation, and if you had been Jewish, and if you had been a Resistant, you would be less *exaltée* about the French." A.J. can't forgive Cohn-Bendit's father, because he chose to go back to Germany: "He wasn't *rancunier*. Well, I am." Think A.J.'s feeling not a matter of being Jewish but a matter of generations. Jews of that generation wish

Cohn-Bendit weren't making himself so damned conspicuous; non-Jews of that generation say, "*Qu'est-ce que c'est que ce petit juif* [or *allemand*]?" But to the kids it simply has no meaning, and that is why I continue to be *exaltée* (in silence). Voices float out: "*Donc ils font l'amour à trois?*" "*Parfaitement. Et avant avec encore une autre. Elle en avait marre, elle s'est suicidée.*" All sounds normal.

Flooded with offers of *liquide*. M.D., Chez Josephine, says he will cash a check "whenever I like," and my *femme de ménage* says that I am to come to her at once if I run short—that her husband keeps the equivalent of about two hundred dollars in cash at all times. As she insists, I say I shall weep. She seems scandalized.

Theme of conversation, over and over: "Would you leave Paris if you could?" "No." Hard for me to realize that, save for the gas shortage, hundreds of thousands of people are not really touched. Think of embassy wife saying, "I'm just not interested." Everyone I know is so involved, so concerned. One of my most conservative friends: "If only the C.P. would take over! *Nous aurions la tranquillité.*" Meaning a very tough law and order, I guess. Read confusing article about something called "talky-walkies," in abandoned newspaper on bench. Have no shame about scavenging papers. They say no magazines will appear next week. Schools still on strike, and today Anne-Marie's little boy finally refused to be locked up. She can't take him to work, so he was passed from hand to hand. I volunteered to take him for a walk as I searched for *Le Monde*. He trotted along, in his teal-blue corduroy velvet *costume Mao* and his soft Chelsea boots—very elegant. Blond Norman child, a bit small for seven. Dark eyes. Plays with a tape measure. I offer conversation about the weather (cool). In front of a toy display, he comes to a halt. His approach is "I suppose I have enough cars." "Which one are you looking at?" A red jeep with a yellow driver, all plastic, in a plastic bag. "What if I got it for you?" "*Je veux bien*." My mind labels it thirty-five cents, but it is about a dollar-thirty, and trashy. He says, "I use these cars for catching *bêtes*." I think he means insects, have vision of cockroaches, beetles. But no. "Lions, camels," he says. A mini-safari. As we part, he says, with a French shrug, "*Merci quand-même, eh?*" That is how he will talk to women when he is thirty.

When you see a knot of people on the street now, you know that newspapers are being sold—piled on the ground, sometimes even on a chair. Search for *Le Monde*. Stop a number of people walking along reading it, but each person always says, "It was the last copy." Find a pile of papers and a boy selling them near the Bon Marché, which has that strange Monday aspect of being shut up.

Lay in modest hoard—two one-half pounds of coffee, and extra batteries for the transistor, which is very hard-worked. I can understand now why people panic over food. Mme. D., the wife of the owner of Chez Josephine, said of the hoarders, "My husband and I laughed at them, but now we begin to wonder if they weren't the intelligent ones." Shopping in the Primistère chain store across the street from Josephine, I see that the shelves of canned goods are empty again—only the prices are left. Third time since Monday the stock has been cleaned out. Nobody buys anything fresh—tomatoes, lettuces untouched. The yogurt and cottage-cheese people on strike—last lot there, in the cold counter. I discover the first impulse to stock—to take countless yogurts, just in case. In case what? Idiotic. Later, I learned that the Basque restaurant along the street will close next week if the strike hasn't ended. The wife of the man in the shoe shop (she carrying what seems to be a ton of bread) says that they may close, too, that de G. has let them down, that she hopes I haven't worn my new shoes in the rain.

Fouchet's statement in the middle of the night last night: "In spite of our sympathy with the students ..." M.L.'s comment: "Giving sympathy with a bulldozer!"

Pharmacy in the Latin Quarter. Man and two women (owners of the place?) sit huddled on three chairs. I ask for eye lotion, because I am bothered by the gas in the streets. Remembering a warning I've read, I say, "Something neutral, not dangerous with tear gas." All three stare at me with *fear* and *hostility*. It is an animal expression. I suddenly realize they think I have been setting fire to cars. I want to say to them, "Why don't you speak up? Why don't you say you hate all this, if you do hate it?" No, they are like dark little animals.

No theatres, no TV, except for the news, and newsmen will probably strike tomorrow; movies may strike next. People driven to reading books (no magazines, either). Driven to reading. God, what a fate! Women more patient, I notice. But inactivity is driving all the men I know off their rockers. E. walked through tear gas and felled trees to buy a Bach record for me at Gibert's. The shop had looked wrecked to me. They must still be doing business inside. Z. down to reading nothing but *Le Monde* and anything she can find about the Commune. Feel claustrophobic; queer cravings—for, for instance, Offenbach (another France?), for Italian poetry (because of claustrophobia, and Italy not France?). Discover I can no longer read it without a dictionary. Gone.

Sit down with pencil and try to make sense of the organized groups called "commandos." Who are trained in armed combat and street fighting? Parachutists. Who know about Molotov cocktails? The O.A.S. did. What clandestine training camps have we heard about in France? The mercenaries'. Matching ingredients, to me. Take my theories down the street to Jacqueline's bookshop. She says her friends have come to same conclusions: extreme right but not intellectuals—no, the bullies, the toughs. The nothing-at-all boys who like being paid (or promised) and like hitting people. Floods of book-buying customers. During the first week of the *contestation*, people came in asking for "something to explain the situation." After that, detective novels. A woman comes in and says, "Something with sun it it—*j'ai besoin de soleil.*" I sit there reading a translation of Painter's *Gide*, and finally am so deep in it I buy it. Jacqueline gives me hilarious account of how the Writers' Union (new) invaded and occupied the Hôtel de Massa and established a "permanent discussion"—as if they needed special quarters for that! She and G.P. and some bewildered students crept out while they (the writers) were still analyzing "from the point of view of various perspectives" every phrase they intended to put in their *déclaration*. Some were Catholics, some Communists, some Marxist-Leninists, some nothing much. She says they must still be talking.

H.T. calls from the Select, comes round, tells me about last night. In Les Halles, the new *manifestants* overturning crates of food, fruit, smashing, spilling. Truck drivers who had brought the food in, trying to maneuver among broken crates, vegetables, "students," finally threaten to run them over. Describes scene out of purgatory: *manifestants*, helmeted, wading in cherries out of crates they've overturned, picking up handfuls, pressing the fruit to their mouths, juice running; stained, spitting; and they are joined by the whores of the quarter, who had lately been driven underground by the police. "Students?" he says. "Impossible. Workers? I saw the real workers in Les Halles." When a tree was cut down on the Right Bank, everyone clapped and cheered. He saw bystanders who laughed and thought it was funny. Parisians don't deserve their beautiful city, he said. Let them all go and live in Roubaix and Lille. Perhaps its beauty was imposed on them. Etc.

Latin Quarter quiet now. Students have a good *service d'ordre*; they are sending away all the tourists and sightseers, holding hands, forming chains, blocking off the side streets, so that the Army can clean up the mess, and so that unnecessary elements won't hang about.

From the children's nursery in the Sorbonne comes a dramatic call for milk and bread. There is plenty of milk and bread in Paris, though their quarter may have run out. You feel they (the parents) are inventing a false siege, imagining they are in the siege of Leningrad. First they create the psychosis, then they create the physical conditions, as if it were part of something needed. I rang up F.W., who is a step from the Sorbonne, who is a granddaughter of a former Rector and whose mother was actually born in the Sorbonne, and who has two babies of her own. Plenty of bread and milk in the quarter. Confirms my theory of siege psychosis. Apart from that, her whole family on the side of the students, against the present Rector; some of them marched May 13th, including her father, a sick man. Her husband night and day at O.R.T.F., on the Reorganization Committee, striking. She part of the teachers' strike. No complaints. Says she has been so nauseated since the hoarding began that her husband thought she was pregnant.

Europe I uses as a signal a recording—American, I imagine—of "Where the Rainbow Ends," someone whistling. A nostalgic, persistent kind of tune. It accompanies, in my mind, burning rubbish in the streets and sad fallen trees.

Find I am asking all my friends: Can you (1) eat, (2) read, (3) work, (4) listen to music? No, no, no, and no, in most cases. In music, I can't stand anything but the pop between news bulletins. Gilbert Bécaud singing "Les cerisiers sont blancs," or the Sinatras we are suddenly flooded with. When I was sixteen, a rather pompous writer said to me, "When bombs fall on New York, I will listen to Mozart." It infuriated me then. Remembering it now, I'd like to say, "I doubt if you could. I just doubt it."

Everyone sick about the trees. The wife of my *marchand de couleurs* in tears.

DEAREST EDITH

Janet Flanner

1929

T HE ARISTOCRATIC Mrs. Edith Wharton was born Jones in a fashionable quarter of New York, arriving appropriately during the quarrel between masters about servants, known as the Civil War. The parents of the novelist were without talent, being mere people of the world. From them into her veins ran Rhinelanders, Stevens, early Howes, and Schermerhorns intact. Her corpuscles were Holland burghers, Colonial colonels, and provincial gentry who with the passage of time had become Avenue patricians—patrons of Protestant church and Catholic grand opera as the two highest forms of public worship, a strict clan making intercellular marriages, attending winter balls, dominating certain smart spots on the eastern seaboard, and unaware of any signs of life further west. In blood they were old, Dutch and British, the only form of being American that they knew. As a child among them, little Miss Jones started living in what Mrs. Wharton later entitled their Age of Innocence—a hard hierarchy of male money, of female modesty and morals.

Moving in high society at this time meant moving but little indeed. Space, outside of Newport for the summer, had not yet been discovered, though stately trips abroad were occasionally taken by bridal couples or dowagers headed for Worth. Fortunately for the impatient authoress, she was repeatedly sent as a child to the Continent, where governesses taught her French, German, and Italian. Something very close to English she had already learned in her correct American home. Thus the future Mrs. Wharton of the book reviews was launched. Thus at an early age she often returned from Europe to her native land, her critical eyes already seeing her New York as America indeed. And thus by her elders she was, in turn, already seen as "that handsome, disagreeable little Pussy Jones, always scribbling." Her first manuscript to reach the outer world was a poem sold at a church fair when she was fifteen.

In the succeeding fifty years she has, according to her harshest critics, moved with unerring failure between two careers—that of a great woman of the world and a great woman novelist. Repeatedly redomiciling herself with elegance in various garden cities of the world, she has always suffered the disadvantage of being an outsider—even in the city of her birth, after she became a popular novelist. For if Boston, the city of her marriage, never forgave her for having been born in New York, her New York never forgave her for having been born in New York and writing about it. As a talented pioneer of professionalism among the domestic women of her class, absolution might have come with the dignity of her fame, had not Mrs. Wharton discovered her sinful skill at sketching from life. Though Thackeray's "Vanity Fair" was the supposed model for her "House of Mirth," many of her contemporaries felt they had unconsciously sat across the space of years for too many of her portraits. And in "The Age of Innocence," certain of the leading innocents connected with the novel's adulteries and banking intrigues were decried, in Four Hundred society, as being this pillar, that pretender, or that déclassé—anyhow all drawn as large as life. The only positive identification which the book afforded, and which, while it gave society at large no more comfort, afforded it even less doubt, was that of Mrs. Wharton herself as the sad, charming, chaste hero, Newland Archer.

For like many novelists, Mrs. Wharton herself is her works. The presence therein of her friends or other characters is only a promenade for principle. They are mere illustrations of her historical report on a manner of living and thinking, often enough (for she is a moralist) bad. Therefore she and her characters in her wake seem too ably to have followed the unfortunate advice of Henry James, once tendered her in a letter of consolation for her domestic infelicities: "Continue making the movements of life." All her heroes and heroines, meeting and sometimes mating under her eye, keep up this pantomime, as perhaps she has, without pleasure. Her books are filled with smart people whose capacity, according to her, for tragedy, wit, houseparties, and divorce, land them nowadays on the front page where vitality belongs. Their activities in her day were regarded not as necessary symptoms of transitional psychology or even news, but as mere decay. She spent her life formally proving that the wages of social sin were social death and lived to see the grandchildren of her characters comfortably and popularly relaxing into open scandals.

———

Though the first to utilize the breakup of the American mold, Mrs. Wharton is still the last to understand it; she saw the plot but never the point. Born for ethics, she ignored the senses. Thus even her most famous character, Lily Bart, though a drug fiend, did not have her heart in her work. For no irresistible Baudelairean visions did she swallow her nightly quota, but as one taking an aspirin tablet, to bring on sleep or ward off a cold. Mrs. Wharton described a trained-nurse murderess, but she was one who killed the wife for professional ethics, not as a passionate means to obtain the husband illegally loved. She even took up the labor problem, but as a banker takes out his typist to dine—a mere excursion out of one's class. It was this emotional emptiness that gave her a success which was half polite incredulity when "The House of Mirth" was translated for the emotional French as "Chez les Heureux de ce Monde." But "Ethan Frome," after its American triumph re-titled as "Sous la Neige," was justly hailed abroad as a chef d'œuvre of sufficient quality to merit a cheap edition and rank with the agrarian tragedies of Balzac and Zola. In this New England tale, small as a chance and tragic rural snapshot which the rich summer visitor leisurely enlarges for her album on returning to town, the worldly Mrs. Wharton gave something like immortality to the sadness of snow which it is likely her nature understood too well. At the age of thirty she was remarked as already cold and handsome. She was then spending her years at fashionable Lenox where the earth, under the many winters, retains a feeling of ice that no spring can thaw. And the rest is under glass…

———

Though she has spent another thirty years writing about human relations, it was in her friendship with Henry James that she really attained her literary height. Their platonic amity lacked none of their style, and contained all the warmth of which she never wrote. As if preparing herself for her own future expatriation, she first fell under his distant tutelage, then under the personal spell of her country's greatest prose exile. He selected her at the expense of Mrs. Humphrey Ward, as his choicest female pupil. When distant in Rye he addressed her in letters as "Dearest Edith," and, when present, introduced her to his London on the precise parabola of his pompous arm. To the literary, correct, meticulous Mrs. Wharton, the affection and approval of the literary, correct, meticulous Mr. James were the real bay leaves which she humbly wore (one imagines him helping adjust them) in her beautiful blond coiffure. Their friendship, which was the greatest and worthiest devotion of her life, covered long years and included, with other friends, Continental motor travels together, briefer always than the interminable charming letters which prepared for, discussed, delayed, and finally concluded them. There was even a houseparty of Whartons, Jameses, and other select souls at the grandiose Villa Medici outside Florence. And when after even that ripe man could ripen no more and so disappeared, there was still, for her, her famous round library in the Rue de Varenne, with its mounting tier of his works and, amidst them, the marble bust of their friend and author, the master American, James.

It was in this aristocratic Parisian quarter that Mrs. Wharton, more than a dozen years ago, began her permanent expatriation. Twice only has she returned to America, once to witness a marriage, and once for a ten days' retreat at the Hotel St. Regis, where she prepared to receive her honorary degree from Yale. Her withdrawal from America was her most American act. She had exhausted New York, and Boston, so it says, always refused to accept her. She had early made with one of its scions what in those inept days was regarded as a brilliant, or happy, marriage (of the type which subsequently has to be legally dissolved). Mr. Edward Wharton was the handsomest man of the class of '73, Harvard, a group which was graduated in virile side-whiskers; but his wife had been born a Rhinelander almost in her own right, wrote books, and had lived in Paris. Boston considered her fast.

So from the Rue de Varenne she finally started her frigid conquest of the *faubourg*, in company only with her mother, who had been Lucretia Rhinelander, and an iron hostess in her day, but was now disgusted with the way Newport was going. Mrs. Wharton was perhaps too formal even for the *faubourg* As one duchesse complained, "*On est trop organizé chez elle.* One can't so much as forget one's umbrella at Madame Wharton's with impunity."

Later, still pursuing her policy of Continental expansion, she purchased a charming Cistercian monastery near Hyrès, on the Mediterranean, where she summers. Finally, for permanent residence, she acquired an eighteenth-century villa, the Pavilion Colombe, at Saint-Brice-sous-Forêt, about eighty motor kilometres from Paris. It was here that she collected her half-dozen adopted war orphans, left from the six hundred she housed during the war when she gave her property to the government and devoted herself to France and little Belgian refugees with a patriotism of which only an expatriated American who dislikes children is capable. For her splendid war work she was decorated by the King of the Belgians and was made an officer of the Légion d'Honneur by France.

She is now a handsome New Yorker of sixty years and immense dignity who has retired into a French country house and solitude. Her pavilion is not without suitability for one who has lived in contemplating the passions of others; the edifice is of the French type lovingly called *une folie*, erected by an amorous banker to house his mistresses, two sisters whose dovelike tenderness gave the property its name. The structure itself has been exquisitely and correctly restored; Mrs. Wharton knows her periods and architecture has long been one of her hobbies. In décors, she has been equally exacting; she spent twenty years searching for some eighteenth-century Chinese Chippendale wall paper of which she originally possessed a fragment.

In all details of life she demonstrates an accuracy of which she alone is capable. Her days are scheduled. The mornings are devoted to writing. The afternoons are devoted to walking in company with small dogs and to gardening, at which she is a tender expert. In all her properties, her flowers have been notable. Her White Garden at Lenox was famous. Moneyed in her own right, she is able to spend her royalties on her blossoms. She travels. She has seen France, Italy, and Spain from a limousine, and the Parthenon from a yacht. She is smartly but decently dressed by Worth who, when she once demanded of him a suitable, chic, black teagown, offered without hesitation a model called Resignation. She is civil rather than cordial as a formal hostess. She no longer smokes, but in the old fashion urges upon the gentlemen their after-dinner cigars. The viands at her table are perfectly served and chosen, though the wines, for which she cares little and which are selected by her butler, are less choice—according to the cigar-smoking gentlemen. Her old French housekeeper, who was Mrs. Wharton's nurse, dominates below stairs and even influences her mistress on the floor above. All of the domestics, legend states, rigorously address each other as "Monsieur" and "Madame."

Her friends are few but of long standing. It is in her character to support the old amities with loyalty. Many of her New York familiars are either dead or gone to Southampton. Her closest connection with her own land is represented by her sister-in-law and lifelong particular friend, Mrs. Cadwalader Jones. Since living in France, her affections have included the Princesse de Poix, the Paul Bourgets, certain of the noble Noailles, and—since the war—the Comte and Comtesse de Beaumont; also certain odd pedants in archeology and horticulture of whom her appreciation is touching and logical. She is herself an omnivorous reader. Among the younger minds she has enrolled Geoffrey Scott, Berenson the Florentine art critic, Percy Lubbock, and others. She also speaks appreciatively of Scott Fitzgerald.

On the whole she finds herself living in a generation in which conversation is lost. She is a dignified little woman set down in the middle of her past. She says that to the greener growths of her day, she must seem like a taffeta sofa under a gas-lit chandelier. Certainly she is old-fashioned in that she reserves her magnanimity for special occasions. In belief she is still nothing of an iconoclast but has become liberal through reflection. Hers is the grand manner which triumphs over a situation where another woman's might save it. With years of living abroad, her anecdotes tend to deplore her tourist compatriots who mistake the Baptistery at Parma for the railway station.

In her long career Mrs. Wharton has published half a hundred short stories, translated Sudermann, written books on Italian gardens and art, a work on Morocco, a trio on France including one of the best on its war, a volume of verse, and more than a dozen novels. She won the Pulitzer Prize with "The Age of Innocence" and was the only woman to receive the gold medal of the National Institute of Arts and Letters. In writing of the sins of society, Mrs. Wharton gave the great public what it wanted and ever since the appearance, in 1905, of "The House of Mirth," each of her novels has remained a bestseller for the period of its commercial life, a remarkable financial triumph. Her earnings must be estimated at approximately seventy-five thousand dollars yearly, of which much, now as in times past, would be for serial rights to magazines with whose feminine readers she is always a heavy favorite. Added to this now would be the play-rights to her old gold nugget, "The Age of Innocence" (1920), this winter's production on Broadway, and already bought for the screen. Her current success, "The

Children," has also been sold for a cinema, was the Book of the Month Club's selection for September past, and reached two hundred thousand copies within a month of publication. In thirty years of writing, Mrs. Wharton's enormous output, with one exception, has been published by two houses, Scribner and Appleton, she not being one to make changes hastily. Her publishers have always found her an enemy of publicity and her standard press photograph shows her in pearls and décolletage, dressed for her public as for a ball.

Mrs. Wharton's real excellencies are never marketed. Even those who love her most come by accident upon her golden qualities. She is regarded as cold. Yet a chord of Bach once recalled to her a moment passed half a century ago with a woman who was ever after to be her fondest companion. And to the same woman she recently wrote, after clipping her garden's roses in the summer dawn, that the ripe sweetness of the flowers personified and brought their amity endearingly to mind. Mrs. Wharton has the tender and reserved sentiments of the truly literate. From many she has earned the title of Dearest Edith and for herself she has perfectly written what she hopes will finally be her epitaph—"She was a friend of Henry James."

EQUAL IN PARIS

James Baldwin

1955

O N THE 19th of December, in 1949, when I had been living in Paris for a little over a year, I was arrested as a receiver of stolen goods and spent eight days in prison. My arrest came about through an American tourist whom I had met twice in New York, who had been given my name and address and told to look me up. I was then living on the top floor of a ludicrously grim hotel on the rue du Bac, one of those enormous dark, cold, and hideous establishments in which Paris abounds that seem to breathe forth, in their airless, humid, stone-cold halls, the weak light, scurrying chambermaids, and creaking stairs, an odor of gentility long long dead. The place was run by an ancient Frenchman dressed in an elegant black suit which was green with age, who cannot properly be described as bewildered or even as being in a state of shock, since he had really stopped breathing around 1910. There he sat at his desk in the weirdly lit, fantastically furnished lobby, day in and day out, greeting each one of his extremely impoverished and *louche* lodgers with a stately inclination of the head that he had no doubt been taught in some impossibly remote time was the proper way for a *propriétaire* to greet his guests. If it had not been for his daughter, an extremely hardheaded *tricoteuse*—the inclination of *her* head was chilling and abrupt, like the downbeat of an axe—the hotel would certainly have gone bankrupt long before. It was said that this old man had not gone farther than the door of his hotel for thirty years, which was not at all difficult to believe. He looked as though the daylight would have killed him.

I did not, of course, spend much of my time in this palace. The moment I began living in French hotels I understood the necessity of French cafés. This made it rather difficult to look me up, for as soon as I was out of bed I hopefully took notebook and fountain pen off to the upstairs room of the Flore, where I consumed rather a lot of coffee and, as evening approached, rather a lot of alcohol, but did not get much writing done. But one night, in one of the cafés of St. Germain des Prés, I was discovered by this New Yorker and only because we found ourselves in Paris we immediately established the illusion that we had been fast friends back in the good old U.S.A. This illusion proved itself too thin to support an evening's drinking, but by that time it was too late. I had committed myself to getting him a room in my hotel the next day, for he was living in one of the nest of hotels near the Gare St. Lazare, where, he said, the *propriétaire* was a thief, his wife a repressed nymphomaniac, the chambermaids "pigs," and the rent a crime. Americans are always talking this way about the French and so it did not occur to me that he meant what he said or that he would take into his own hands the means of avenging himself on the French Republic. It did not occur to me, either, that the means which he *did* take could possibly have brought about such dire results, results which were not less dire for being also comic-opera.

———

It came as the last of a series of disasters which had perhaps been made inevitable by the fact that I had come to Paris originally with a little over forty dollars in my pockets, nothing in the bank, and no grasp whatever of the French language. It developed, shortly, that I had no grasp of the French character either. I considered the French an ancient, intelligent, and cultured race, which indeed they are. I did not know, however, that ancient glories imply, at least in the middle of the present century, present fatigue and, quite probably, paranoia; that there is a limit to the role of the intelligence in human affairs; and that no people come into possession of a culture without having paid a heavy price for it. This price they cannot, of course, assess, but it is revealed in their personalities and in their institutions. The very word "institutions," from my side of the ocean, where, it seemed to me, we suffered so cruelly from the lack of them, had a pleasant ring, as of safety and order and common sense; one had to come into contact with these institutions in order to understand that they were also outmoded, exasperating, completely impersonal, and very often cruel. Similarly, the personality which had seemed from a distance to be so large and free had to be dealt with before one could see that, if it was large, it was also inflexible and, for the foreigner, full of strange, high, dusty rooms which could not be inhabited. One had, in short, to come into contact with an alien culture in order to understand that a culture was not a community basket-weaving project, nor yet an act of God; was something neither desirable nor undesirable in itself, being inevitable, being nothing more or less than the recorded and visible effects on a body of people of the vicissitudes with which they had been forced to deal. And their great men are revealed as simply another of these vicissitudes, even if, quite against their will, the brief battle of their great men with them has left them richer.

When my American friend left his hotel to move to mine, he took with him, out of pique, a bedsheet belonging to the hotel and put it in his suitcase. When he arrived at my hotel I borrowed the sheet, since my own were filthy and the chambermaid showed no sign of bringing me any clean ones, and put it on my bed. The sheets belonging to *my* hotel I put out in the hall, congratulating myself on having thus forced on the attention of the Grand Hôtel du Bac the unpleasant state of its linen. Thereafter, since, as it turned out, we kept very different hours— I got up at noon, when, as I gathered by meeting him on the stairs one day, he was only just getting in—my new-found friend and I saw very little of each other.

On the evening of the 19th I was sitting thinking melancholy thoughts about Christmas and staring at the walls of my room. I imagine that I had sold something or that someone had sent me a Christmas present, for I remember that I had a little money. In those days in Paris, though I floated, so to speak, on a sea of acquaintances, I knew almost no one. Many people were eliminated from my orbit by virtue of the fact that they had more money than I did, which placed me, in my own eyes, in the humiliating role of a freeloader; and other people were eliminated by virtue of the fact that they enjoyed their poverty, shrilly insisting that this wretched round of hotel rooms, bad food, humiliating concierges, and unpaid bills was the Great Adventure. It couldn't, however, for me, end soon enough, this Great Adventure; there was a real question in my mind as to which would end soonest, the Great Adventure or me. This meant, however, that there were many evenings when I sat in my room, knowing that I couldn't work there, and not knowing what to do, or whom to see. On this particular evening I went down and knocked on the American's door.

There were two Frenchmen standing in the room, who immediately introduced themselves to me as policemen; which did not worry me. I had got used to policemen in Paris bobbing up at the most improbable times and places, asking to see one's *carte d'identité*. These policemen, however, showed very little interest in my papers. They were looking for something else. I could not imagine what this would be and, since I knew I certainly didn't have it, I scarcely followed the conversation they were having with my friend. I gathered that they were looking for some kind of gangster and since I wasn't a gangster and knew that gangsterism was not, insofar as he had one, my friend's style, I was sure that the two policemen would presently bow and say *Merci, messieurs*, and leave. For by this time, I remember very clearly, I was dying to have a drink and go to dinner.

I did not have a drink or go to dinner for many days after this, and when I did my outraged stomach promptly heaved everything up again. For now one of the policemen began to exhibit the most vivid interest in me and asked, very politely, if he might see my room. To which we mounted, making, I remember, the most civilized small talk on the way and even continuing it for some moments after we were in the room in which there was certainly nothing to be seen but the familiar poverty and disorder of that precarious group of people of whatever age, race, country, calling, or intention which Paris recognizes as *les étudiants* and sometimes, more ironically and precisely, as *les nonconformistes*. Then he moved to my bed, and in a terrible flash, not quite an instant before he lifted the bedspread, I understood what he was looking for. We looked at the sheet, on which I read, for the first time, lettered in the most brilliant scarlet I have ever seen, the name of the hotel from which it had been stolen. It was the first time the word *stolen* entered my mind. I had certainly seen the hotel monogram the day I put the sheet on the bed. It had simply meant nothing to me. In New York I had seen hotel monograms on everything from silver to soap and towels. Taking things from New York hotels was practically a custom, though, I suddenly realized, I had never known anyone to take a *sheet*. Sadly, and without a word to me, the inspector took the sheet from the bed, folded it under his arm, and we started back downstairs. I understood that I was under arrest.

And so we passed through the lobby, four of us, two of us very clearly criminal, under the eyes of the old man and his daughter, neither of whom said a word, into the streets where a light rain was falling. And I asked, in French, "But is this very serious?"

For I was thinking, it is, after all, only a sheet, not even new.

"No," said one of them. "It's not serious."

"It's nothing at all," said the other.

I took this to mean that we would receive a reprimand at the police station and be allowed to go to dinner. Later on I concluded that they were not being hypocritical or even trying to comfort us. They meant exactly what they said. It was only that they spoke another language.

In Paris everything is very slow. Also, when dealing with the bureaucracy, the man you are talking to is never the man you have to see. The man you have to see has just gone off to Belgium, or is busy with his family, or has just discovered that he is a cuckold; he will be in next Tuesday at three o'clock, or sometime in the course of the afternoon, or possibly tomorrow, or, possibly, in the next five minutes. But if he is coming in the next five minutes he will be far too busy to be able to see you today. So that I suppose I was not really astonished to learn at the commissariat that nothing could possibly be done about us before The Man arrived in the morning. But no, we could not go off and have dinner and come back in the morning. Of course he knew that we *would* come back—that was not the question. Indeed, there was no question: we would simply have to stay there for the night. We were placed in a cell which rather resembled a chicken coop. It was now about seven in the evening and I relinquished the thought of dinner and began to think of lunch.

I discouraged the chatter of my New York friend and this left me alone with my thoughts. I was beginning to be frightened and I bent all my energies, therefore, to keeping my panic under control. I began to realize that I was in a country I knew nothing about, in the hands of a people I did not understand at all. In a similar situation in New York I would have had some idea of what to do because I would have had some idea of what to expect. I am not speaking now of legality which, like most of the poor, I had never for an instant trusted, but of the temperament of the people with whom I had to deal. I had become very accomplished in New York at guessing and, therefore, to a limited extent manipulating to my advantage the reactions of the white world. But this was not New York. None of my old weapons could serve me here. I did not know what they saw when they looked at me. I knew very well what Americans saw when they looked at me and this allowed me to play endless and sinister variations on the role which they had assigned me; since I knew that it was, for them, of the utmost importance that they never be confronted with what, in their own personalities, made this role so necessary and gratifying to them, I knew that they could never call my hand or, indeed, afford to know what I was doing; so that I moved into every crucial situation with the deadly and rather desperate advantages of bitterly accumulated perception, of pride and contempt. This is an awful sword and shield to carry through the world, and the discovery that, in the game I was playing, I did myself a violence of which the world, at its most ferocious, would scarcely have been capable, was what had driven me out of New York. It was a strange feeling, in this situation, after a year in Paris, to discover that my weapons would never again serve me as they had.

It was quite clear to me that the Frenchmen in whose hands I found myself were no better or worse than their American counterparts. Certainly their uniforms frightened me quite as much, and their impersonality, and the threat, always very keenly felt by the poor, of violence, was as present in that commissariat as it had ever been for me in any police station. And I had seen, for example, what Paris policemen could do to Arab peanut vendors. The only difference here was that I did not understand these people, did not know what techniques their cruelty took, did not know enough about their personalities to see danger coming, to ward it off, did not know on what ground to meet it. That evening in the commissariat I was not a despised black man. They would simply have laughed at me if I had behaved like one. For them, I was an American. And here it was they who had the advantage, for that word, *Américain*, gave them some idea, far from inaccurate, of what to expect from me. In order to corroborate none of their ironical expectations I said nothing and did nothing—which was not the way any Frenchman, white or black, would have reacted. The question thrusting up from the bottom of my mind was not *what* I was, but *who*. And this question, since a *what* can get by with skill but a *who* demands resources, was my first real intimation of what humility must mean.

In the morning it was still raining. Between nine and ten o'clock a black Citroën took us off to the Ile de la Cité, to the great, gray Préfecture. I realize now that the questions I put to the various policemen who escorted us were always answered in such a way as to corroborate what I wished to hear. This was not out of politeness, but simply out of indifference—or, possibly, an ironical pity—since each of the policemen knew very well that nothing would speed or halt the machine in which I had become entangled. They knew I did not know this and there was certainly no point in their telling me. In one way or another I would certainly come out at the other side—for they also knew that being found with a stolen bedsheet in one's possession was not a crime punishable by the guillotine. (They had the advantage over me there, too, for there were certainly moments later on when I was not so sure.) If I did *not* come out at the other side—well, that was just too bad. So, to my question, put while we were in the Citroën—"Will it be over today?"—I received a *"Oui, bien sûr."* He was not lying. As it turned out, the *procès-verbal* was over that day. Trying to be realistic, I dismissed, in the Citroën, all thoughts of lunch and pushed my mind ahead to dinner.

At the Préfecture we were first placed in a tiny cell, in which it was almost impossible either to sit or to lie down. After a couple of hours of this we were taken down to an office, where, for the first time, I encountered the owner of the bedsheet and where the *procès-verbal* took place. This was simply an interrogation, quite chillingly clipped and efficient (so that there was, shortly, no doubt in one's own mind that one *should* be treated as a criminal), which was recorded by a secretary. When it was over, this report was given to us to sign. One had, of course, no choice but to sign it, even though my mastery of written French was very far from certain. We were being held, according to the law in France, incommunicado, and all my angry demands to be allowed to speak to my embassy or to see a lawyer met with a stony *"Oui, oui. Plus tard."* The *procès-verbal* over we were taken back to the cell, before which, shortly, passed the owner of the bedsheet. He said he hoped we had slept well, gave a vindictive wink, and disappeared.

By this time there was only one thing clear: that we had no way of controlling the sequence of events and could not possibly guess what this sequence would be. It seemed to me, since what I regarded as the high point—the *procès-verbal*—had been passed and since the hotelkeeper was once again in possession of his sheet, that we might reasonably expect to be released from police custody in a matter of hours. We had been detained now for what would soon be twenty-four hours, during which time I had learned only that the official charge against me was *receleur*. My mental shifting, between lunch and dinner, to say nothing of the physical lack of either of these delights, was beginning to make me dizzy. The steady chatter of my friend from New York, who was determined to keep my spirits up, made me feel murderous; I was praying that some power would release us from this freezing pile of stone before the impulse became the act. And I was beginning to wonder what was happening in that beautiful city, Paris, which lived outside these walls. I wondered how long it would take before anyone casually asked, "But where's Jimmy? He hasn't been around"—and realized, knowing the people I knew, that it would take several days.

Quite late in the afternoon we were taken from our cells; handcuffed, each to a separate officer; led through a maze of steps and corridors to the top of the building; finger-printed; photographed. As in movies I had seen, I was placed against a wall, facing an old-fashioned camera, behind which stood one of the most completely cruel and indifferent faces I had ever seen, while someone next to me and, therefore, just outside my line of vision, read off in a voice from which all human feeling, even feeling of the most base description, had long since fled, what must be called my public characteristics—which, at that time and in that place, seemed anything but that. He might have been roaring to the hostile world secrets which I could barely, in the privacy of midnight, utter to myself. But he was only reading off my height, my features, my approximate weight, my color—that color which, in the United States, had often, odd as it may sound, been my salvation—the color of my hair, my age, my nationality. A light then flashed, the photographer and I staring at each other as though there was murder in our hearts, and then it was over. Handcuffed again, I was led downstairs to the bottom of the building, into a great enclosed shed in which had been gathered the very scrapings off the Paris streets. Old, old men, so ruined and old that life in them seemed really to prove the miracle of the quickening power of the Holy Ghost—for clearly their life was no longer their affair, it was no longer even their burden, they were simply the clay which had once been touched. And men not so old, with faces the color of lead and the consistency of oatmeal, eyes that made me think of stale *café-au-lait* spiked with arsenic, bodies which could take in food and water—any food and water—and pass it out, but which could not do anything more, except possibly, at midnight, along the riverbank where rats scurried, rape. And young men, harder and crueler than the Paris stones, older by far than I, their chronological senior by some five to seven years. And North Africans, old and young, who seemed the only living people in this place because they yet retained the grace to be bewildered. But they were not bewildered by being in this shed: they were simply bewildered because they were no longer in North Africa. There was a great hole in the center of this shed, which was the common toilet. Near it, though it was impossible to get very far from it, stood an old man with white hair, eating a piece of camembert. It was at this point, probably, that thought, for me, stopped, that physiology, if one may say so, took over. I found myself incapable of saying a word, not because I was afraid I would cry but because I was afraid I would vomit. And I did not think any longer of the city of Paris but my mind flew back to that home from which I had fled. I was sure that I would never see it anymore. And it must have seemed to me that my flight from home was the cruelest trick I had ever played on myself, since it had led me here, down to a lower point than any I could ever in my life have imagined—lower, far, than anything I had seen in that Harlem which I had so hated and so loved, the escape from which had soon become the greatest direction of my life. After we had been here an hour or so a functionary came and opened the door and called out our names. And I was sure that *this* was my release. But I was handcuffed again and led out of the Préfecture into the streets—it was dark now, it was still raining—and before the steps of the Préfecture stood the great police wagon, doors facing me, wide open. The handcuffs were taken off, I entered the wagon, which was peculiarly constructed. It was divided by a narrow aisle, and on each side of the aisle was a series of narrow doors. These doors opened on a narrow cubicle, beyond which was a door which opened onto another narrow cubicle: three or four cubicles, each private, with a locking door. I was placed in one of them; I remember there was a small vent just above my head which let in a little light. The door of my cubicle was locked from the outside. I had no idea where this wagon was taking me and, as it began to move, I began to cry. I suppose I cried all the way to prison, the prison called Fresnes, which is twelve kilometers outside of Paris.

For reasons I have no way at all of understanding, prisoners whose last initial is A, B, or C are always sent to Fresnes; everybody else is sent to a prison called, rather cynically it seemed to me, La Santé. I will, obviously, never be allowed to enter La Santé, but I was told by people who certainly seemed to know that it was infinitely more unbearable than Fresnes. This arouses in me, until today, a positive storm of curiosity concerning what I promptly began to think of as The Other Prison. My colleague in crime, occurring lower in the alphabet, had been sent there and I confess that the minute he was gone I missed him. I missed him because he was not French and because he was the only person in the world who knew that *the* story I told was true.

For, once locked in, divested of shoelaces, belt, watch, money, papers, nailfile, in a freezing cell in which both the window and the toilet were broken, with six other adventurers, the story I told of *l'affaire du drap de lit* elicited only the wildest amusement or the most suspicious disbelief. Among the people who shared my cell the first three days no one, it is true, had been arrested for anything much more serious—or, at least, not serious in my eyes. I remember that there was a boy who had stolen a knitted sweater from a *monoprix*, who would probably, it was agreed, receive a six-month sentence. There was an older man there who had been arrested for some kind of petty larceny. There were two North Africans, vivid, brutish, and beautiful, who alternated between gaiety and fury, not at the fact of their arrest but at the state of the cell. None poured as much emotional energy into the fact of their arrest as I did; they took it, as I would have liked to take it, as simply another unlucky happening in a very dirty world. For, though I had grown accustomed to thinking of myself as looking upon the world with a hard, penetrating eye, the truth was that they were far more realistic about the world than I, and more nearly right about it. The gap between us, which only a gesture I made could have bridged, grew steadily, during thirty-six hours, wider. I could not make any gesture simply because they frightened me. I was unable to accept my imprisonment as a fact, even as a temporary fact. I could not, even for a moment, accept my present companions as *my* companions. And they, of course, felt this and put it down, with perfect justice, to the fact that I was an American.

There was nothing to do all day long. It appeared that we would one day come to trial but no one knew when. We were awakened at seven-thirty by a rapping on what I believe is called the Judas, that small opening in the door of the cell which allows the guards to survey the prisoners. At this rapping we rose from the floor—we slept on straw pallets and each of us was covered with one thin blanket—and moved to the door of the cell. We peered through the opening into the center of the prison, which was, as I remember, three tiers high, all gray stone and gunmetal steel, precisely that prison I had seen in movies, except that, in the movies, I had not known that it was cold in prison.

I had not known that when one's shoelaces and belt have been removed one is, in the strangest way, demoralized. The necessity of shuffling and the necessity of holding up one's trousers with one hand turn one into a rag doll. And the movies fail, of course, to give one any idea of what prison food is like. Along the corridor, at seven-thirty, came three men, each pushing before him a great garbage can, mounted on wheels. In the garbage can of the first was the bread—this was passed to one through the small opening in the door. In the can of the second was the coffee. In the can of the third was what was always called *la soupe*, a pallid paste of potatoes which had certainly been bubbling on the back of the prison stove long before that first, so momentous revolution. Naturally, it was cold by this time and, starving as I was, I could not eat it. I drank the coffee—which was not coffee—because it was hot, and spent the rest of the day, huddled in my blanket, munching on the bread. It was not the French bread one bought in bakeries. In the evening the same procession returned. At ten-thirty the lights went out. I had a recurring dream, each night, a nightmare which always involved my mother's fried chicken. At the moment I was about to eat it came the rapping at the door. Silence is really all I remember of those first three days, silence and the color gray.

I am not sure now whether it was on the third or the fourth day that I was taken to trial for the first time. The days had nothing, obviously, to distinguish them from one another. I remember that I was very much aware that Christmas Day was approaching and I wondered if I was really going to spend Christmas

Day in prison. And I remember that the first trial came the day before Christmas Eve.

On the morning of the first trial I was awakened by hearing my name called. I was told, hanging in a kind of void between my mother's fried chicken and the cold prison floor, "*Vous préparez. Vous êtes extrait*"—which simply terrified me, since I did not know what interpretation to put on the word "*extrait*," and since my cellmates had been amusing themselves with me by telling terrible stories about the inefficiency of French prisons, an inefficiency so extreme that it had often happened that someone who was supposed to be taken out and tried found himself on the wrong line and was guillotined instead. The best way of putting my reaction to this is to say that, though I knew they were teasing me, it was simply not possible for me to totally disbelieve them. As far as I was concerned, once in the hands of the law in France, anything could happen. I shuffled along with the others who were *extrait* to the center of the prison, trying, rather, to linger in the office, which seemed the only warm spot in the whole world, and found myself again in that dreadful wagon, and was carried again to the Ile de la Cité, this time to the Palais de Justice. The entire day, except for ten minutes, was spent in one of the cells, first waiting to be tried, then waiting to be taken back to prison.

For I was *not* tried that day. By and by I was handcuffed and led through the halls, upstairs to the courtroom where I found my New York friend. We were placed together, both stage-whisperingly certain that this was the end of our ordeal. Nevertheless, while I waited for our case to be called, my eyes searched the courtroom, looking for a face I knew, hoping, anyway, that there was someone there who knew *me*, who would carry to someone outside the news that I was in trouble. But there was no one I knew there and I had had time to realize that there was probably only one man in Paris who could help me, an American patent attorney for whom I had worked as an office boy. He could have helped me because he had a quite solid position and some prestige and would have testified that, while working for him, I had handled large sums of money regularly, which made it rather unlikely that I would stoop to trafficking in bedsheets. However, he was somewhere in Paris, probably at this very moment enjoying a snack and a glass of wine and as far as the possibility of reaching him was concerned, he might as well have been on Mars. I tried to watch the proceedings and to make my mind a blank. But the proceedings were not reassuring. The boy, for example, who had stolen the sweater *did* receive a six-month sentence. It seemed to me that all the sentences meted out that day were excessive; though, again, it seemed that all the people who were sentenced that day had made, or clearly were going to make, crime their career. This seemed to be the opinion of the judge, who scarcely looked at the prisoners or listened to them; it seemed to be the opinion of the prisoners, who scarcely bothered to speak in their own behalf; it seemed to be the opinion of the lawyers, state lawyers for the most part, who were defending them. The great impulse of the courtroom seemed to be to put these people where they could not be seen—and not because they were offended at their crimes, unless, indeed, they were offended that the crimes were so petty, but because they did not wish to know that their society could be counted on to produce, probably in greater and greater numbers, a whole body of people for whom crime was the only possible career. Any society inevitably produces its criminals, but a society at once rigid and unstable can do nothing whatever to alleviate the poverty of its lowest members, cannot present to the hypothetical young man at the crucial moment that so-well-advertised right path. And the fact, perhaps, that the French are the earth's least sentimental people and must also be numbered among the most proud aggravates the plight of their lowest, youngest, and unluckiest members, for it means that the idea of rehabilitation is scarcely real to them. I confess that this attitude on their part raises in me sentiments of exasperation, admiration, and despair, revealing as it does, in both the best and the worst sense, their renowned and spectacular hard-headedness.

Finally our case was called and we rose. We gave our names. At the point that it developed that we were American the proceedings ceased, a hurried consultation took place between the judge and what I took to be several lawyers. Someone called out for an interpreter. The arresting officer had forgotten to mention our nationalities and there was, therefore, no interpreter in the court. Even if our French had been better than it was we would not have been allowed to stand trial without an interpreter. Before I clearly understood what was happening, I was handcuffed again and led out of the courtroom. The trial had been set back for the 27th of December.

I have sometimes wondered if I would *ever* have got out of prison if it had not been for the older man who had been arrested for the mysterious petty larceny. He was acquitted that day and when he returned to the cell—for he could not be released until morning—he found me sitting numbly on the floor, having just been prevented, by the sight of a man, all blood, being carried back to *his* cell on a stretcher, from seizing the bars and screaming until they let me out. The sight of the man on the stretcher proved, however, that screaming would not do much for me. The petty-larceny man went around asking if he could do anything in the world outside for those he was leaving behind. When he came to me I, at first, responded, "No, nothing"—for I suppose I had by now retreated into the attitude, the earliest I remember, that of my father, which was simply (since I had lost his God) that nothing could help me. And I suppose I will remember with gratitude until I die the fact that the man now insisted: "*Mais, êtes-vous* sûr?" Then it swept over me that he was going *outside* and he instantly became my first contact since the Lord alone knew how long with the outside world. At the same time, I remember, I did not really believe that he would help me. There was no reason why he should. But I gave him the phone number of my attorney friend and my own name.

So, in the middle of the next day, Christmas Eve, I shuffled downstairs again, to meet my visitor. He looked extremely well fed and sane and clean. He told me I had nothing to worry about any more. Only not even he could do anything to make the mill of justice grind any faster. He would, however, send me a lawyer of his acquaintance who would defend me on the 27th, and he would himself, along with several other people, appear as a character witness. He gave me a package of Lucky

Strikes (which the turnkey took from me on the way upstairs) and said that, though it was doubtful that there would be any celebration in the prison, he would see to it that I got a fine Christmas dinner when I got out. And this, somehow, seemed very funny. I remember being astonished at the discovery that I was actually laughing. I was, too, I imagine, also rather disappointed that my hair had not turned white, that my face was clearly not going to bear any marks of tragedy, disappointed at bottom, no doubt, to realize, facing him in that room, that far worse things had happened to most people and that, indeed, to paraphrase my mother, if this was the worst thing that ever happened to me I could consider myself among the luckiest people ever to be born. He injected—my visitor—into my solitary nightmare common sense, the world, and the hint of blacker things to come.

The next day, Christmas, unable to endure my cell, and feeling that, after all, the day demanded a gesture, I asked to be allowed to go to Mass, hoping to hear some music. But I found myself, for a freezing hour and a half, locked in exactly the same kind of cubicle as in the wagon which had first brought me to prison, peering through a slot placed at the level of the eye at an old Frenchman, hatted, overcoated, muffled, and gloved, preaching in this language which I did not understand, to this row of wooden boxes, the story of Jesus Christ's love for men.

The next day, the 26th, I spent learning a peculiar kind of game, played with match-sticks, with my cellmates. For, since I no longer felt that I would stay in this cell forever, I was beginning to be able to make peace with it for a time. On the 27th I went again to trial and, as had been predicted, the case against us was dismissed. The story of the *drap de lit*, finally told, caused great merriment in the courtroom, whereupon my friend decided that the French were "great." I was chilled by their merriment, even though it was meant to warm me. It could only remind me of the laughter I had often heard at home, laughter which I had sometimes deliberately elicited. This laughter is the laughter of those who consider themselves to be at a safe remove from all the wretched, for whom the pain of the living is not real. I had heard it so often in my native land that I had resolved to find a place where I would never hear it any more. In some deep, black, stony, and liberating way, my life, in my own eyes, began during that first year in Paris, when it was borne in on me that this laughter is universal and never can be stilled.

MEMOIRS OF
A FEEDER IN FRANCE

A GOOD APPETITE

A.J. Liebling

1959

T HE PROUST *madeleine* phenomenon is now as firmly established in folklore as Newton's apple or Watt's steam kettle.
The man ate a tea biscuit, the taste evoked memories, he wrote
a book. This is capable of expression by the formula TMB,
for Taste > Memory > Book. Some time ago, when I began to
read a book called "The Food of France," by Waverley Root, I
had an inverse experience: BMT, for Book > Memory > Taste.
Happily, the tastes that "The Food of France" re-created for
me—small birds, stewed rabbit, stuffed tripe, Côte Rôtic, and
Tavel—were more robust than that of the *madeleine*, which
Larousse defines as "a light cake made with sugar, flour, lemon
juice, brandy, and eggs." (The quantity of brandy in a *madeleine*
would not furnish a gnat with an alcohol rub.) In the light of
what Proust wrote with so mild a stimulus, it is the world's loss
that he did not have a heartier appetite. On a dozen Gardiners
Island oysters, a bowl of clam chowder, a peck of steamers,
some bay scallops, three sautéed soft-shelled crabs, a few ears

of fresh-picked corn, a thin swordfish steak of generous area, a pair of lobsters, and a Long Island duck, he might have written a masterpiece.

The primary requisite for writing well about food is a good appetite. Without this, it is impossible to accumulate, within the allotted span, enough experience of eating to have anything worth setting down. Each day brings only two opportunities for field work, and they are not to be wasted minimizing the intake of cholesterol. They are indispensable, like a prize-fighter's hours on the road. (I have read that the late French professional gourmand Maurice Curnonsky ate but one meal a day—dinner. But that was late in his life, and I have always suspected his attainments anyway; so many mediocre witticisms are attributed to him that he could not have had much time for eating.) A good appetite gives an eater room to turn around in. For example, a non-professional eater I know went to the Restaurant Pierre, in the Place Gaillon, a couple of years ago, his mind set on a sensibly light meal: a dozen, or possibly eighteen, oysters, and a thick chunk of steak topped with beef marrow, which M. Pierre calls a "Délice de la Villette"—the equivalent of a "Stock-yards' Delight." But as he arrived, he heard M. Pierre say to his headwaiter, "Here comes Monsieur L. Those two portions of *cassoulet* that are left—put them aside for him." A *cassoulet* is a substantial dish, of a complexity precluding its discussion here. (Mr. Root devotes three pages to the great controversy over what it should contain.) M. Pierre is the most amiable of restaurateurs, who prides himself on knowing in advance what his friends will like. A client of limited appetite would be obliged either to forgo his steak or to hurt

M. Pierre's feelings. Monsieur L., however, was in no difficulty. He ate the two *cassoulets*, as was his normal practice; if he had consumed only one, his host would have feared that it wasn't up to standard. He then enjoyed his steak. The oysters offered no problem, since they present no bulk.

In the heroic age before the First World War, there were men and women who ate, in addition to a whacking lunch and a glorious dinner, a voluminous *souper* after the theatre or the other amusements of the evening. I have known some of the survivors, octogenarians of unblemished appetite and unfailing good humor—spry, wry, and free of the ulcers that come from worrying about a balanced diet—but they have had no emulators in France since the doctors there discovered the existence of the human liver. From that time on, French life has been built to an increasing extent around that organ, and a niggling caution has replaced the old recklessness; the liver was the seat of the Maginot mentality. One of the last of the great around-the-clock gastronomes of France was Yves Mirande, a small, merry author of farces and musical-comedy books. In 1955, Mirande celebrated his eightieth birthday with a speech before the curtain of the Théâtre Antoine, in the management of which he was associated with Mme. B., a protégée of his, forty years younger than himself. But the theatre was only half of his life. In addition, M. Mirande was an unofficial director of a restaurant on the Rue Saint-Augustin, which he had founded for another protégée, also forty years younger than himself; this was Mme. G., a Gasconne and a magnificent cook. In the restaurant on the Rue Saint-Augustin, M. Mirande would dazzle his juniors, French and American, by dispatching a lunch of raw Bayonne ham and fresh figs, a hot sausage in crust, spindles of filleted pike in a rich rose *sauce Nantua*, a leg of lamb larded with anchovies, artichokes on a pedestal of foie gras, and four or five kinds of cheese, with a good bottle of Bordeaux and one of champagne, after which he would call for the Armagnac and remind Madame to have ready for dinner the larks and ortolans she had promised him, with a few *langoustes* and a turbot—and, of course, a fine *civet* made from the *marcassin*, or young wild boar, that the lover of the leading lady in his current production had sent up from his estate in the Sologne. "And while I think of it," I once heard him say, "we haven't had any woodcock for days, or truffles baked in the ashes, and the cellar is becoming a disgrace—no more '34s and hardly any '37s. Last week, I had to offer my publisher a bottle that was far too good for him, simply because there was nothing between the insulting and the superlative."

M. Mirande had to his credit a hundred produced plays, including a number of great Paris hits, but he had just written his first book for print, so he said "my publisher" in a special mock-impressive tone. "An informal sketch for my definitive autobiography," he would say of this production. The informal sketch, which I cherish, begins with the most important decision in Mirande's life. He was almost seventeen and living in the small Breton port of Lannion—his offstage family name was Le Querrec—when his father, a retired naval officer, said to him, "It is time to decide your future career. Which will it be, the Navy or the Church?" No other choice was conceivable in

Lannion. At dawn, Yves ran away to Paris. There, he had read a thousand times, all the famous wits and cocottes frequented the tables in front of the Café Napolitain, on the Boulevard des Capucines. He presented himself at the café at nine the next morning—late in the day for Lannion—and found that the place had not yet opened. Soon he became a newspaperman. It was a newspaper era as cynically animated as the corresponding period of the Bennett-Pulitzer-Hearst competition in New York, and in his second or third job he worked for a press lord who was as notional and niggardly as most press lords are; the publisher insisted that his reporters be well turned out, but did not pay them salaries that permitted cab fares when it rained. Mirande lived near the fashionable Montmartre cemetery and solved his rainy-day pants-crease problem by crashing funeral parties as they broke up and riding, gratis, in the carriages returning to the center of town. Early in his career, he became personal secretary to Clemenceau and then to Briand, but the gay theatre attracted him more than politics, and he made the second great decision of his life after one of his political patrons had caused him to be appointed *sous-préfet* in a provincial city. A *sous-préfet* is the administrator of one of the districts into which each of the ninety *départements* of France is divided, and a young *sous-préfet* is often headed for a precocious rise to high positions of state. Mirande, attired in the magnificent uniform that was then de rigueur, went to his "capital," spent one night there, and then ran off to Paris again to direct a one-act farce. Nevertheless, his connections with the serious world remained cordial. In the restaurant on the Rue Saint-Augustin, he introduced me to Colette, by that time a national glory of letters.

The regimen fabricated by Mirande's culinary protégée, Mme. G., maintained him *en pleine forme*. When I first met him, in the restaurant during the summer of the Liberation, he was a sprightly sixty-nine. In the spring of 1955, when we renewed a friendship that had begun in admiration of each other's appetite, he was as good as ever. On the occasion of our reunion, we began with a *truite au bleu*—a live trout simply done to death in hot water, like a Roman emperor in his bath. It was served up doused with enough melted butter to thrombose a regiment of Paul Dudley Whites, and accompanied, as was right, by an Alsatian wine—a Lacrimae Sanctae Odiliae, which once contributed slightly to my education. Long ago, when I was very young, I took out a woman in Strasbourg, and, wishing to impress her with my knowledge of local customs, ordered a bottle of Ste. Odile. I was making the same mistake as if I had taken out a girl in Boston and offered her baked beans. "How quaint!" the woman in Strasbourg said. "I haven't drunk that for years." She excused herself to go to the telephone, and never came back.

After the trout, Mirande and I had two meat courses, since we could not decide in advance which we preferred. We had a magnificent *daube provençale*, because we were faithful to *la cuisine bourgeoise*, and then *pinta-dous*—young guinea hens, simply and tenderly roasted—with the first asparagus of the year, to show our fidelity to *la cuisine classique*. We had clarets with both courses—a Pétrus with the *daube*, a Cheval Blanc with the guineas. Mirande said that his doctor had discounselled Burgundies. It was the first time in our acquaintance that I had heard him admit he had a doctor, but I was reassured when he drank a bottle and a half of Krug after luncheon. We had three bottles between us—one to our loves, one to our countries, and one for symmetry, the last being on the house.

Mirande was a small, alert man with the face of a Celtic terrier—salient eyebrows and an upturned nose. He looked like an intelligent Lloyd George. That summer, in association with Mme. B., his theatrical protégée, he planned to produce a new play of Sartre's. His mind kept young by the theatre of Mme. B., his metabolism protected by the restaurant of Mme. G., Mirande seemed fortified against all eventualities for at least another twenty years. Then, perhaps, he would have to recruit new protégées. The Sunday following our reunion, I encountered him at Longchamp, a racecourse where the restaurant does not face the horses, and diners can keep first things first. There he sat, radiant, surrounded by celebrities and champagne buckets, sending out a relay team of commissionaires to bet for him on the successive tips that the proprietors of stables were ravished to furnish him between races. He was the embodiment of a happy man. (I myself had a nice thing at 27–1.)

The first alteration in Mirande's fortunes affected me so directly that I did not at once sense its gravity for him. Six weeks later, I was again in Paris. (That year, I was shuttling frequently between there and London.) I was alone on the evening I arrived, and looked forward to a pleasant dinner at Mme. G.'s, which was within two hundred metres of the hotel, in the Square Louvois, where I always stop. Madame's was more than a place to eat, although one ate superbly there. Arriving, I would have a bit of talk with the proprietress, then with the waitresses—Germaine and Lucienne—who had composed the original staff. Waiters had been added as the house prospered, but they were of less marked personality. Madame was a bosomy woman—voluble, tawny, with a big nose and lank black hair—who made one think of a Saracen. (The Saracens reached Gascony in the eighth century.) Her conversation was a chronicle of letters and the theatre—as good as a subscription to *Figaro Littéraire*, but more advanced. It was somewhere between the avant-garde and the main body, but within hailing distance of both and enriched with the names of the great people who had been in recently—M. Cocteau, Gene Kelly, la Comtesse de Vogüé. It was always well to give an appearance of listening, lest she someday fail to save for you the last order of larks *en brochette* and bestow them on a more attentive customer. With Germaine and Lucienne, whom I had known when we were all younger, in 1939, the year of the *drôle de guerre*, flirtation was now perfunctory, but the *carte du jour* was still the serious topic—for example, how the fat Belgian industrialist from Tournai had reacted to the *caille vendangeuse*, or quail potted with fresh grapes. "You know the man," Germaine would say. "If it isn't dazzling, he takes only two portions. But when he has three, then you can say to yourself…" She and Lucienne looked alike—compact little women, with high foreheads and cheekbones and solid, muscular legs, who walked like *chasseurs à pied*, a hundred and thirty steps to the minute. In 1939, and again in 1944, Germaine had been a brunette and Lucienne a blonde, but in 1955 Germaine had become a blonde, too, and I found it hard to tell them apart.

Among my fellow-customers at Mme. G.'s I was always likely to see some friend out of the past. It is a risk to make an engagement for an entire evening with somebody you haven't seen for years. This is particularly true in France now. The almost embarrassingly pro-American acquaintance of the Liberation may be by now a Communist Party-line hack; the idealistic young Resistance journalist may have become an editorial writer for the reactionary newspaper of a textile magnate. The Vichy apologist you met in Washington in 1941, who called de Gaulle a traitor and the creation of the British Intelligence Service, may now tell you that the General is the best thing ever, while the fellow you knew as a de Gaulle aide in London may now compare him to Sulla destroying the Roman Republic. As for the women, who is to say which of them has resisted the years? But in a good restaurant that all have frequented, you are likely to meet any of them again, for good restaurants are not so many nowadays that a Frenchman will permanently desert one—unless, of course, he is broke, and in that case it would depress you to learn of his misfortunes. If you happen to encounter your old friends when they are already established at their tables, you have the opportunity to greet them cordially and to size them up. If you still like them, you can make a further engagement.

On the ghastly evening I speak of—a beautiful one in June—I perceived no change in the undistinguished exterior of Mme. G.'s restaurant. The name—something like Prospéria—was the same, and since the plate-glass windows were backed with scrim, it was impossible to see inside. Nor, indeed, did I notice any difference when I first entered. The bar, the tables, the banquettes covered with leatherette, the simple décor of mirrors and pink marble slabs were the same. The premises had been a business employees' bar-and-café before Mme. G., succeeding a long string of obscure proprietors, made it illustrious. She had changed the fare and the clientele but not the cadre. There are hundreds of identical fronts and interiors in Paris, turned out by some mass producer in the late twenties. I might have been warned by the fact that the room was empty, but it was only eight o'clock and still light outdoors. I had come unusually early because I was so hungry. A man whom I did not recognize came to meet me, rubbing his hands and hailing me as an old acquaintance. I thought he might be a waiter who had served me. (The waiters, as I have said, were not the marked personalities of the place.) He had me at a table before I sensed the trap.

"Madame goes well?" I asked politely.

"No, Madame is lightly ill," he said, with what I now realize was a guilty air.

He presented me with a *carte du jour* written in the familiar purple ink on the familiar wide sheet of paper with the name and telephone number of the restaurant at the top. The content of the menu, however, had become Italianized, the spelling had deteriorated, and the prices had diminished to a point where it would be a miracle if the food continued distinguished.

"Madame still conducts the restaurant?" I asked sharply.

I could now see that he was a Piedmontese of the most evasive description. From rubbing his hands he had switched to twisting them.

"Not exactly," he said, "but we make the same cuisine."

I could not descry anything in the smudged ink but misspelled noodles and unorthographical *"escaloppinis;"* Italians writing French by ear produce a regression to an unknown ancestor of both languages.

"Try us," my man pleaded, and, like a fool, I did. I was hungry. Forty minutes later, I stamped out into the street as purple as an *aubergine* with rage. The minestrone had been cabbage scraps in greasy water. I had chosen *côtes d'agneau* as the safest item in the mediocre catalogue that the Prospéria's prospectus of bliss had turned into overnight. They had been cut from a tired Alpine billy goat and seared in machine oil, and the *haricots verts* with which they were served resembled decomposed whiskers from a theatrical-costume beard.

"The same cuisine?" I thundered as I flung my money on the falsified *addition* that I was too angry to verify. "You take me for a jackass!"

I am sure that as soon as I turned my back the scoundrel nodded. The restaurant has changed hands at least once since then.

In the morning, I telephoned Mirande. He confirmed the disaster. Mme. G., ill, had closed the restaurant. Worse, she had sold the lease and the good will, and had definitely retired.

"What is the matter with her?" I asked, in a tone appropriate to fatal disease.

"I think it was trying to read Simone de Beauvoir," he said. "A syncope."

Mme G. still lives, but Mirande is dead. When I met him in Paris the following November, his appearance gave no hint of decline. It was the season for his sable-lined overcoat à *l'im-presario*, and a hat that was a furry cross between a porkpie and a homburg. Since the restaurant on the Rue Saint-Augustin no longer existed, I had invited him to lunch with me at a very small place called the Gratin Dauphinois, on the Rue Chabanais, directly across from the building that once housed the most celebrated sporting house in Paris. The Rue Chabanais is a short street that runs from the Square Louvois to the Rue des Petits Champs—perhaps a hundred yards—but before the reform wave stimulated by a Municipal Councillor named Marthe Richard at the end of the Second World War, the name Chabanais had a cachet all its own. Mme. Richard will go down in history as the Carry Nation of sex. Now the house is closed, and the premises are devoted to some low commercial purpose. The walls of the midget Gratin Dauphinois are hung with cartoons that have a nostalgic reference to the past glories of the street.

Mirande, when he arrived, crackled with jokes about the locale. He taunted me with being a criminal who haunts the scene of his misdeeds. The fare at the Gratin is robust, as it is in Dauphiné, but it did not daunt Mirande. The wine card, similarly, is limited to the strong, rough wines of Arbois and the like, with a couple of Burgundies for clients who want to show off. There are no clarets; the proprietor hasn't heard of them. There are, of course, a few champagnes, for wedding parties or anniversaries, so Mirande, with Burgundies discounselled by his doctor, decided on champagne throughout the meal. This was a *drôle* combination with the mountain food, but I had forgotten about the lack of claret when I invited him.

We ordered a couple of dozen *escargots en pots de chambre* to begin with, These are snails baked and served, for the client's convenience, in individual earthenware crocks, instead of being forced back into shells. The snail, of course, has to be taken out of his shell to be prepared for cooking. The shell he is forced back into may not be his own. There is thus not even a sentimental justification for his reincarceration. The frankness of the service *en pot* does not improve the preparation of the snail, nor does it detract from it, but it does facilitate and accelerate his consumption. (The notion that the shell proves the snail's authenticity, like the head left on a woodcock, is invalid, as even a suburban housewife knows nowadays; you can buy a tin of snail shells in a supermarket and fill them with a mixture of nutted cream cheese and chopped olives.)

Mirande finished his dozen first, meticulously swabbing out the garlicky butter in each *pot* with a bit of bread that was fitted to the bore of the crock as precisely as a bullet to a rifle barrel. Tearing bread like that takes practice. We had emptied the first bottle of champagne when he placed his right hand delicately on the point of his waistcoat farthest removed from his spinal column.

"Liebling," he said, "I am not well."

It was like the moment when I first saw Joe Louis draped on the ropes. A great pity filled my heart. "*Maître*," I said, "I will take you home."

The dismayed *patronne* waved to her husband in the kitchen (he could see her through the opening he pushed the dishes through) to suspend the preparation of the *gendarme de Morteau*—the great smoked sausage in its tough skin—that we had proposed to follow the snails with. ("Short and broad in shape, it is made of pure pork and ... is likely to be accompanied ... by hot potato salad."—Root, page 217.) We had decided to substitute for the *pommes à l'huile* the *gratin dauphinois* itself. ("Thinly sliced potatoes are moistened with boiled milk and beaten egg, seasoned with salt, pepper, and nutmeg, and mixed with grated cheese, of the Gruyère type. The potatoes are then put into an earthenware dish which has been rubbed with garlic and then buttered, spotted with little dabs of butter, and sprinkled with more grated cheese. It is then cooked slowly in not too hot an oven."—Root, page 228.) After that, we were going to have a fowl in cream with *morilles*—wild black mushrooms of the mountains. We abandoned all.

I led Mirande into the street and hailed a taxi.

"I am not well, Liebling," he said. "I grow old."

He lived far from the restaurant, beyond the Place de l'Etoile, in the Paris of the successful. From time to time on our way, he would say, "It is nothing. You must excuse me. I am not well."

The apartment house in which he and Mme. B. lived resembled one of the chic modern museums of the quarter, with entrance gained through a maze of garden patches sheathed in glass. Successive metal grilles swung open before us as I pushed buttons that Mirande indicated—in these modern palaces there are no visible flunkies—until we reached an elevator that smoothly shot us upward to his apartment, which was rather larger in area than the Square Louvois. The décor, with basalt columns and floors covered with the skins of jumbo Siberian tigers—a special strain force-fed to supply old-style movie stars—reminded me of the sets for "Belphégor," a French serial of silent days that I enjoyed when I was a student at the Sorbonne in 1926. (It was, I think, about an ancient Egyptian high priest who came to life and set up bachelor quarters in Paris in the style of the Temple of Karnak.) Three or four maids rushed to relieve Mirande of his sable-lined coat, his hat, and his cane, topped with the horn of an albino chamois. I helped him to a divan on which two Theda Baras could have defended their honor simultaneously against two villains of the silents without either couple's getting in the other's way. Most of the horizontal surfaces in the room were covered with sculpture and most of the vertical ones with large paintings. In pain though he was, Mirande called my attention to these works of art.

"All the sculptures are by Renoir," he said. "It was his hobby. And all the paintings are by Maillol. It was his hobby. If it were the other way around, I would be one of the richest chaps in France. Both men were my friends. But then one doesn't give one's friends one's bread and butter. And, after all, it's less banal as it is."

After a minute, he asked me to help him to his bedroom, which was in a wing of the apartment all his own. When we got there, one of the maids came in and took his shoes off.

"I am in good hands now, Liebling," he said. "Farewell until next time. It is nothing."

I telephoned the next noon, and he said that his doctor, who was a fool, insisted that he was ill.

Again I left Paris, and when I returned, late the following January, I neglected Mirande. A Father William is a comforting

companion for the middle-aged—he reminds you that the best
is yet to be and that there's a dance in the old dame yet—but
a sick old man is discouraging. My conscience stirred when I
read in a gossip column in *France-Dimanche* that Toto Mirande
was convalescing nicely and was devouring caviar at a great
rate—with champagne, of course. (I had never thought of
Mirande as Toto, which is baby slang for "little kid," but from
then on I never referred to him in any other way; I didn't want
anybody to think I wasn't in the know.) So the next day I sent
him a pound of fresh caviar from Kaspia, in the Place de la
Madeleine. It was the kind of medication I approved of.

I received a note from Mirande by tube next morning,
reproaching me for spoiling him. He was going better, he wrote,
and would telephone in a day or two to make an appointment
for a return bout. When he called, he said that the idiotic doctor
would not yet permit him to go out to a restaurant, and he invited
me, instead, to a family dinner at Mme. B.'s. "Only a few old
friends, and not the cuisine I hope to give you at Maxim's next
time," he said. "But one makes out."

On the appointed evening, I arrived early—or on time, which
amounts to the same thing—*chez* Mme. B.; you take taxis when
you can get them in Paris at the rush hours. The handsome
quarter overlooking the Seine above the Trocadéro is so dull
that when my taxi deposited me before my host's door, I had
no inclination to stroll to kill time. It is like Park Avenue or the
near North Side of Chicago. So I was the first or second guest to
arrive, and Mme. B.'s fourteen-year-old daughter, by a past marriage, received me in the Belphégor room, apologizing because
her mother was still with Toto—she called him that. She need

not have told me, for at that moment I heard Madame, who is famous for her determined voice, storming at an unmistakable someone: "You go too far, Toto. It's disgusting. People all over Paris are kind enough to send you caviar, and because you call it monotonous, you throw it at the maid! If you think servants are easy to come by…"

When they entered the room a few minutes later, my old friend was all smiles. "How did you know I adore caviar to such a point?" he asked me. But I was worried because of what I had heard; the Mirande I remembered would never have been irritated by the obligation to eat a few extra kilos of fresh caviar. The little girl, who hoped I had not heard, embraced Toto. "Don't be angry with *Maman!*" she implored him. It was a gathering so familial that it recalled the home scenes in "Gigi."

My fellow-guests included the youngish new wife of an old former Premier, who was unavoidably detained in Lille at a congress of the party he now headed; it mustered four deputies, of whom two formed a Left Wing and two a Right Wing. ("If they had elected a fifth at the last election, or if, by good luck, one had been defeated, they could afford the luxury of a Center," Mirande told me in identifying the lady. "*C'est malheureux*, a party without a Center. It limits the possibilities of maneuver.") There was also an amiable couple in their advanced sixties or beginning seventies, of whom the husband was the grand manitou of Veuve Clicquot champagne. Mirande introduced them by their right name, which I forget, and during the rest of the evening addressed them as M. and Mme. Clicquot. There was a forceful, black-haired man from the Midi, in the youth of middle age—square-shouldered, stocky, decisive, blatantly virile—who, I was told, managed Mme. B.'s vinicultural enterprises in Provence. There were two guests of less decided individuality, whom I barely remember, and filling out the party were the young girl—shy, carefully unsophisticated and unadorned—Mme. B., Mirande, and me. Mme. B. had a strong triangular face on a strong triangular base—a strong chin, high cheekbones, and a wide, strong jaw, but full of stormy good nature. She was a woman who, if she had been a man, would have wanted to be called Honest John. She had a high color and an iron handgrip, and repeatedly affirmed that there was no affectation about her, that she was *sans façon*, that she called her shots as she saw them. "I won't apologize," she said to me. "I know you're a great feeder, like Toto here, but I won't offer you the sort of menu he used to get in that restaurant you know of, where he ruined his plumbing. Oh, that woman! I used to be so jealous. I can offer only a simple home dinner." And she waved us toward a marble table about twenty-two feet long. Unfortunately for me, she meant it. The dinner began with a kidney-and-mushroom mince served in a giant popover—the kind of thing you might get at a literary hotel in New York. The inner side of the pastry had the feeling of a baby's palm, in the true tearoom tradition.

"It is savory but healthy," Madame said firmly, setting an example by taking a large second helping before starting the dish on its second round. Mirande regarded the untouched doughy fabric on his plate with diaphanously veiled horror, but he had an excuse in the state of his health. "It's still a little rich for me, darling," he murmured. The others, including me, delivered salvos of compliments. I do not squander my moral courage on minor crises. M. Clicquot said, "Impossible to obtain anything like this *chez* Lapérouse!" Mme. Clicquot said, "Not even at the Tour d'Argent!"

"And what do you think of my little wine?" Mme. B. asked M. Clicquot. "I'm so anxious for your professional opinion—as a rival producer, you know."

The wine was a thin *rosé* in an Art Nouveau bottle with a label that was a triumph of lithography; it had spires and monks and troubadours and blondes in wimples on it, and the name of the *cru* was spelled out in letters with Gothic curlicues and pennons. The name was something like Château Guillaume d'Aquitaine, *grand vin.*

"What a madly gay little wine, my dear!" M. Clicquot said, repressing, but not soon enough, a grimace of pain.

"One would say a Tavel of a good year," I cried, "if one were a complete bloody fool." I did not say the second clause aloud.

My old friend looked at me with new respect. He was discovering in me a capacity for hypocrisy that he had never credited me with before.

The main course was a shoulder of mutton with white beans—the poor relation of a gigot, and an excellent dish in its way, when not too dry. This was.

For the second wine, the man from the Midi proudly produced a red, in a bottle without a label, which he offered to M. Clicquot with the air of a tomcat bringing a field mouse to its master's feet. "Tell me what you think of this," he said as he filled the champagne man's glass.

M. Clicquot—a veteran of such challenges, I could well imagine—held the glass against the light, dramatically inhaled the bouquet, and then drank, after a slight stiffening of the features that indicated to me that he knew what he was in for. Having emptied half the glass, he deliberated.

"It has a lovely color," he said.

"But what is it? What is it?" the man from the Midi insisted.

"There are things about it that remind me of a Beaujolais," M. Clicquot said (he must have meant that it was wet), "but on the whole I should compare it to a Bordeaux" (without doubt unfavorably).

Mme. B.'s agent was beside himself with triumph. "Not one or the other!" he crowed. "It's from the *domaine*—the Chateau Guillaume d'Aquitaine!"

The admirable M. Clicquot professed astonishment, and I, when I had emptied a glass, said that there would be a vast market for the wine in America if it could be properly presented. "Unfortunately," I said, "the cost of advertising…" and I rolled my eyes skyward.

"Ah, yes," Mme. B. cried sadly. "The cost of advertising!"

I caught Mirande looking at me again, and thought of the Pétrus and the Cheval Blanc of our last meal together *chez* Mme. G. He drank a glass of the red. After all, he wasn't going to die of thirst.

For dessert, we had a simple fruit tart with milk—just the thing for an invalid's stomach, although Mirande didn't eat it.

M. Clicquot retrieved the evening, oenologically, by producing two bottles of a wine "impossible to find in the cellars of any restaurant in France"—Veuve Clicquot '19. There is at present a great to-do among wine merchants in France and the United States about young wines, and an accompanying tendency to cry down the "legend" of the old. For that matter, hardware clerks, when you ask for a can opener with a wooden handle that is thick enough to give a grip and long enough for leverage, try to sell you complicated mechanical folderols, and, when you go on insisting, tell you that effectual things are out of fashion. The motivation in both cases is the same—simple greed. To deal in wines of varied ages requires judgment, the sum of experience and flair. It involves the risk of money, because every lot of wine, like every human being, has a life span, and it is this that the good vintner must estimate. His object should be to sell his wine at its moment of maximum value—to the drinker as well as the merchant. The vintner who handles only young wines is like an insurance company that will write policies only on children; the unqualified dealer wants to risk nothing and at the same time wants to avoid tying up his money. The client misled by brochures warning him off clarets and champagnes that are over ten years old and assuring him that Beaujolais should be drunk green will miss the major pleasures of wine drinking. To deal wisely in wines and merely to sell them are things as different as being an expert in ancient coins and selling Indian-head pennies over a souvenir counter.

Despite these convictions of mine about wine, I should never have tried a thirty-seven-year-old champagne on the recommendation of a lesser authority than the blessed M. Clicquot. It is the oldest by far that I have ever drunk. (H. Warner Allen, in "The Wines of France," published circa 1924, which is my personal wine bible, says, "In the matter of age, champagne is a capricious wine. As a general rule, it has passed its best between fifteen and twenty, yet a bottle thirty years old may

prove excellent, though all its fellows may be quite undrinkable."
He cites Saintsbury's note that "a Perrier Jouet of 1857 was
still majestical in 1884," adding, "And all wine-drinkers know
of such amazing discoveries." Mr. Root, whose book is not a
foolish panegyric of everything French, is hard on champagne, in
my opinion. He falls into a critical error more common among
writers less intelligent: he attacks it for not being something else.
Because its excellences are not those of Burgundy or Bordeaux,
he underrates the peculiar qualities it does not share with them,
as one who would chide Dickens for not being Stendhal, or
Marciano for not being Benny Leonard.)

The Veuve Clicquot '19 was tart without brashness—a
refined but effective understatement of younger champagnes,
which run too much to rhetoric, at best. Even so, the force was
all there, to judge from the two glasses that were a shade more
than my share. The wine still had a discreet *cordon*—the ring of
bubbles that forms inside the glass—and it had developed the
color known as "partridge eye." I have never seen a partridge's
eye, because the bird, unlike woodcock, is served without the
head, but the color the term indicates is that of serous blood
or a maple leaf on the turn.

"How nice it was, life in 1919, eh, M. Clicquot?" Mirande
said as he sipped his second glass.

After we had finished M. Clicquot's offering, we played a
game called lying poker for table stakes, each player being
allowed a capital of five hundred francs, not to be replenished
under any circumstances. When Mme. B. had won everybody's
five hundred francs, the party broke up. Mirande promised me
that he would be up and about soon, and would show me how

men revelled in the heroic days of *la belle époque*, but I had a feeling that the bell was cracked.

I left Paris and came back to it seven times during the next year, but never saw him. Once, being in his quarter in the company of a remarkably pretty woman, I called him up, simply because I knew he would like to look at her, but he was too tired. I forget when I last talked to him on the telephone. During the next winter, while I was away in Egypt or Jordan or someplace where French papers don't circulate, he died, and I did not learn of it until I returned to Europe.

When Mirande first faltered, in the Rue Chabanais, I had failed to correlate cause and effect. I had even felt a certain selfish alarm. If eating well was beginning to affect Mirande at eighty, I thought, I had better begin taking in sail. After all, I was only thirty years his junior. But after the dinner at Mme. B.'s, and in the light of subsequent reflection, I saw that what had undermined his constitution was Mme. G.'s defection from the restaurant business. For years, he had been able to escape Mme. B.'s solicitude for his health by lunching and dining in the restaurant of Mme. G., the sight of whom Mme. B. could not support. Entranced by Mme. G.'s magnificent food, he had continued to live "like a cock in a pie"—eating as well, and very nearly as much, as when he was thirty. The organs of the interior—never very intelligent, in spite of what the psycho-somatic quacks say—received each day the amount of pleasure to which they were accustomed, and never marked the passage of time; it was the indispensable roadwork of the prizefighter.

When Mme. G., good soul, retired, moderation began its fatal inroads on his resistance. My old friend's appetite, insufficiently stimulated, started to loaf—the insidious result, no doubt, of the advice of the doctor whose existence he had revealed to me by that slip of the tongue about why he no longer drank Burgundy. Mirande commenced, perhaps, by omitting the fish course after the oysters, or the oysters before the fish, then began neglecting his cheeses and skipping the second bottle of wine on odd Wednesdays. What he called his pipes (*"ma tuyauterie"*), being insufficiently exercised, lost their tone, like the leg muscles of a retired champion. When, in his kindly effort to please me, he challenged the *escargots en pots de chambre*, he was like an old fighter who tries a comeback without training for it. That, however, was only the revelation of the rot that had already taken place. What always happens happened. The damage was done, but it could so easily have been averted had he been warned against the fatal trap of abstinence.

MEMOIRS OF
A FEEDER IN FRANCE

JUST ENOUGH MONEY

A.J. Liebling

1959

I F, as I was saying not long ago in discussing Waverley Root's
book "The Food of France," the first requisite for writing
well about food is a good appetite, the second is to put in your
apprenticeship as a feeder when you have enough money to
pay the check but not enough to produce indifference to the
size of the total. (I also meant to say, previously, that Root has
a good appetite, but I never got around to it.) The optimum
financial position for a serious apprentice feeder is to have
funds in hand for three more days, with a reasonable, but not
certain, prospect of reinforcements thereafter. The student at
the Sorbonne waiting for his remittance, the newspaperman
waiting for his salary, the free-lance writer waiting for a check
that he has cause to believe is in the mail—all are favorably
situated to learn. (It goes without saying that it is essential to be
in France.) The man of appetite who will stint himself when he
can see three days ahead has no vocation, and I dismiss from
consideration, as manic, the fellow who will spend the lot on

one great feast and then live on fried potatoes until his next increment; Tuaregs eat that way, but only because they never know when they are going to come by their next sheep. The clearheaded voracious man learns because he tries to compose his meals to obtain an appreciable quantity of pleasure from each. It is from this weighing of delights against their cost that the student eater (particularly if he is a student at the University of Paris) erects the scale of values that will serve him until he dies or has to reside in the Middle West for a long period. The scale is different for each eater, as it is for each writer.

Eating is highly subjective, and the man who accepts say-so in youth will wind up in bad and overtouted restaurants in middle age, ordering what the maître d'hôtel suggests. He will have been guided to them by food-snob publications, and he will fall into the habit of drinking too much before dinner to kill the taste of what he has been told he should like but doesn't. An illustration: For about six years, I kept hearing of a restaurant in the richest shire of Connecticut whose proprietor, a Frenchman, had been an assistant of a disciple of the great Escoffier. Report had it that in these wilds—inhabited only by executives of the highest grade, walking the woods like the King of Nemi until somebody came on from Winnetka to cut their throats—the restaurateur gave full vent to the creative flame. His clients took what he chose to give them. If they declined, they had to go down the pike to some joint where a steak cost only twelve dollars, and word would get around that they felt their crowns in danger—they had been detected economizing. I finally arranged to be smuggled out to the place disguised as a *Time-Life* Executive Vice-Publisher in Charge of Hosannas with the mission of entertaining the advertising manager of the Hebrew National Delicatessen Corporation. When we arrived, we found the Yale-blue vicuña rope up and the bar full of couples in the hundred-thousand-dollar bracket, dead drunk as they waited for tables; knowing that this would be no back-yard cookout, they had taken prophylactic anesthesia. But when I tasted the food, I perceived that they had been needlessly alarmed. The Frenchman, discouraged because for four years no customers had tasted what they were eating, had taken to bourbon-on-the-rocks. In a morose way, he had resigned himself to becoming dishonestly rich. The food was no better than Howard Johnson's, and the customers, had they not been paralyzed by the time they got to it, would have liked it as well. The *spécialité de la maison*, the unhappy patron said when I interrogated him, was jellied oysters dyed red, white, and blue. "At least they are aware of that," he said. "The colors attract their attention." There was an on-the-hour service of Brink's armored cars between his door and the night-deposit vault of a bank in New York, conveying the money that rolled into the *caisse*. The wheels, like a juggernaut's, rolled over his secret heart. His intention in the beginning had been noble, but he was a victim of the system.

The reference room where I pursued my own first earnest researches as a feeder without the crippling handicap of afflu-ence was the Restaurant des Beaux-Arts, on the Rue Bonaparte, in 1926–27. I was a student, in a highly generalized way, at the Sorbonne, taking targets of opportunity for study. Eating soon developed into one of my major subjects. The franc was at twenty-six to the dollar, and the researcher, if he had only a certain sum—say, six francs—to spend, soon established for himself whether, for example, a half bottle of Tavel *supérieur*, at three and a half francs, and braised beef heart and yellow turnips, at two and a half, gave him more or less pleasure than a *contre-filet* of beef, at five francs, and a half bottle of *ordinaire*, at one franc. He might find that he liked the heart, with its strong, rich flavor and odd texture, nearly as well as the beef, and that since the Tavel was overwhelmingly better than the cheap wine, he had done well to order the first pair. Or he might find that he so much preferred the generous, sanguine *contre-filet* that he could accept the undistinguished *picrate* instead of the Tavel. As in a bridge tournament, the learner played duplicate hands, making the opposite choice of fare the next time the problem presented itself. (It was seldom as simple as my example, of course, because a meal usually included at least an hors d'oeuvre and a cheese, and there was a complexity of each to choose from. The arrival, in season, of fresh asparagus or venison further complicated matters. In the first case, the investigator had to decide what course to omit in order to fit the asparagus in, and, in the second, whether to forgo all else in order to afford venison.)

A rich man, faced with this simple sumptuary dilemma, would have ordered both the Tavel *and* the *contre-filet*. He would then never know whether he liked beef heart, or whether an *ordinaire* wouldn't do him as well as something better. (There are people to whom wine is merely an alcoholized sauce, although they may have sensitive palates for meat or pastries.) When one considers the millions of permutations of foods and wines to test, it is easy to see that life is too short for the formulation of dogma. Each eater can but establish a few general principles that are true only for him. Our hypothetical rich *client* might even have ordered a Pommard, because it was listed at a higher price than the Tavel, and because he was more likely to be acquainted with it. He would then never have learned that a good Tavel is better than a fair-to-middling Pommard—better than a fair-to-middling almost anything, in my opinion. In student restaurants, renowned wines like Pommard were apt to be mediocre specimens of their kind, since the customers could never have afforded the going prices of the best growths and years. A man who is rich in his adolescence is almost doomed to be a dilettante at table. This is not because all millionaires are stupid but because they are not impelled to experiment. In learning to eat, as in psychoanalysis, the customer, in order to profit, must be sensible of the cost.

There is small likelihood that a rich man will frequent modest restaurants even at the beginning of his gustatory career; he will patronize restaurants, sometimes good, where the prices are high and the repertory is limited to dishes for which it is conventionally permissible to charge high prices. From this list, he will order the dishes that in his limited experience he has already found agreeable. Later, when his habits are formed, he will distrust the originality that he has never been constrained to develop. A diet based chiefly on game birds and oysters becomes a habit as easily as a diet of jelly doughnuts and hamburgers. It is a better habit, of course, but restrictive just the same. Even in Paris, one can dine in the costly restaurants for years without learning that there are fish other than sole, turbot, salmon (in season), trout, and the Mediterranean *rouget* and *loup de mer*. The fresh herring or sardine *sauce moutarde*; the *colin froid mayonnaise*; the conger eel *en matelote*; the small fresh-water fish of the Seine and the Marne, fried crisp and served *en buisson*; the whiting *en colère* (his tail in his mouth, as if contorted with anger); and even the skate and the *dorade*—all these, except by special and infrequent invitation, are out of the swim. (It is a standing tourist joke to say that the fishermen on the quays of the Seine never catch anything, but in fact they often take home the makings of a nice fish fry, especially in winter. In my hotel on the Square Louvois, I had a room waiter—a Czech naturalized in France—who used to catch hundreds of *goujons* and *ablettes* on his days off. He once brought a shoe box of them to my room to prove that Seine fishing was not pure whimsey.) All the fish I have mentioned have their habitats in humbler restaurants, the only places where the aspirant eater can become familiar with their honest fishy tastes and the decisive modes of accommodation that suit them. Personally, I like tastes that know their own minds. The reason that people who detest fish often tolerate sole is that sole doesn't taste very much like fish, and even this degree of resemblance disappears when it is submerged in the kind of sauce that patrons of Piedmontese restaurants in London and New York think characteristically French. People with the same apathy toward decided flavor relish "South African lobster" tails—frozen as long as the Siberian mammoth—because they don't taste lobstery. ("South African lobsters" are a kind of sea crayfish, or *langouste*, but that would be nothing against them if they were fresh.) They prefer processed cheese because it isn't cheesy, and synthetic vanilla

extract because it isn't vanillary. They have made a triumph of
the Delicious apple because it doesn't taste like an apple, and of
the Golden Delicious because it doesn't taste like anything. In a
related field, "dry" (non-beery) beer and "light" (non-Scotchlike)
Scotch are more of the same. The standard of perfection for
vodka (no color, no taste, no smell) was expounded to me long
ago by the then Estonian consul-general in New York, and it
accounts perfectly for the drink's rising popularity with those
who like their alcohol in conjunction with the reassuring tastes
of infancy—tomato juice, orange juice, chicken broth. It is the
ideal intoxicant for the drinker who wants no reminder of how
hurt Mother would be if she knew what he was doing.

The consistently rich man is also unlikely to make the
acquaintance of meat dishes of robust taste—the hot *andouille*
and *andouillette*, which are close-packed sausages of smoked
tripe, and the *boudin*, or blood pudding, and all its relatives that
figure in the pages of Rabelais and on the menus of the market
restaurants. He will not meet the *civets*, or dark, winy stews of
domestic rabbit and old turkey. A tough old turkey with plenty
of character makes the best *civet*, and only in a *civet* is turkey good
to eat. Young turkey, like young sheep, calf, spring chicken, and
baby lobster, is a pale preliminary phase of its species. The pig,
the pigeon, and the goat—as suckling, squab, and kid—are the
only animals that are at their best (to eat) when immature. The
first in later life becomes gross through indolence; the second
and third grow muscular through overactivity. And the world
of tripery is barred to the well-heeled, except for occasional
exposure to an expurgated version of *tripes à la mode de Caen*.
They have never seen *gras-double* (tripe cooked with vegetables,

principally onions) or *pieds et paquets* (sheep's tripe and calves' feet with salt pork). In his book, Waverley Root dismisses tripe, but he is no plutocrat; his rejection is deliberate, after fair trial. Still, his insensibility to its charms seems to me odd in a New Englander, as he is by origin. Fried pickled honeycomb tripe used to be the most agreeable feature of a winter breakfast in New Hampshire, and Fall River, Root's home town, is in the same cultural circumscription.

Finally, to have done with our rich man, seldom does he see even the simple, well-pounded *bifteck* or the *pot-au-feu* itself—the foundation glory of French cooking. Alexandre Dumas the elder wrote in his "Dictionary of Cuisine," of which Simon & Schuster last fall published an English translation, "French cooking, the first of all cuisines, owes its superiority to the excellence of French bouillon. This excellence derives from a sort of intuition with which I shall not say our cooks but our women of the people are endowed." This bouillon is one of the two end products of the *pot*. The other is the material that has produced it—beef, carrots, parsnips, white turnips, leeks, celery, onions, cloves, garlic, and cracked marrowbones, and, for the dress version, fowl. Served *in* some of the bouillon, this constitutes the dish known as *pot-au-feu*. Dumas is against poultry "unless it is old," but advises that "an old pigeon, a partridge, or a rabbit roasted in advance, a crow in November or December" works wonders. He postulates "seven hours of sustained simmering," with constant attention to the "scum" that forms on the surface and to the water level. ("Think twice before adding water, though if your meat actually rises above the level of the bouillon it is necessary to add boiling water to cover it.") This supervision demands the full-time presence of the cook in the kitchen throughout the day, and the maintenance of the temperature calls for a considerable outlay in fuel. It is one reason that the *pot-au-feu* has declined as a chief element of the working-class diet in France. Women go out to work, and gas costs too much. For a genuinely good *pot-au-jeu*, Dumas says, one should take a fresh piece of beef—"a twelve-to-fifteen-pound rump"—and simmer it seven hours in the bouillon of the beef that you simmered seven hours the day before. He does not say what good housekeepers did with the first piece of beef—perhaps cut it into sandwiches for the children's lunch. He regrets that even when he wrote, in 1869, excessive haste was beginning to mar cookery; the demanding ritual of the *pot* itself had been abandoned. This was "a receptacle that never left the fire, day or night," Dumas writes. "A chicken was put into it as a chicken was withdrawn, a piece of beef as a piece was taken out, and a glass of water whenever a cup of broth was removed. Every kind of meat that cooked in this bouillon gained, rather than lost, in flavor." *Pot-au-feu* is so hard to find in chic restaurants nowadays that every Saturday evening there is a mass pilgrimage from the fashionable quarters to Chez Benoit, near the Châtelet—a small but not cheap restaurant that serves it once a week. I have never found a crow in Benoit's *pot*, but all the rest is good.

A drastically poor man, naturally, has even less chance than a drastically rich one to educate himself gastronomically. For him eating becomes merely a matter of subsistence; he can exercise no choice. The chief attraction of the cheapest student restaurants in my time was advertised on their largest placards:

"*Pain à Discrétion*" ("All the Bread You Want"). They did not graduate discriminating eaters. During that invaluable year, I met a keen observer who gave me a tip: "If you run across a restaurant where you often see priests eating with priests, or sporting girls with sporting girls, you may be confident that it is good. Those are two classes of people who like to eat well and get their money's worth. If you see a priest eating with a layman, though, don't be too sure about the money's worth. The fellow *en civil* may be a rich parishioner, and the good Father won't worry about the price. And if the girl is with a man, you can't count on anything. It may be her kept man, in which case she won't care what she spends on him, or the man who is keeping her, in which case she won't care what he spends on her."

Failing the sure indications cited above, a good augury is the presence of French newspapermen.

The Restaurant des Beaux-Arts, where I did my early research, was across the street from the Ecole des Beaux-Arts, and not, in fact, precisely in my quarter, which was that of the university proper, a good half mile away, on the other side of the Boulevard Saint-Germain. It was a half mile that made as much difference as the border between France and Switzerland. The language was the same, but not the inhabitants. Along the Rue Bonaparte there were antiquarians, and in the streets leading off it there were practitioners of the ancillary arts—picture framers and bookbinders. The bookshops of the Rue Bonaparte, of which there were many, dealt in fine editions and rare books, instead of the used textbooks and works of erudition that predominated around the university. The students of the Beaux-Arts were only a small element of the population of the neighborhood, and they were a different breed from the students of the Boulevard Saint-Michel and its tributaries, such as the Rue de l'Ecole de Médecine, where I lived. They were older and seemingly in easier circumstances. I suspected them of commercial art and of helping Italians to forge antiques. Because there was more money about, and because the quarter had a larger proportion of adult, experienced eaters, it was better territory for restaurants than the immediate neighborhood of the Sorbonne. I had matriculated at the Faculté des Lettres and at the Ecole des Chartes, which forms medievalists, but since I had ceased attending classes after the first two weeks, I had no need to stick close to home. One of the chief joys of that academic year was that it was one long cut without fear of retribution.

I chanced upon the Restaurant des Beaux-Arts while strolling one noon, and tried it because it looked neither chic nor sordid, and the prices on the menu were about right for me: *pâté maison*, 75 centimes; sardines, 1 franc; artichoke, 1.25; and so on. A legend over the door referred to the proprietor as a M. Teyssedre, but the heading of the bill of fare called him Balazuc. Which name represented a former proprietor and which the current one I never learned. I had a distaste for asking direct questions, a practice I considered ill-bred. This had handicapped me during my brief career as a reporter in Providence, Rhode Island, but not as much as you might think. Direct questions tighten a man up, and even if he answers, he will not tell you anything you have not asked him. What you want is to get him to tell you his story. After he has, you can ask clarifying questions, such as "How did you come to have the axe in your hand?" I had interrupted this journalistic grind after one year, at the suggestion of my father, a wise man. "You used to talk about wanting to go to Europe for a year of study," he said to me one spring day in 1926, when I was home in New York for a weekend. "You are getting so interested in what you are doing that if you don't go now you never will. You might even get married."

I sensed my father's generous intention, and, fearing that he might change his mind, I told him that I didn't feel I should go, since I was indeed thinking of getting married. "The girl is ten years older than I am," I said, "and Mother might think she is kind of fast, because she is being kept by a cotton broker from Memphis, Tennessee, who only comes North once in a while. But you are a man of the world, and you understand that a woman can't always help herself. Basically..." Within the week, I had a letter of credit on the Irving Trust for two thousand dollars, and a reservation on the old Caronia for late in the summer, when the off-season rates would be in effect. It was characteristic of my father that even while doing a remarkably generous thing he did not want to waste the difference between a full-season and an off-season passage on a one-class boat. (He never called a liner anything but a boat, and I always found it hard to do otherwise myself, until I stopped trying. "Boat" is an expression of affection, not disrespect; it is like calling a woman a girl. What may be ships in proportion to Oxford, where the dictionary is written, are boats in proportion to New York, where they nuzzle up to the bank to feed, like the water-fowl in Central Park.)

While I continued to work on the Providence paper until the rates changed, Father, with my mother and sister, embarked for Europe on a Holland-America boat—full-season rate and first class—so that my sister might take advantage of her summer holiday from school. I was to join them for a few days at the end of the summer, after which they would return to the United States and I would apply myself to my studies. Fortunately, I discovered that the titulary of a letter of credit can draw on it at the issuing bank as easily as abroad. By the time I sailed, I was eight hundred dollars into the letter, and after a week in Paris at a hotel off the Champs-Elysées I found, without astonishment, that I had spent more than half of the paternal fellowship that was intended to last me all year. The academic year would not begin until November, and I realized that I would be lucky to have anything at all by then. At this juncture, the cotton broker's girl came to my rescue in a vision, as an angel came to Constantine's. I telegraphed to my parents, who were at Lake Como, that I was on my way to join them. From my attitude when I got there—reserved, dignified, preoccupied—my father sensed that I was in trouble. The morning after my arrival, I proposed that we take a walk, just the two of us, by the lake. Soon we felt thirst, and we entered the trellised arbor of a hotel more modest than ours and ordered a bottle of rustic wine that recalled the stuff that Big Tony, my barber in Providence, used to manufacture in his yard on Federal Hill. Warmed by this homelike glow, I told my father that I had dilapidated his generous gift; I had dissipated in riotous living seventy-two per cent of the good man's unsolicited benefaction. Now there was only one honorable thing for me to do—go back to work, get married, and settle down. "She is so noble that she wouldn't tell me," I said, "but I'm afraid I left her in the lurch."

"God damn it," he said, "I knew I should never have given you that money in one piece. But I want you to continue your education. How much will you need every month?"

"Two hundred," I said, moderately. Later, I wished I had asked for fifty more; he might have gone for it. "You stay in Paris," he said—he knew I had chosen the Sorbonne—"and I'll have the Irving send you two hundred dollars every month. No more lump sums. When a young man gets tangled up with that kind of women, they can ruin his whole life."

That was how I came to be living in Paris that academic year in a financial situation that facilitated my researches. Looking back, I am sure my father knew that I wanted to stay on, and that there was no girl to worry about. But he also understood that I couldn't simply beg; for pride's sake, I had to offer a fake *quid pro quo* and pretend to myself that he believed me. He had a very good idea of the value of leisure, not having had any until it was too late to become accustomed to it, and a very good idea of the pleasure afforded by knowledge that has no commercial use, having never had time to acquire more than a few odd bits. His parents had brought him to America when he was eight years old; he went to work at ten, opened his own firm at twenty-one, started being rich at thirty, and died broke at sixty-five—a perfect Horatio Alger story, except that Alger never followed his heroes through. At the moment, though, he had the money, and he knew the best things it would buy.

———

The great day of each month, then, was the one when my draft arrived at the main office of the Crédit Lyonnais—the Irving's correspondent bank—on the Boulevard des Italiens. It was never even approximately certain what day the draft would get there; there was no airmail, and I could not be sure what ship it was on. The Crédit, on receiving the draft, would notify me, again by ordinary mail, and that would use up another day. After the second of the month, I would begin to be haunted by the notion that the funds might have arrived and that I could save a day by walking over and inquiring. Consequently, I walked a good many times across the river and the city from the Rue de l'Ecole de Médecine to the Boulevard des Italiens, via the Rue Bonaparte, where I would lunch at the Maison Teyssedre or Balazuc. There were long vertical black enamel plaques on either side of the restaurant door, bearing, in gold letters, such information as "Room for Parties," "Telephone," "Snails," "Specialty of Broils," and, most notably, "Renowned Cellar, Great Specialty of Wines of the Rhone." The Great Specialty dated back to the regime of a proprietor anteceding M. Teyssedre-Balazuc. This prehistoric *patron*, undoubtedly an immigrant from Languedoc or Provence, had set up a bridgehead in Paris for the wines of his region of origin.

The wines of the Rhone each have a decided individuality, viable even when taken in conjunction with *brandade de morue*—a delightful purée of salt codfish, olive oil, and crushed garlic—which is their compatriot. *Brandade*, according to Root, is "definitely not the sort of dish that is likely to be served at the Tour d'Argent." "Subtlety," that hackneyed wine word, is a cliché seldom employed in writing about Rhone wines; their appeal is totally unambiguous. The Maison Teyssedre-Balazuc had the whole gamut, beginning with a rough, faintly sour Côtes du Rhône—which means, I suppose, anything grown along that river as it runs its three-hundred-and-eighty-mile course through France. It continued with a Tavel and then a Tavel *supérieur*. The proprietor got his wines in barrel and bottled them in the Renowned Cellar; the plain Tavel came to the table in a bottle with a blue wax seal over the cork, the *supérieur* in a bottle with a purple seal. It cost two cents more a pint. I do not pretend to remember every price on the card of the Restaurant des Beaux-Arts, but one figure has remained graven in my heart like "Constantinople" in the dying Czar's. A half bottle of Tavel *supérieur* was 3.50; I can still see the figure when I close my eyes, written in purple ink on the cheap, grayish paper of the *carte*. This is a mnemonic testimonial to how good the wine was, and to how many times I struggled with my profligate tendencies at that particular point in the menu, arguing that the unqualified Tavel, which was very good, was quite good enough; two cents a day multiplied by thirty, I frequently told myself, mounted up to fifteen francs a month. I don't think I ever won the argument; my spendthrift palate carried the day. Tavel has a rose-cerise *robe*, like a number of well-known racing silks, but its taste is not thin or acidulous, as that of most of its mimics is. The taste is warm but dry, like an enthusiasm held under restraint, and there is a tantalizing suspicion of bitterness when the wine hits the top of the palate. With the second glass, the enthusiasm gains; with the third, it is overpowering. The effect is generous and calorific, stimulative of cerebration and the social instincts. "An apparently light but treacherous *rosé*," Root calls it, with a nuance of resentment that hints at some old misadventure.

Tavel is from a place of that name in Languedoc, just west of the Rhone. In 1926, there were in all France only two well-known wines that were neither red nor white. One was Tavel, and the other Arbois, from the Jura—and Arbois is not a rose-colored but an "onion-peel" wine, with russet and purple glints. In the late thirties, the *rosés* began to proliferate in wine regions where they had never been known before, as growers discovered how marketable they were, and to this day they continue to pop up like measles on the wine map. Any normally white wine can be converted into a *rosé* simply by leaving the new wine in contact with the grapeskins for a bit longer than is customary. In 1926 and 1927, for example, I never heard of Anjou *rosé* wine, although I read wine cards every day and spent a week of purposeful drinking in Angers, a glorious white-wine city. Alsace is another famous white-wine country that now lends its name to countless cases of a pinkish cross between No-Cal and vinegar; if, in 1926, I had crossed the sacred threshold of Valentin Sorg's restaurant in Strasbourg and asked the sommelier for a *rosé d'Alsace*, he would have, quite properly, kicked me into Germany. The list is endless now; flipping the coated-paper pages of any dealer's brochure, you see *rosés* from Bordeaux, Burgundy, all the South of France, California, Chile, Algeria, and heaven knows where else. Pink champagne, colored by the same procedure, has existed for a century and was invented for the African and Anglo-Saxon trade. The "discovery" of the demand for pink wine approximately coincided with the repeal of prohibition in the United States. (The American housewife is susceptible to eye and color appeal.) In England, too, in the same period, a new class of wine buyer was rising with the social revolution. Pink worked its miracle there, and also in France itself, where many families previously limited to the cheapest kind of bulk wine were beginning to graduate to "nice things." Logically, there is no reason any good white-wine region should not produce equally good *rosé*, but in practice the proprietors of the good vineyards have no cause to change the nature of their wines; they can sell every drop they make. It is impossible to imagine a proprietor at Montrachet, or Chablis, or Pouilly, for example, tinting his wine to make a Bourgogne *rosé*. It is almost as hard to imagine it of a producer of first-rate Alsatian or Angevin wines. The wines converted to *rosé* in the great-wine provinces are therefore, I suspect, the worst ones—a suspicion confirmed by almost every experience I have had of them. As for the *rosés* from the cheap-wine provinces, they are as bad as their coarse progenitors, but are presented in fancy bottles of untraditional form—a trick learned from the perfume industry. The bottles are generally decorated with art labels in the style of Robida's illustrations for Rabelais, and the wines are peddled at a price out of all proportion to their inconsiderable merits. There is also behind their gruesome spread the push of a report, put out by some French ad man, that while white wine is to be served only with certain aliments, and red wine only with certain others, *rosé* "goes with everything," and so can be served without embarrassment by the inexperienced hostess. The truth is, of course, that if a wine isn't good it doesn't "go" with anything, and if it is it can go in any company. Tavel, though, is the good, the old, and, as far as I am concerned, still the only worthy *rosé*.

At the Restaurant des Beaux-Arts, the Tavel *supérieur* was as high on the list as I would let my eyes ascend until I felt that the new money was on its way. When I had my first supersensory intimation of its approach, I began to think of the prizes higher on the card—Côte Rôtie, Châteauneuf-du-Pape, and white as well as red Hermitage, which cost from three to five francs more, by the half bottle, than my customary Purple Seal. Racing men like to say that a great horse usually has a great name—impressive and euphonious—and these three wines bear similar cachets. The Pope's new castle and the Hermitage evoke medieval pomp and piety, but the name Côte Rôtie—the hillside roasted in the sun—is the friendliest of the three, as is the wine, which has a cleaner taste than Châteauneuf and a warmer one than Hermitage. Châteauneuf often seems to be a wine that there is too much of to be true, and it varies damnably in all respects save alcoholic content, which is high. Red Hermitage is certainly distinguished; as its boosters like to say, of all Rhône wines it most resembles a great Burgundy, but perhaps for that reason it was hardest for a young man to understand. It was least like a *vin du Rhône*. As for the scarce white Hermitage, of which I haven't encountered a bottle in many years, it left a glorious but vague memory. Côte Rôtie was my darling. Drinking it, I fancied I could see that literally roasting but miraculously green hillside, popping with goodness, like the skin of a roasting duck, while little wine-colored devils chased little nymphs along its simmering rivulets of wine. (Thirty years later, I had a prolonged return match with Côte Rôtie, when I discovered it on the wine card of Prunier's, in London. I approached it with foreboding, as you return to a favorite author whom you haven't read for a long time, hoping that he will be as good as you remember. But I need have had no fear. Like Dickens, Côte Rôtie meets the test. It is no Rudyard Kipling in a bottle, making one suspect a defective memory or a defective cork.)

On days when I merely suspected money to be at the bank, I would continue from the Restaurant des Beaux-Arts to the Boulevard des Italiens by any variation of route that occurred to me, looking in the windows of the rare-book dealers for the sort of buy I could afford only once a month. Since on most of my trips I drew a blank at the Crédit Lyonnais, I had plenty of time for window-shopping and for inspection of the bookstalls on the quays. To this I attribute my possession of some of the best books I own—the "Moyen de Parvenir," for example, printed at Chinon in the early seventeenth century, with the note on its title page "New edition, corrected of divers faults that weren't there, and augmented by many others entirely new."

On the *good* day, when I had actually received the notification, I had to walk over again to collect, but this time I had a different stride. Simply from the way I carried myself when I left my hotel on the Rue de l'Ecole de Médecine, my landlord, M. Perès, knew that I would pay my bill that night, together with the six or seven hundred francs I invariably owed him for personal bites. He would tap cheerfully on the glass of the window that divided his well-heated office and living quarters from the less well-heated entrance hall, and wave an arm with the gesture that he had probably used to pull his company out of the trenches for a charge at Verdun. He was a *grand blessé* and a Chevalier of the Legion of Honor, *à titre militaire*, with a silver plate in his head that lessened his resistance to liquor, as he frequently reminded Madame when she bawled him out for drinking too much. "One little glass, and you see how I am!" he would say mournfully. In fact, he and I had usually had six each at the Taverne Soufflet, and he convived with other lodgers as well—notably with an Irishman named O'Hea, who worked in a bank, and a spendthrift Korean, who kept a girl.

At the restaurant, I would drink Côte Rôtie, as I had pre-meditated, and would have one or two Armagnacs after lunch. After that, I was all business in my trajectory across Paris, pausing only nine or ten times to look at the water in the river, and two or three more to look at girls. At the Crédit, I would be received with scornful solemnity, like a suitor for the hand of a miser's daughter. I was made to sit on a bare wooden bench with other wretches come to claim money from the bank, all feeling more like culprits by the minute. A French bank, by the sombre intensity of its addiction to money, establishes an emotional claim on funds in transit. The client feels in the moral position of a wayward mother who has left her babe on a doorstep and later comes back to claim it from the foster parents, who now consider it their own. I would be given a metal check with a number on it, and just as I had begun to doze off from the effects of a good lunch, the Côte Rôtie, the brisk walk, and the poor ventilation, a *huissier* who had played Harpagon in repertoire at Angers would shake me by the shoulder. I would advance toward a grille behind which another Harpagon, in an alpaca coat, held the draft, confident that he could riddle my pretensions to the identity I professed. Sometimes, by the ferocity of his distrust, he made me doubt who I was. I would stand fumbling in the wrong pocket for my *carte d'identité*, which had a knack of passing from one part of my apparel to another, like a prestidigitator's coin, and then for my passport, which on such occasions was equally elusive. The sneer on Harpagon's cuttlefish bone of a face would grow triumphant, and I expected him to push a button behind his grille that would summon a squad of detectives. At last, I would find my fugitive credentials and present them, and he would hand over the draft. Then he would send me back to the bench, a *huissier* would present me with another number, and it all had to be done over again—this time with my Kafka impersonation enacted before another Harpagon, at another grille, who would hand out the substantive money. Finally, with two hundred times twenty-six francs, minus a few deductions for official stamps, I would step out onto the Boulevard des Italiens—a once-a-month Monte Cristo. "Taxi!" I would cry. There was no need to walk back.

WOLCOTT GIBBS

E.B. White

1958

T HE DEATH of Wolcott Gibbs on August 16th in his house
on Fire Island was, of course, reported in the papers,
and his stature as a drama critic noted. Here at the magazine
we tend to think of him in an earlier phase, before the theatre
became his chief concern. He came to *The New Yorker* in 1927,
from the top of a boxcar on the Long Island Rail Road, where
he had been employed, and of all the early arrivals, in those
days when the magazine watched the skies for signs of salvation,
he seemed somehow the most promising. He had the manner
and appearance and speech of a native New Yorker; he dressed
appropriately; he seemed uninterested in, if not scornful of,
any other city; he was young, talented, humorous; and he was
obviously a pro, able to do his work without regard to the many
difficulties that prevailed. Even more implausible was the fact
that he appeared to be (and turned out to be) professionally
ambidextrous: a natural editor, a prolific and good and versatile
writer—gifts rarely combined in one person.

Long before Gibbs slipped into the critic's seat at the play-
house, he was turning in an editor-writer performance at *The
New Yorker* that has never been equalled. His judgment on humor,
on fiction, and on art helped form the magazine and shape

its course. He was a stern critic of manuscripts, just as, later, he became a stern critic of plays, but he was a friendly and a humorous one, and writers found him kind, helpful, amusing and amused. Often the Editor would have been far happier to publish a Gibbs opinion sheet than the manuscript to which it was attached. In fact, if these spontaneous and unguarded written opinions of his could he released to the world (and they most assuredly can't be), they would make probably a funnier and sounder critique of creative writing in the late twenties and early thirties than has ever been assembled.

Gibbs filled our gaping pages with satirical sketches, profiles, parodies, reminiscences, and comments. All of his stuff was good, much of it was superb—sharp, memorable, and funny. His style had a brilliance that was never flashy, he was self-critical as well as critical, and he had absolute pitch, which enabled him to become a parodist of the first rank. The parodies are in a class by themselves: Huxley, Hemingway, Marquand, Saroyan, Lewis, Pegler, Maxwell Anderson, the rewrite men of *Time*—a long list. Luckily, these great parodies, together with some other material, will soon reappear, in a new book; Gibbs was studying an advance copy of this book, cigarette in hand, when he died. Parody was his favorite form, because it was the most challenging. ("I found them harder and more rewarding to do than anything else.") It is safe to predict that this will be the most distinguished collection of parodies in American letters to date, and it will certainly be the funniest.

Wolcott Gibbs was too high-strung to live at peace with the world; he exhausted himself fighting rear-guard actions in private, inescapable wars of the mind and spirit. He was a tortured man. ("There was a hard ball of panic in his stomach," he wrote of one of his characters, who could only have been himself.) He enjoyed the society of cats and the relatively tranquil companionship of a few well-tempered friends. Of late years, he fought against the odds of poor health. Two important things happened to him about twenty years ago: he fell under the spell of the theatre and began contributing the reviews that won him the respect of the theatrical world and the gratitude of paying customers, and he fell desperately in love with Fire Island, where the sun and the wind and the untidy civilization of that relaxed and accessible sandbar supplied him with ingredients missing in Manhattan. Fire Island was his Riviera, his Left Bank, his South Sea Island. We who knew and loved him felt particularly grateful that he managed to be there when he died, where he most liked to be, right in the middle of his season in the sun.

When he was a youngster attending the Riverdale Country School, Gibbs once strode the boards; he played Puck in "A Midsummer Night's Dream," wearing a costume covered with tiny bells. The director gave him explicit instructions for portraying the part; "I want you to be a little whirlwind," he said, and the young actor soberly accepted the assignment. He leaped and shook continuously throughout the show, his bells effectively drowning out the voices of all the other members of the cast. This episode came back to us, remembering Gibbs as we used to know him in his first flights of editorial duty. He was a singularly restless co-worker, a sheet of copy paper always in his machine, and the rapid bursts of composition audible as you passed his door. He was, in all truth, a whirlwind; and in these offices can still be heard the pure and irreplaceable sound of his wild bells.

HAROLD ROSS

A RECOLLECTION

S.M. Behrman

1966

THE LAST TASK that Harold Ross, the founder and first editor of *The New Yorker*, worked on was a profile I wrote of a baffling and fascinating character named Gabriel Pascal. Pascal had achieved sudden fame because, in some mysterious way, he had persuaded Bernard Shaw to give him the exclusive rights to film his plays. The various theories to account for this remarkable arrangement are described in the profile itself, which appears in this volume. However, it is a fact that Shaw made the arrangement—a dazzling and ultimately inexplicable fact. Pascal's own account of it varied with his mood, as his accounts of everything varied with his moods. Every great film company in the world— at a time when there *were* great film companies—had been importuning Shaw for years to sell them these rights. The terms they offered had been fabulous. He nevertheless gave them, finally, to Pascal, a penniless and obscure Hungarian adventurer whom, evidently, he found irresistible. When I was working with Ross on this profile, in 1951, I did not realize how very ill he was. My last conference with Ross on Pascal took place in Ross's rooms in the Algonquin Hotel, a week before his death.

This is not the place for a memoir of Ross. I hope, one day, to write one. I will simply say that what I have read about him—including Thurber's book—seems to me very wide of the mark. He is, for example, generally described as "protean," as having been all things to all men—mercurial, unpredictable, capricious. Actually, Ross was one of the most single-minded, dedicated, and coherent men I have ever known. He was always the same. He was himself incapable of affectation and quick to detect it. He had one passion, and it animated his every action and thought: to maintain the excellence of *The New Yorker*. No artist absorbed in a work-in-progress could be more passionate than Ross was in the perfection of his magazine. Wolcott Gibbs once told me that when Ross wrote, opposite a paragraph Gibbs had written, "Is this interesting?" Gibbs was invariably forced to admit to himself, after he had got over his preliminary irritation, that the paragraph really wasn't very interesting. In 1944, Ross practically forced me to go to London, where the V-2s were falling, to write an impression of wartime England ("The Suspended Drawing Room," which is also contained in this volume). In 1946, he asked me to go again. I protested. "But Ross," I said, "I've been. I've done it." "Write me a cold piece on London," he said. I went. London was indeed cold. The resulting piece was called "It's Cold at Lady Windermere's." It was a singular mission: to register frigidity. Ross's instinct was sound.

No one I have ever known had a shrewder sense of his own limitations. But Ross had no intention of allowing *The New Yorker* to be hemmed in by these limitations. His own "social conscience"—as an abstraction—was not acute. When he found himself badgered by radio-bullying on commuter trains, his rebellion crystallized in a successful crusade in *The New Yorker* columns to free the captive audience. But, for example, the Spanish Civil War did not impinge on him. Somewhere in his consciousness he felt that perhaps it should, but it didn't. He felt that *The New Yorker* must reflect the moral sense it abraded in others. He therefore nurtured one of the most sensitive social consciences in this country, that of E.B. White, and gave him the run of the magazine in matters involving social conscience. In effect, he substituted E.B. White's conscience for his own. As long as the conscience of *The New Yorker* was all right, he rested easy.

Several years before I had worked on the Pascal, Ross had been after me to do another project: a profile of Chaim Weizmann, who was to be the first President of Israel. I had seen as much as I could of Dr. Weizmann during his frequent visits here in the years before the State of Israel came into being. I had talked a lot about him to Ross, and had told him of my fascination with this extraordinary man. The Near East was no more in Ross's purview than was Spain. He was not a Zionist—he was not even a non-Zionist. About all that his mind was *tabula rasa*. But he sniffed something important in the ambiance of Weizmann, some portent. He began urging me to write a profile of this statesman without portfolio, this phenomenal man who went about the world, as Sir Isaiah Berlin has pointed out, with the authority and the dignity of a head of state, although he had no army, no navy, and no state. Ross never let up on Weizmann. "You can let it run as long as you like," he said. I had many letters from him on the subject. One reached me in Hollywood. "For God's sake," he wrote, "get out of Hollywood and come to Zion." It was a singular plea to receive from a man who was not even a non-Zionist. As it happened, Dr. Weizmann was in Hollywood when Ross's letter arrived. I showed it to him. He was amused. He consented to sit for me and invited me to accompany him to Arrowhead, where he was spending the weekend. This weekend I have described in the piece on Dr. Weizmann contained in this book. The piece never appeared in *The New Yorker*; it was printed in the *Festschrift* volume presented to Dr. Weizmann on his seventieth birthday. But it had its genesis with Ross. Because of his insistence, I had begun taking notes for a profile long before that weekend in Arrowhead.

Professor Harold Laski, of the London School of Economics, was a friend of mine, and I always visited him when I was in London. Like many of his colleagues at the University, Laski was a great admirer of *The New Yorker*. The University, apparently, could afford only one copy; by unwritten law, equal time was allotted each member of the faculty. One day, Laski told me, a colleague came up to him, panting with indignation, and said, "Professor X has had it for more than an *hour!*" On one of his visits here, Laski asked to meet Ross. The meeting was arranged for a lunch at 21. Ross came in all spruced up and tidy, as is becoming when you are meeting a professor. Somewhere in his past, Ross had picked up and read a volume of *The Autobiography of Herbert Spencer,* and he mentioned this feat casually. "I happened to be reading the autobiography of Herbert Spencer the other day," said Ross dreamily—an opening he felt appropriate for a professor. Laski's eyes lit up behind his glasses. He sized up Ross at once as a Herbert Spencer man. He warmed to Ross and plunged at once into an intimate discourse, as one Spencerian to another. I saw panic in Ross's eyes as it dawned on him that Spencer had written other books besides the autobiography and that, regrettably, Laski seemed to be familiar with them. When Laski stopped for breath, Ross switched abruptly to a visit he had had the day before from Noel Coward. By this sudden shift of terrain, Ross forced Laski to the defensive, since Laski was less at home in Coward than he was in Spencer. As a result of this lunch, with all its ups and downs, Ross got a book review out of Laski.

Another Englishman, a friend of Laski's, equally eminent but considerably different, also asked to meet Ross. This gentleman is one of the most brilliant talkers in the world, but his utterance has a breakneck velocity and a uniqueness of intonation that force you to hang onto his sentences as they race by, as to a rope on an Alpine climb. At one point, Ross asked to shift chairs so as to be nearer his guest, but, alas, proximity did not bring clarification. As I walked away from the restaurant with Ross, he said mournfully, "I didn't understand a goddam word your friend said, but he can write anything for us that he likes."

The profile of Pascal was one I had begun many years before Ross's death. I had promised Gabby, as he was known to his innumerable acquaintances, that I would not publish it without letting him see it and without getting his approval. I had made such promises to profile subjects before. Theretofore, without exception, these subjects had proved amenable. Usually, they were so pleased to be written about at all that they did not hear whatever overtones of denigration there may have been. But Pascal was hurt by my portrait of him. I reported this to Ross, who brushed it aside. "It's a very friendly profile," he said. "Let me meet Pascal. I'll fix it up with him." I arranged for the three of us to have dinner in the Oak Room at the Plaza. I had been telling Ross all this time how genial Gabby was. And he usually was. He had a fluorescent smile, which slowly lit up the wide expanse of his swarthy face, till it reached the tips of his ears. But there was nothing fluorescent about Pascal when he came to our table at the Plaza. His expression was grim. I introduced him to Ross. It was like the first encounter between Lord Halifax and Molotov in San Francisco—Lord Halifax smiling, Molotov stony-faced. I could see that Ross was taken aback. Pascal and I were on a first-name basis; he pronounced mine "Som." Before even sitting down, Pascal delivered himself of a short address: "Schopenhauer say it is fine dividing-line which separate char-la-*tan* from genius. Som has put me on the wrong side of line."

It was inauspicious. Ross looked at me, an expression of bewilderment in his blue eyes. "Where is the genial character you have been telling me about?" he seemed to be asking. During the meal, Pascal never brightened. His vanity was inordinate, and I had wounded it by suggesting that the first Shavian film he had made, *Pygmalion*, had really been directed not by him—although it had been so announced in the credit-titles—but by Leslie

Howard, who played Higgins. I had not made this statement lightly. I had talked to everyone connected with the filming of *Pygmalion*, and this was the consensus. Pascal vehemently rejected this notion. "I would hate for Charlotte to see this," he said. He was referring to Shaw's wife. I could see that what I had written was a threat to him. The first solid ground under his feet that he had ever known was this relationship he had achieved with Shaw. He felt that it was being eroded. I knew that Mrs. Shaw did not entirely share her husband's delight in Gabby. I offered at once to delete the offending sentence. Pascal was momentarily appeased, but he was not really comforted. He began to harangue Ross with a list of his achievements from early childhood—all intended to persuade him that he was not char-la-*tan*, as I had invidiously suggested. "When I was sixteen, I was already genius," he assured Ross. In the course of this persuasion, he dropped the names of his friends and prospective collaborators on films—Sir Basil Zaharoff, Eamon De Valera, and Gandhi. Among several lavish offers he had already made to me were proposals that we go to see these eminent pals of his with a view to filming their lives. I could see Ross stumbling to find a pathway through the thicket of Pascal's ecumenical projects. All Ross wanted to do was to persuade Pascal that my piece was "friendly." Pascal remained obdurate. He insisted that he couldn't bear the idea of having Charlotte see what I had written. He didn't mind so much about "the sweet Irish Pope" (his sobriquet for GBS); it was Charlotte he was sensitive about. I suppose he felt sure that nothing any scribbler wrote could possibly dislodge the love and esteem Shaw felt for him but that my hints might give Mrs. Shaw a talking-point. I saw myself depriving Pascal of a lifeline. In my mind, right then, I gave up the project The dinner was certainly a failure. Ross and I both promised to have another go at the piece, and to see whether we could get it into such shape that it would not disillusion Charlotte Shaw. Years passed, and both Shaw and his wife died, but Ross continued to be enthusiastic about the Pascal project. To the end, Ross insisted that Pascal must come to see that my piece on him was friendly. Had Ross lived for another meeting with him, perhaps Pascal would have yielded.

When I got out of college, I tried for years to make my living as a prose writer. I contributed to various magazines—especially to *The Smart Set*, edited by H.L. Mencken and George Jean Nathan. But there was no living in it. One day, in a moment of despair, I dramatized a short story of mine that had appeared in *The Smart Set*. The play opened and was a success. I was then caught up in a whirl of motion-picture writing and in other plays. All this time it was a frustration for me that I wasn't writing prose. One day—I don't precisely remember where or when—I met Ross. He asked me to write for him. I did a short, juvenile profile of George Gershwin, which he accepted. From then on, I was seeing him all the time and writing for him the pieces now contained in this book. He released for me a dammed-up means of expression. I am greatly indebted to him, also, for the exhilaration and delight of his company, from the moment I met him to the evening I spent with him a week before his death.

H.W. ROSS

E.B. White

1951

R OSS DIED in Boston, unexpectedly, on the night of
December 6th, and we are writing this in New York
(unexpectedly) on the morning of December 7th. This is known,
in these offices that Ross was so fond of, as a jam. Ross always
knew when we were in a jam and usually got on the phone to
offer advice and comfort and support. When our phone rang
just now, and in that split second before the mind focusses, we
thought, "Good! Here it comes!" But this old connection is
broken beyond fixing. The phone has lost its power to explode
at the right moment and in the right way.

Actually, things are not going as badly as they might; the sheet
of copy paper in the machine is not as hard to face as we feared.
Sometimes a love letter writes itself, and we love Ross so, and
bear him such respect, that these quick notes, which purport to
record the sorrow that runs through here and dissolves so many
people, cannot possibly seem overstated or silly. Ross, even on
this terrible day, is a hard man to keep quiet; he obtrudes—his
face, his voice, his manner, even his amused interest in the critical
proceedings. If he were accorded the questionable privilege of
stopping by here for a few minutes, he would gorge himself on
the minor technical problems that a magazine faces when it

must do something in a hurry and against some sort of odds—in this case, emotional ones of almost overpowering weight. He would be far more interested in the grinding of the machinery than in what was being said about him.

All morning, people have wandered in and out of our cell, some tearfully, some guardedly, some boisterously, most of them long-time friends in various stages of repair. We have amused ourself thinking of Ross's reaction to this flow. "Never bother a writer" was one of his strongest principles. He used to love to drop in, himself, and sit around, but was uneasy the whole time because of the carking feeling that if only he would get up and go away, we might settle down to work and produce something. To him, a writer at work, whether in the office or anywhere in the outside world, was an extraordinarily interesting, valuable, but fragile object; and he half expected it to fall into a thousand pieces at any moment.

The report of Ross's death came over the telephone in a three-word sentence that somehow managed to embody all the faults that Ross devoted his life to correcting. A grief-stricken friend in Boston, charged with the task of spreading the news but too dazed to talk sensibly, said, "It's all over." He meant that Ross was dead, but the listener took it to mean that the operation was over. Here, in three easy words, were the ambiguity, the euphemistic softness, the verbal infirmity that Harold W. Ross spent his life thrusting at. Ross regarded every sentence as the enemy, and believed that if a man watched closely enough, he would discover the vulnerable spot, the essential weakness. He devoted his life to making the weak strong—a rather specialized form of blood transfusion, to be sure, but one that he believed in with such a consuming passion that his spirit infected others and inspired them, and lifted them. Whatever it was, this contagion, this vapor in these marshes, it spread. None escaped it. Nor is it likely to be dissipated in a hurry.

His ambition was to publish one good magazine, not a string of successful ones, and he thought of *The New Yorker* as a sort of movement. He came equipped with not much knowledge and only two books—Webster's Dictionary and Fowler's "Modern English Usage." These books were his history, his geography, his literature, his art, his music, his everything. Some people found Ross's scholastic deficiencies quite appalling, and were not sure they had met the right man. But he was the right man, and the only question was whether the other fellow was capable of being tuned to Ross's vibrations. Ross had a thing that is at least as good as, and sometimes better than, knowledge: he had a sort of natural drive in the right direction, plus a complete respect for the work and ideas and opinions of others. It took a little while to get on to the fact that Ross, more violently than almost anybody, was proceeding in a good direction, and carrying others along with him, under torrential conditions. He was like a boat being driven at the mercy of some internal squall, a disturbance he himself only half understood, and of which he was at times suspicious.

In a way, he was a lucky man. For a monument he has the magazine to date—one thousand three hundred and ninety-nine issues, born in the toil and pain that can be appreciated only by those who helped in the delivery room. These are his. They stand, unchangeable and open for inspection. We are, of course, not in a position to estimate the monument, even if we were in the mood to. But we are able to state one thing unequivocally: Ross set up a great target and pounded himself to pieces trying to hit it square in the middle. His dream was a simple dream; it was pure and had no frills: he wanted the magazine to be good, to be funny, and to be fair.

We say he was lucky. Some people cordially disliked him. Some were amused but not impressed. And then, last, there are the ones we have been seeing today, the ones who loved him and had him for a friend—people he looked after, and who looked after him. These last are the ones who worked close enough to him, and long enough with him, to cross over the barrier reef of noisy shallows that ringed him, into the lagoon that was Ross himself—a rewarding, and even enchanting, and relatively quiet place, utterly trustworthy as an anchorage. Maybe these people had all the luck. The entrance wasn't always easy to find.

He left a note on our desk one day apropos of something that had pleased him in the magazine. The note simply said, "I am encouraged to go on." That is about the way we feel today, because of his contribution. We are encouraged to go on.

When you took leave of Ross after a calm or stormy meeting, he always ended with the phrase that has become as much a part of the office as the paint on the walls. He would wave his limp hand, gesturing you away. "All right," he would say. "God bless you." Considering Ross's temperament and habits, this was a rather odd expression. He usually took God's name in vain if he took it at all. But when he sent you away with this benediction, which he uttered briskly and affectionately, and in which he and God seemed all scrambled together, it carried a warmth and sincerity that never failed to carry over. The words are so familiar to his helpers and friends here that they provide the only possible way to conclude this hasty notice and to take our leave. We cannot convey his manner. But with much love in our heart, we say, for everybody, "All right, Ross. God bless you!"

LETTERS FROM
THE NEW YORKER
ARCHIVES

August 11, 1947

To the Messrs. Gibbs, Thurber, White:

Greetings. A writer named Allen Churchill, heretofore unknown to me, is doing a piece on *The New Yorker* for *Cosmopolitan* and has the idea that he wants to quote some interoffice memos in it, being under the impression that these are interesting as hell. He seems to have been told so. The fact is that certain notes written at various times by you gentlemen, among others, *would* be interesting, I believe, and also entertaining, and doubtless many of them are around. How do you stand about letting him have some of yours? They could be dug up and shown to you first.

I deplore such projects as this story, but don't know what to do about them, other than to be decently cooperative. This organization has been bothering everybody in New York for twenty years and I'm ashamed to do otherwise.

Please let me know.

There is always Gibbs's note on the proofs of Max Eastman's book, that "... he got American humor down and broke its arm."

H.W. Ross

February 21, 1925

To Contributors:

The first issue virtually sold out in New York City in the first thirty-six hours and we were as surprised as the next one. We printed 30,000 of which 18,000 were distributed in town. Reports from outside New York are encouraging. Amount of mere curiosity, non-repeat sale unknown. The print order on the second issue is 40,000.

We had not intended to look so much like a humorous magazine and regret that the appearance, together with the contents, tend to give a wrong impression. We are changing our make-up somewhat and are trying to be a little more serious and purposeful.

It is hoped that the early issues will give a better idea of what we want. We are going to try to be exceedingly topical. We will go to press on Wednesday and be on sale the following Tuesday morning, which will help. Short stuff may be taken even on a Thursday. Longer material will have to be got in a week or two earlier than this.

Most of the departmental stuff will be done by staff writers although contributions are wanted for the "Talk of the Town" department, anecdotes about people more or less well known, new stories, etc.

If these are roughly set down as notes it will be acceptable. Items for "In Our Midst" also are sought.

The paragraph department ("In Our Midst") has been weak and offerings are earnestly sought. We want to say something in this department and at the same time keep it more or less entertaining and bright.

We hope to give a prompt reading in the future (admitting and apologizing for some derelection in the past due to getting the early issues to press).

We also want humorous drawings and cartoons, and ideas for same.

Harold Ross advises early editor Ralph Ingersoll on how to squeeze writer Alexander Woollcott.

[1926]

Ingersoll:

On the rate. Try this–pay him for one of the pieces, the longer one. If he complains tell him bookkeeping error, other not paid for yet. He will get over the fifteen cent [per word] idea soon. I will get him over it if necessary. You have got to take the brunt on Wooll. Alibi vaguely, or what you think of. He will write more....

———

Letter from Harold Ross to Dorothy Parker, one of the magazine's first defining voices.

February 26 1927

Dorothy:

The verses came and God Bless Me: if I never do anything else I can say I ran a magazine that printed some of your stuff. Tearful thanks. Check, proof etc. to follow. We want to use one of the verses under the title that the ones now appearing. Think this a good idea. Is it satisfactory? If not please say so and we will jump in the lake. It is better, though, to spread your stuff out because it reminds people of you oftener and will help sell your book. I'm nothing if not practical, and one of the leading men in New York although still in my early thirties.

Ross

In 1936 Harold Ross financed a Hollywood restaurant launched by his pal Dave Chasen. He queries the menu as strictly as an article, his advice creating a Hollywood institution that lasted 59 years.

October 4th, 1937

Dear Dave:

A few brief remarks following the telephone conversation, hurriedly put down:

The salmon will be ordered tomorrow (Monday) and I'll get right to work on the lobsters. I'll order some sent out if I can find where to get them—which I can if they're obtainable.

You missed my point on the French menu business. I wasn't advocating that you change your dishes at all; I was pointing out that there isn't a single French dish that can't be described in English and a God damned sight better than it can be described in French and that you might consider dropping the French language in a place like yours and putting an end to a lot of nonsensical posing that has been going on in American restaurants for decades. I said this for what it is worth, but use your own judgment of course, and you'll hear no more out of me, or not much. But for Christ's sake, if you're going to use French use it right and don't have a menu printed that would be an acute pain between the shoulders for anyone who is the least bit literate. Even if your customers don't look at your menu, or can't read French, or English, either, I might want to send someone in sometime and I wouldn't want to be embarrassed. I enclose a sheet pointing out fourteen errors in your, or your printer's reproduction of the French language. If you're going to use French use it. Get someone who knows the language to go over the printers' proof of the menu. And tell your printer to get French accent marks and use them, or get another printer. You

328

can't print French without accent marks. They're part of the language. You can't even do this in Hollywood. Suppose Sam Goldwyn should come in.

And when you get around to it, get a decent looking menu. The one I have is the most offensively ugly typographical job I've seen in twenty years. And have your English copy read, too. Don't (in your ad on the back, say: "Dave Chasen Maitre d' Airline for…" Say "Dave Chasen, Maitre d'Airline". Put in the comma and no space after "d' ". Don't say "New York Meats— used exclusively". Say "New York Meats Used Exclusively". Or, at most "New York Meats, used exclusively."

I'll let you know about the lobster right away.

Sincerely,

P.S. Why list three kinds of herring, all at the same price? Why not get the best herring and serve it and let it go at that? Who the hell knows the difference? Why serve Columbia River salmon at all, if you can get the best? Why not serve tree-ripened olives, or green-ripe, as I think they're called on the can, one of the greatest delicacies in the world?

H.W.R.

P.S. #2 About the insurance: It doesn't matter what company you take it out through, I should say. If Dan has any objection to your going to any outfit you want I'll have him write you. Otherwise go ahead. This taking out insurance is the customary thing under the circumstances; moreover, if you get hit by a truck, or the old gal comes back, I don't want to be tangled up trying to manage a restaurant in California with just Ellis in charge.

H.W.R.

P.S. #3 Maybe you ought to give an anniversary party for the bunch that was at your opening, and possibly more (including your lawyer friend).

H.W.R.

Writer Geoffrey Hellman spent most of his five decade career at The New Yorker, *as both a journalist and a humorist.*

March 16, 1942

Hellman:

All I know is what I read in the papers, and from these I learn that George White is your wife's former husband's lawyer. He was my first wife's lawyer, and a man I bitterly resent. I am ready to gang him at any time you say.

Ross

———

Editor Gus Lobrano, along with Katharine White, helped define the magazine's fiction aesthetic.

July 9, 1942

Dear Mr. Lobrano:

This letter is to commit to paper our oral understanding in the matter of your activities in connection with possible military service by yourself. The New Yorker recognizes that many men in your position, facing the possibility of eventually being drafted and thereafter feeling the prospect of supporting their families largely on their service pay, are seeking commissions in the armed service for purposes of insuring a larger income. In view of your not doing so, but awaiting the decision of your draft board as to your service, The New Yorker agrees that, if you eventually are drafted into the Army it will, for a period of two years from the date of your induction, pay you the difference between whatever pay you actually receive from the Army and the base pay of a Captain in the Army, these payments to be made monthly to you, or to your wife if you so direct, or to anyone else you nominate.

Sincerely yours,

H.W. Ross

July 9, 1942

Dear Mr. Lobrano:

This letter is to commit to paper our oral understanding in the matter of your activities in connection with possible military service by yourself. The New Yorker recognizes that many men in your position, facing the possibility of eventually being drafted and thereafter feeling the prospect of supporting their families largely on their service pay, are seeking commissions in the armed service for purposes of insuring a larger income. In view of your not doing so, but awaiting the decision of your draft board as to your service, The New Yorker agrees that, if you eventually are drafted into the Army it will, for a period of two years from the date of your induction, pay you the difference between whatever pay you actually receive from the Army and the base pay of a Captain in the Army, these payments to be made monthly to you, or to your wife if you so direct, or to anyone else you nominate.

Sincerely yours,

H. W. Ross

Mr. G. S. Lobrano

Letter from Ross to E.B. White about Reader's Digest *publisher De Witt Wallace.*

May 7th [1943]

White:

After a brief spell of breathlessness, I had several loud chuckles over your defiance of Wallace, and I continue to have them. I am carrying your note around with me and referring to it whenever life seems grim. My admiration for your boldness is unbounded. You have defied the biggest giant in the business and, by God, it's the first time I ever heard of anyone turning down his big dough.

Whatever Wallace may think of your merits and your wordage, he cannot exceed me in the former, and as for the latter, I have never seen you use an unnecessary word. I am willing to take an oath to this effect. Take your Comments this week, exactly right as to length. You are a man who should not be digested; hydrochloric acid should never be applied....

Ross

Harold Ross persisted with ideas he believed in. This follow-up to Shawn evolved into a 6-year journey for S.N. Behrman, profiling art dealer Lord Joseph Duveen.

April 19, 1945

Mr. Shawn:

I talked to Liebling and he did not take seriously my idea of his doing a series on art dealers, so the field is clear for Behrman. If Behrman doesn't want to do it, though, I want to put it up to Liebling again. I have remind so it won't get lost entirely.

H.W. Ross

Hobart 'Hobie' Weekes spent nearly half a century as a writer and editor at The New Yorker.

August 23, 1945

Dear Weekes:

I got your telegram and was heartened. I hope you come up, and I hope to Jesus that you are in a mood to go to work soon, because you are the only man around who would relieve Shawn appreciably and he has taken more than any other man I know of in this war, and that goes for General Marshall and a lot of others I can name. He has done two-and-a-half jobs for four years, working every night practically and every weekend, having been driven in a most inhuman manner. It is heart-rending.

I am in a position to swing a big lump of dough your way, and will do so, but I want to talk to you.

As ever,
H.W. Ross

Roald Dahl's first experience with The New Yorker's *editing process captures the love-hate dynamic shared by many writers. He published a total of ten stories at the magazine over the course of a decade.*

July 13th 1949

Dear Mr. Lobrano:

I had written you off as a bunch of cantankerous bums who try to get their own way and then refuse to play when they find they can't. Then your letter came; and a very nice letter it was.

I return the galleys, practically unaltered, and I approve of your publishing the story as it now stands. There are one or two very minor adjustments, as you will see, and I'll be grateful if you would allow them.

The story has, of course, been cut in certain places more than I should wish, with a subsequent slight loss of suspense, particularly in the passage where Klausner hesitates to swing the axe the second time; but on the other hand, you have come such a long way to meet me that it would be foolish and presumptious of me not to go along a little way with you as well.

I hasten to admit, also, that the story, in its present form, is a better one than that which you received in the very first instance. I'm grateful for the plot-change suggestion which Mr. Moss made originally.

But on the other hand it is time to say that I was so goddamn bloody mad about the cutting and changing which was done in the first galley, and so discouraged by the attitude of magazine editors in general, that I have been unable to write anything since I decided that I didn't want all the sorrow and heart boiling which editors cause, not any more any way, and I decided that I would give up whole time writing for the time being and earn my living as a bookmaker instead.

That is a curious transition, but it is taking place. I am setting up a bookmaker's office in London right now, and soon, each day, I shall plod up there to take the telephones and the bets and watch the ticker tick. In the evenings I shall write. I shall still write. But I want to be in a position where I have another livelihood upon which I can depend and consequently where I can tell all the editors and publishers in the world to go and stuff themselves if I feel inclined.

So if I'm a successful bookie, I shall have the New Yorker to thank, and all the editors (including Mr. Moss!) will get a free bet on next year's English derby.

I've written some bad stories, but some I like immensely. This one you've bought is one. Another is a very short one which Ann Watkins is hawking unsuccessfully around the place and which was broadcast over here several times. I should have thought it was just your stuff, but I believe you've turned it down. Have you yourself read it. It's called "People Nowadays". You know, if you wished to make a nice public repudiation of Mr. Spender's views, you should publish my first angry letter to Mr. Moss and your last letter to me.

But thank you for your help. You have made me a happier man.

Yours sincerely,

s/Roald Dahl

Ross's request for something less "psychopathic" from Truman Capote is typical of his awkward locutions around anything sexual. Ironically, the biggest success Capote and the magazine would have together was In Cold Blood, *a story of two actual psychopaths, with a homoerotic subtext.*

July 27, 1949

Mr. Lobrano:

A reminder that you said you would ask Mr. Henderson to suggest, over the telephone, to Miss Ives, Truman Capote's agent, that we would like to see any Capote stories that aren't too psychopathic.

H.W. Ross

———

Dorothy Parker writing the ever loyal Ross from Hollywood.

DEC 5 1949

Dear Harold, could you please possibly like this?

Loves and hopes—

Dorothy

While Ross was generous with his praise of A.J. Liebling, they battled constantly, typically over expenses. This rare letter from Liebling about politics captures the generation gap between Liebling and the older Ross.

March 7

Dear Harold,

In one of your notes on the second part of the Bradley piece you wrote that one paragraph (which, incidentally, you misread) looked to you like just a lot of "sneering leftist dope." This pointed up a misunderstanding which has begun to worry me. When in the past you made occasional cracks about how "left" I was I alwyas thought you were ~~in~~ simply trying to needle me. When you said at lunch the other day that I "never wrote a story without having an axe to grind," you succeeded. It occurred to me then that you really think I am some sort of crypto-~~commie~~ communist, and have completely forgotten (or chosen to ignore) my point of view expressed in print during the past 15 years, which has never changed at all.

In 1938 I published a book, "Back Where I Came From," composed partly of New Yorker pieces. It got good reviews except in the Daily Worker and New Masses, which slammed it. The New Masses reviewer Rovere, was particularly contemptuous of the anti-Marxian, New Yorkerish superficiality of the job.

In the summer of 1939, as you must remember, I was eager to go to France for what the Communists here were denouncing as an imperialist war, and I was so much in favor of that war that I am afraid it impaired my reporting. I wrote, in the New Yorker, of how Communists had been sab-otaging the French war effort, and in 1940 I hinted strongly, in the New Yorker Paris Letter, that the United States Army Air Corps should intervene against the Russians in Finland. This may have been silly, but it

listened to them, ----- The two propaganda groups had taken the xxxxxxx
same line[against intervention] --- Robert "Maynard Hutchins of the Univ
-ersity of Chicago who was the accredited intellect of the money people,
hit exactly the same note on that as the New Masses.-----

"June 22, (1941) when the news of the invasion of Russia got around in
New York,was a hot Sunday. I walked up through Union Square,where the
free-style catch-as-catch-can "Marxist arguers hang out,and all the boys
who two days earlier had been howling for Churchill's blood were now
screaming for us to get right into the war. 'Wee Well,' I thought,'we xx
are now on thesame side of a question for once,anyway.' Somehow, I remembered my old French general who had said to his estranged friend,'I
will shake hands if you have arrived at better sentiments.''
       xxxxxxxxly pertinent,
   Most xxxxxxxxpointxinxhisxargxmxxx,I wrote:

"I think I must say here what I believe myself," because if you a
are going to see a war through a man's eyes you ought to know what there
is behind them, I think democracy a most precious thing,not because any
democratic state is perfect,but because it is perfectible. It sounds heartb
breakingly banal,but I believe that you cannot even fool most of the people
most of the time, They are quite likely to vote in their own interest. I
also believe that since a democracy is made up of individual electors,the
electors will protect the rights of the individual, A democracy may sometimes grant too little power to its government and at others allow government to infringe on the rights of the individual - Prohibition is
example enough - but the vote always offers the means of correcting imbalance,and the repeal of prohibition is an example of that. Any system that
is run by a few,whether they sit in a Fascist Grand Council or at the
pinnacle of a pyramid of holding companies,is a damned bad system,and Italy
is a fine example of that,but unfortunately we didn't have its finish to
point to in 1940-41. And so much for my ideology,"

   Road Back to Paris,p 335
   I xxxxxxx have never seen reason to change any of thatxxxxxxxxxxx
xxxxxxxxxxxxxxxxxxxxxxxxxxxxxxxxxxxxxxxxxxxxxxxxxxxxxxxxx

   I went back to the war and then in 1943 wrote a long piece you may
remember called Colonel "Brenoff and the "newspaper PM,about the Russ
colonel I roomed with in Tunisia,who feared I was about to xxxxxx accuse
him of stealing my xxxxxxx lost watch. He helped me understand why the
Russians as a nation,just as individuals,were so damned suspicious,but
I dxxt think my piece was any boost for him ot them, In the fall of 1948
when you sprang your famous scheme of sending me to Russia,they wouldn't
have me.

sure was early. During the war the FBI used to talk of "premature anti-Fascism." Mine was premature anti-Communism.

In 1943, when I was home from my third round-trip to the war, I ~~wore~~ wrote in my book The Road Back to Paris:

"Although I believed that in the United States, as in France, the para-Fascists were more dangerous than the Communists, the latter caused me considerably more personal annoyance, because a number of my friends had listened to them. ----- The two propaganda groups had taken the ~~same lin~~ same line [against intervention] --- Robert Maynard Hutchins of the University of Chicago who was the accredited intellect of the money people, hit exactly the same note on that as the New Masses. -----

"June 22, (1941) when the news of the invasion of Russia got around in New York, was a hot Sunday. I walked up through Union Squarre, where the free-style catch-as-catch-can Marxist arguers hang out, and all the boys who two days earlier had been howling for Churchill's blood were now screaming for us to get right into the war. '~~Wee~~ Well,' I thought, 'we ~~are~~ are now on thesame side of a question for once, anyway.' Somehow, I remembered my old French general who had said to his estranged friend, 'I will shake hands if you have arrived at better sentiments.'"

~~pertinently~~ pertinent,

Most ~~to the point in his argument~~, I wrote:

"I think I must say here what I believe myself, because if you ~~a~~ are going to see a war through a man's eyes you ought to know what there is behind them. I think democracy a most precious thing, not because any democratic state is perfect, but because it is perfectible. It sounds heart~~b~~ breakingly banal, but I believe that you cannot even fool most of the people most of the time. They are quite likely to vote in their own interest. I also believe that since a democracy is made up of individual electors, the electors will protect the rights of the individual. A democracy may sometimes grant too little power to its government and at others allow government to infringe on the rights of the individual – Prohibition is example enough – but the vote always offers the means of correcting imbalance, and the repeal of prohibition is an example of that. Any system that is run by a few, whether they sit in a Fascist Grand Council or at the pinnacle of a pyramid of holding companies, is a damned bad system, and Italy is a fine example of that, but unfortunately we didn't have its finish to point to in 1940–41. And so much for my ideology."

Road Back to Paris, p.120

I ~~seen~~ have never seen reason to change any of that, ~~and only people who would like a system run by a few – the Howards, Hearsts, Luces etc. Peglers, etc. who are vocally or tacitly tacitly anti-democratic can possibly disagree.~~

I went back to the war and then in 1945 wrote a long piece you may remember called Colonel Baranoff and the Newspaper PM, about the Russ colonel I roomed with in Tunisia, who feared I was about to ~~frame~~ accuse him of stealing my ~~watch~~ lost watch. He helped me understand why the Russians as a nation, just as individuals, were so damned suspicious, but I don't think my piece was any boost for him or them. In the fall of 1946 when you sprang your famous scheme of sending me to Russia, they wouldn't have me.

After I began writing the Wayward Press my way, however, I began to get the elbow, old bastards writing in to me and saying I had been a fine war correspondent, but needling newspapers was revolution. ~~I also~~ ~~sex more approving letters than out of any~~ ~~other kind of stuff I xxxxx for the New Year~~. Noting this response from the Ed Jameses etc. I wrote in that subversive publication,

After I began writing the Wayward Press or war,however,I began to get the elbow,old bastards writing in to me saying I had been a fine war correspondent, but needling newspapers was revolution. Noting this response from the Ed Jameses etc. I wrote in that subversive publication,the Dartmouth Alumni Weekly,in March,1947.

"Every now and then I write a piece for the New Yorker under the head -ing of the Wayward Press (a title for the department invented by the late Robert Benchley when he started it early in the New Yorker's hectic history). In this I concern myself not with big general thoughts about Trends (my boss wouldn't stand for such),but with the treatment of special fic stories by the daily press. I am a damned sight kinder about news- papers than Colonel Glick is about the theatre, but while nobody accuses him of sedition when he rags a play,I get letters calling me a little pal of Stalin when I sneer at the New York Sun. This reflects a pitch & that newspaper publishers make to the effect that they are part of the great American heritage with a right to travel wrapped in in the folds of the flag like a bell weevil in a cotton ball. Political theatrical prof -essors and book publishers,apparently,pertake of this sacred character. This was four years ago. In 1943 I xxxthatlikexxxTrumanxxix re- signed fromtthe Committee of the Arts,Sciences and Professions,which had been organized to campaign for Roosevelt in 1944 and afterwards xx xxxxxx. I wrote a letter to PM,which published it,giving my reasons. the Progressives in combatting Wallace would simply split the Truman vote and help elect whatever sonofabitch the Republicans put up. I pointed out that this was the way the German Communists,back by refus- ing to vote for Bruening,had helped elect bring in Hitler, In the compign I took the line,as Truman did,that the Republicans were bring- ing in a lot of unimportant crap in order to steal the election. We were right,we win. That is subversive about Truman?

338

the Dartmouth Alumni ~~Monthly~~ Magazine, in March, 1947,

"Every now and then I write a piece for the New Yorker under the heading of the Wayward Press (a title for the department invented by the late Robert Benchley when he started it early in the New Yorker's ~~histor~~ history). In this I concern myself not with big general thoughts about trends (my boss wouldn't stand for such), but with the treatment of specific stories by the daily press. I am a damned sight kinder about newspapers than Wolcott Gibbs is about the theatre, but while nobody accuses him of sedition when he raps a play, I get letters calling me a little pal of Stalin when I sneer at the New York Sun. This reflects a pitch ~~s~~ that newspaper~~s~~ publishers make to the effect that they are part of the great American heritage with a right to travel wrapped in in the folds of the flag like a boll weevil in a cotton boll. Neither theatrical producers nor book publishers, apparently, partake of this sacred character."

This was four years ago. In January 1948 I ~~took the line, as Truman did~~ resigned from the Committee of the Arts, Sciences and Professions, which had been organized to campaign for Roosevelt in 1944 ~~and which I had heard xxx thing~~. I wrote a letter to PM, which published it, giving my reasons: the Progressives in nominating Wallace would simply split the Truman vote and help elect whatever sonofabitch the Republicans put up. I pointed out that this was the way the German Communists, ~~had~~ by refusing to vote for Bruening, had helped ~~elect~~ bring in Hitler. In the campaign I took the line, as Truman did, that the Republicans were bringing in a lot of unimportant crap in order to steal the election. We were right, we win. What is subversive about Truman?

In the spring of 1948 you evidently were already hearing knocks on me because I remember that before I went to Norway you told me, over in the Algonquin, not to grind my axe in favor of Finland, an ~~iorem~~ iron-curtain country where I wasn't going. I had said that if anybody could get along with both Russia and us, and incidentally find a way for us to get along with the Russians, it would be the Norwegians. I found, and reported in your honored mag, that the Norwegians had given up on the Russians as hopeless, and that they were ready to fight and then take to their ships if invaded. This was the best reporting on Norway done up to that time.

In all my pieces on the Hiss-Chambers business I carefully abstained from saying Hiss was innocent – although I firmly believe he is – but I said that he was entitled to a fair hearing, that the newspapers made a fair s econd trial impossible by the way they blackguarded the first ~~jud~~ judge and hjusrors, that Chambers was a fantastic liar (which he admitted cheerfully in court) that Parnell Thomas denied civil rights, that there was no way of making explosives from garbage, hence no secret formula, etc., etc. I was abundantly right on ~~eqeh~~ each of these counts.

The climate of the times has changed, although not so much as the Armos and Peglers would ~~have~~ like to believe. But for Christ's sake don't let anybody sell you the line that the sure proof any guy is a communist is that he never seemed to be one (for example ,me) while the only one you can trust not to be a commie is an ex-commie (Arthur ~~Koestl~~ Koestler, Whittaker Chambers, etc.) By that standard you'd be a commie yourself.

I am annoyed,
Joe Liebling

October 10, 1950

Mr. Shawn:

Precautionary note on Part IV Duveen.

In my notes I expressed wonderment as to how Berenson acquired so much wealth—his estate, library, painting collection, etc., which would seem to be of great value. What I didn't thoughtlessly realize, was that most if not all of this came through his arrangement, his partnership, with Duveen, which is obvious on second thought. On the other hand, Behrman was thoughtless in not indicating that the Berenson arrangement with Duveen was highly—if not enormously—profitable, and in giving some idea of the arrangement and of the fruits to Berenson.

The trouble is that Behrman presents Berenson as such a high-principled, non-commercial, detached person that the reader is lulled into forgetting that, after all, he wasn't a Christ or a Father Divine who just went along with no worldly goods of his own and never accumulated anything.

H. W. Ross

cc Wigglesworth

A warning from Ross to Shawn after three parts of Behrman's Duveen profile had already run.

October 10, 1950

Mr. Shawn:

Precautionary note on part IV Duveen.

In my notes I expressed wonderment as to how Berenson acquired so much wealth—his estate, library, painting collection, etc., which would seem to be of great value. What I didn't thoughtlessly realize, was that most if not all of this came through his arrangement, his partnership, with Duveen, which is obvious on second thought. On the other hand, Behrman was thoughtless in not indicating that the Berenson arrangement with Duveen was highly—if not enormously—profitable, and in giving some idea of the arrangement and of the fruits to Berenson.

The trouble is that Behrman presents Berenson as such a high-principled, non-commercial, detached person that the reader is lulled into forgetting that, after all, he wasn't a Christ or a Father Divine who just went along with no worldly goods of his own and never accumulated anything.

H.W. Ross

Letter from Simon & Schuster co-founder Richard Simon praising the November 4, 1950 issue, which featured Nathaniel Benchley, Alfred Kazin, and Janet Flanner, among others.

November 6, 1950

Dear Harold:

It's a wonderful issue of <u>The New Yorker</u> this week. After reading it I remembered a fascinating thing you told me about publishing when you and Andrea and I were driving to New York a while ago.

You said for a magazine to succeed it must bring out one or two good issues a year, and every five years it has to bring out a superlative issue. It seems to me that the current <u>New Yorker</u> is just about the best single issue I have ever read. One of the highspots is the piece about Hitler's photographer; another is Alfred Kazin's review of Budd Schulberg's book.

Sincerely yours,
Dick

no hu

January 2, 1951

Dear Ashton:

Your tele ras arrived, and your thoughtfulness
is appreciated.

What is getting me is the frequency of this
sort of thing these days—Ring Lardner, Clarence
Day, Helen Hokinson, Alva Johnston, Mencken (he
can't write any more), and so on. People talk
of the first stories we run by new writers and
the first pictures by new artists, but what is
getting me down is the number of last pieces and
pictures of old-timers we run.

Anyhow, a happy new year.

As ever,

H. W. Ross

Mr. Ashton Stevens
Chicago Herald American
326 West Madison Street
Chicago, Illinois

rp

*Response to a condolence note from Ashton Stevens,
Dean of America's drama critics in the first half of
the 20th century. Orson Welles said Stevens inspired
Joseph Cotton's character Jed in* Citizen Kane.

January 2, 1951

Dear Ashton:

Your telegram arrived, and your thoughtfulness is appreciated.

What is getting me is the frequency
of this sort of thing these days—Ring
Lardner, Clarence Day, Helen Hokinson,
Alva Johnston, Mencken (he can't write any
more), and so on. People talk of the first
stories we run by new writers and the first
pictures by new artists, but what is getting
me down is the number of <u>last</u> pieces and
pictures of old-timers we run.

Anyhow, a happy new year.

As ever,
H.W. Ross

———

*'Done + Done'—one of Harold Ross's favorite
'Rossisms.'*

———

*Condolence telegram from film director and early
Chasen's chum Frank Capra.*

WESTERN UNION

NA073 PD=FALLBROOK CALIF 17 1135A=
=THE NEWYORKER MAGAZINE=

THE NEW YORK HAS LOST ITS FATHER,
MOTHER AND LOVER AND THE MAGAZINE
WORLD ITS MOST BRILLIANT EDITOR
STOP IN THE LIFE OF HIS FRIENDS HE
LEFT A BIG HOLE FOR THIS HOMELY,
SOPHISTICATED WARM HEARTED IMP
TOOK UP A LOT OF ROOM IN LIVING STOP
ONLY ONE THING HE COULDNT DO. HE
COULDNT BE BORING=
FRANK CAPRA=

WESTERN
UNION

NA073 PD=FALLBROOK CALIF 17 1135A=
THE NEWYORKER MAGAZINE=

THE NEW YORK HAS LOST ITS FATHER, MOTHER AND LOVER AND THE
MAGAZINE WORLD ITS MOST BRILLIANT EDITOR STOP IN THE LIFE
OF HIS FRIENDS HE LEFT A BIG HOLE FOR THIS HOMELY,
SOPHISTICATED WARM HEARTED IMP TOOK UP A LOT OF ROOM IN
LIVING STOP ONLY ONE THING HE COULDNT DO. HE COULDNT
BE BORING=
FRANK CAPRA=

December 19, 1951

Dear Sir:

This is in appreciation to the writer who turned in the obit on Harold Ross. It is a beautiful and a moving piece of writing and I know that many share my gratitude for it.

We have known many great editors, and in my book he is among the greatest. I knew him once as "Hobo" Ross, at the time he slaved in that ancient salt mine, the San Francisco Call — later to become a hyphenated adjunct of the Hearst empire. (The newspaper, I mean.)

He was quite a guy. Neil Hitt revived an antique hilarious anecdote covering the evening when Hobo matched adjectives with Corporal Duffy of the SF Police in last year's edition of the SF Press Club's annual, Scoop.

My agent attempted at various times to foist scripts of mine on Hobo, always correctly meeting with a flat rejection. Hobo was a damn good editor, and a damn fine drinking man. That's the way we remember him in San Francisco. God rest his sparkling soul.

(S) Richard Dermody

312 North San Mateo Drive
San Mateo, California
December 19, 1951

Editor, New Yorker
25 West 43rd Street
New York, N.Y.

Dear Sir:

This is in appreciation to the writer who turned in the obit on Harold Ross. It is a beautiful and a moving piece of writing and I know that many share my gratitude for it.

We have known many great editors, and in my book he is among the greatest. I knew him once as "Hobo" Ross, at the time he slaved in that ancient salt mine, the San Francisco Call — later to become a hyphenated adjunct of the Hearst empire. (The newspaper, I mean.)

He was quite a guy. Neil Hitt revived an antique hilarious anecdote covering the evening when Hobo matched adjectives with Corporal Duffy of the SF Police in last year's edition of the SF Press Club's annual, Scoop.

My agent attempted at various times to foist scripts of mine on Hobo, always correctly meeting with a flat rejection. Hobo was a damn good editor, and a damn fine drinking man. That's the way we remember him in San Francisco. God rest his sparkling soul.

(S) Richard Dermody

Announcement of William Shawn's appointment as Editor by primary New Yorker *shareholder Raoul Fleischmann.*

January 21, 1952.

Office of the Publisher

William Shawn has accepted the position of editor of The New Yorker, effective today.

R.H. Fleischmann

Letter from longtime Paris correspondent Janet 'Genêt' Flanner to her intimate friend, book editor Natalia Danesi Murray. January 23rd, 1952.

Just this minute received a cable from Raoul Fleischman announcing with pleasure that Shawn had accepted to be editor-in-chief of *New Yorker*. I am so glad, so proud for him. I had taken it for granted. How nice of Raoul to wire me.

I feel the magazine's loss can be explained like this: we have lost Ross and there is nobody to take his place; Shawn will make a place for himself as he already has, and nobody can replace him either – or even aid him sufficiently. It is bad enough that we only had one Ross. In a way, it is more alarming that in twenty-seven years we have only found one Shawn. Bless him. I know how satisfied you will be also at this choice which is no less satisfying because they might have tried to bring in some outsider which would have been fatal perhaps...

*Brendan Gill's father urged him to spend his inherit-
ance while young and Gill heeded the advice. His
pleas to Shawn for $1,200–$1,500 (10k–12k
in 2020 dollars) arrived with regularity and wit.*

Dear Master:

　The money that I make with one hand
I spend with the other. Ross said years ago
that I must learn to manage my affairs and I
am so glad that he never learned to manage
his. Do you suppose I could possibly have
fifteen hundred dollars, to keep me out
of the pen?

Yours,

B.G

October 9th, 1961

Dear Master:

　If agreeable to management, I'd dearly
like an

ADVANCE

AGAINST

FUTURE

DIRT

　　OF, say, fifteen hundred?

Your morbid friend,

B.G.

April 3rd, 1964

Dear Master:

As usual, jail threatens, and I would dearly like to stay out of it, if Harding Mason can get up fifteen hundred in scratch for me.

I mean to hand in the Chaplin review this week, by the way, in case you thought I'd forgotten about it.

Yrs., in penury,

Brendan

Monday, November 2nd, 1964

Dear Master:

As usual, jail threatens, and I would dearly like to stay out of it, if Harding Mason can get up fifteen hundred in scratch for me.

I mean to hand in the Chaplin review this week, by the way, in case you thought I'd forgotten about it.

Yrs., in penury,

Brendan

Monday, November 2nd, 1964

Mavis Gallant submits her raw notebooks to the magazine, which would be published in two parts as The Events In May.

Monday 17th June

Dear Mrs. Mackenzie:

Here is the last lot. I stopped it the morning of June 5th because the worst of it was over, and one has to stop somewhere. Actually, what is happening now in France is horribly ugly. If I were still in Paris I would be even more depressed than I am today.

This afternoon I had a letter from Bill, written June 4, to say that five pages posted from Brussels had turned up, no more. This means that I was let down by the girls going to Germany and by the ex-paratrooper gasoline smuggler. You should have, along with this, two lots from Belgium, one from Germany, and one from Italy.

I have just received a bookpost with the May 25 New York and Janet Flanner's <u>perfect</u> piece covering about May 3 to May 24, and so I cannot imagine you will have any use for this. Anyway, it is no good trying to read it unless you have the whole thing fromthe beginning. You will see that the pages are not numbered. You just put it together by dates.

Some of it may look like second guessing on my part, or being wise after the event, but I can assure you it is authentically almost hour-by-hour as written at the time. I guessed about the mercenaries, and that de G had done a horse-trade with the Army. Now we know what he promised. It is all very uglyand sad. I have learned from this that nothing is sadder than one fragment of a revolution. You keep feeling that for better or worse (as I wrote little Kate Maxwell) something was missed. But then everyone would have to want the same thing.

I am sending you Nancy Mitford's Journal, which made me want to throw paving stones. You might like to see another point of view. Could I please have it back some time? I am keeping a sort of dossier.

It is possible that the German and the paratroop envelopes were never sent at all, but dumped by the wayside. Would you please tell me when you get this letter if you are at all interested in reading the whole thing? In that case, I shall send my carbon copy, which is complete from beginning to end. But if you don't want to read it I shan't bother. Do please let me know.*

As I said in my letter, this is not a professionally-written journal, it is merely what Ikept for myself.

Yours ever,

Mavis Gallant

*   The rest may never have been sent at
all – I never saw the two people again.
So no good waiting

this that nothing is sadder than one fragment of a revolution.
You keep feeling that for better or worse (as i wrote little Kate
Maxwell) something was missed. But then everyone would have to want
the same thing.

I am sending you nancy Mitford's Journal, which made me want to
throw paving stones. You might like to see another point of view.
Could i please have it back some time? I am keeping a sort of
dossier.

It is possible that the German and the paratroop envelopes were
never sent at all, but dumped by the wayside. Would you please tell
me when you get this letter if you are at all interested in reading
the whole thing? In that case, I shall send my carbon copy, which is
complete from beginning to end. But if you don't want to read it
I shan't bother. So please let me know*

As i said in my letter, this is not a professionally-written journal,
it is merely what ikept for myself.

                    Yours ever,
                    Mavis Gallant

* The rest may never have been sent at all - I
never saw the two people again. So no good
waiting

Letter from Mavis Gallant to editor William 'Bill' Maxwell.

Paris, Friday

Dear Bill,

Yes, this seems fine.

About France -- what is worrying me is the xenophobia that has been caused by all this, and that is deliberately worked up on T.V. and in the government papers. The only balanced paper at the moment is the comic one, the Canard Euchainé (I am serious.) People I've known over fifteen years suddenly look upon me as Winsten Churchill and tell me how they hate the English. I don't care about the English and never have, but I care about the hate. The deliberate mistakes in reporting I told you about were all in good papers. (As you must have guessed by now I am passionately interested in politics. I read -- for pleasure -- three newspapers a day and more when travelling -- plus all the weeklies. Alas, the Pope has never consulted me.)

Much love,

M.

WESTERN UNION TELEGRAM
THE NEW YORKER

Mavis Gallant
Petit Mas de St. Joseph
Colline de l'Annunciade
06 Menton
France

There is still time to ask Shawn to change back anything made wrong in editing. Please do it.

Bill

February 12, 1987

Dear colleagues, dear friends:

My feelings at this perplexed moment are too strong for farewells. I will miss you terribly, but I can be grateful to have had your companionship for part of my journey through the years. Whatever our individual roles at <u>The New Yorker</u>, whether on the eighteenth, nineteenth, or twentieth floor, we have built something quite wonderful together. Love has been the controlling emotion, and love is the essential word. We have done our work with honesty and love. <u>The New Yorker</u>, as a reader once said, has been the gentlest of magazines. Perhaps it has also been the greatest, but that matters far less. What matters most is that you and I, working together, taking strength from the inspiration that our first editor, Harold Ross, gave us, have tried constantly to find and say what is true. I must speak of love once more. I love all of you, and will love you as long as I live.

William Shawn

ACKNOWLEDGMENTS

We would like to thank the staff of the Brooke Russell Astor Reading Room at the New York Public Library, Octavia Peissel, Jeremy Dawson, Susan Morrison and Erin Overbey.

The essays and articles in this anthology are reprinted from the following books and journals, all by permission of the publishers listed unless stated otherwise. The unpublished correspondence was discovered in The New York Public Library by the editors, and the relevant agents, estate and rights holders were consulted for their permission. Every effort has been made to trace the copyright holders of the materials published in this book. The editor and publisher apologises if any material has been included without permission or without the appropriate acknowledgment, and would be glad to be told of anyone who has not been consulted.

Thanks are due to all the copyright holders cited below for their kind permission:

James Baldwin, *Notes of a Native Son*, Copyright © 1949, 1950, 1951, 1953, 1954, 1955 by James Baldwin, Reprinted with permission from Beacon Press, Boston Massachusetts and the Estate of James Baldwin.

Sam Behrman, "Harold Ross: A Recollection" by S.N. Behrman. Copyright © 1965 by S.N. Behrman. From *The Suspended Drawing Room*, by S.N. Behrman. Used by permission of Brandt & Hochman Literary Agents, Inc. All rights reserved.

"The Days of Duveen: A Legendary Art Dealer and His Clients", by S.N. Behrman, copyright © 1951, 1952 by S.N. Behrman. Originally in *The New Yorker*, and later appeared in "The Days of Duveen" by S.N. Behrman. Used by permission of Brandt & Hochman Literary Agents, Inc. All rights reserved.

Frank Capra, unpublished correspondence, © 1951 Frank Capra Productions, Inc. Used by kind permission of the Estate of Frank Capra.

Roald Dahl, unpublished correspondence from Roald Dahl to *The New Yorker* © The Roald Dahl Story Company Limited, with kind permission from David Higham Associates Limited

Richard Dermody, 'Letters to the Editor' correspondence (December 1951), by permission of *The New Yorker*.

Janet Flanner, *Paris Was Yesterday, 1925–1939* (Harcourt Publishers Ltd; 1st Harvest Ed edition, 1998).

Raoul Fleischmann, unpublished correspondence by permission of *The New Yorker*.